SHOWING THE FLAG

THE WEST COAST TUG & BARGE INDUSTRY

Offshore and Overseas Operations

S.C. Heal

WEST COAST MARITIME SERIES
#4

Book layout and design by Jean Robinson, Victoria, B.C.
Cover design by Jim Scammell, Victoria, B.C.
Photo technical work by Pat Monty, Vancouver, B.C.
Printed and bound in Canada

Back cover photos:

    Top left, *Bei Hei 102,* Chinese deep-sea tug makes up a tow for China (Rick Garcia photo)
    Top right, *Dahlia,* Japanese deep-sea tug arrives Vancouver towing new dry dock (WMG Archives)
    Lower left, *Rivtow Lion,* former British wartime salvage tug enters Vancouver Harbour (Author's collection)
    Lower right, *Sundancer,* after salvage, enters Vancouver in charge of Seaspan tugs (WMG Archives)

"Genstar's *Genmar 104* loads a rig at Port Arthur, Texas"
Cover photo by Sven Stokke

National Library of Canada Cataloguing in Publication Data

Heal, S. C. (Syd C.)
 Showing the flag : the west coast tug & barge industry, offshore & overseas
operations / S.C. Heal. -- 2nd ed.

(West coast maritime series ; 4)
Includes bibliographical references and index.
ISBN 1-895590-27-2

 1. Marine towing--Canada.. 2. Tugboats--Canada. I. Title. II. Series: Heal,
S. C. (Syd C.) West coast maritime series ; 4.
HE566.T8H32 2003   387.2'32'0971   C2003-911046-X

SECOND EDITION
Published by Cordillera Books
8415 Granville Street, Box 46
Vancouver, B.C. V6P 4Z9
604-261-1695
richbook@ca.inter.net

TABLE OF CONTENTS

WEST COAST MARITIME SERIES

ACKNOWLEDGEMENTS
WEST COAST MARITIME SERIES

This series of books is the product of accumulated and sometimes hands-on knowledge and experience of others as well as my own. I personally back it with a formidable memory and a tendency to be a rat-packer of books, plans, photos and information that might be useful "at some time in the future."

It would not have been possible, however, to fully develop its multiple themes without the willing and forth-right co-operation of others. Opinions expressed are my own for which I take full responsibility. They do not imply endorsement by others even though their opinions might have helped refine my own. The aim of this book is to demonstrate the linkages between the primary industries and the tug, barge and coastal shipping industries in a largely historical setting. A great many personalities thread their way through the history of the industry and many have not been mentioned. How could they be? There are simply too many to cover, many worthy people and full coverage would need many large books.

A guideline in preparing this book has been accuracy above all and while care has been taken in assembling factual information, I apologise for any inadvertent error or omission which might show up, or the failure to make specific mention of an individual, a company or vessel which might rightly be considered a part of the historical mosaic.

Thanks are due to a considerable number of people, some are in or retired from the industry, others are dedicated industry watchers, but all are in possession of a healthy interest in a vital and fascinating industry. People who made significant contributions to the text in written form include Dick Doerksen, J. Bigelow and Captains J.P. Brown, Nick Roman and Peter Tull. People who gave me time for interviews and in some instances read vital segments of the manuscript or openly discussed issues faced by the industry include retired tugboat executives Donald B. Elworthy, James S. Byrn, Norman Cosulich, Lucille Johnstone, Peter Shields, Elmer Leard, Mrs. Margaret Jorgensen (McKenzie), Vern Logan and Captains, Jim Stewart, Fred Collins, Dick Tolhurst, Sven Stokke, Bob Fulton, Doug Rust, Wayne Lusk and Alan Gray. Others who have allowed me to pick their brains include Captains Don Mackenzie, Don Rose, Frank Wright, Dave Hirtle, Ted Wilson and David Martin-Smith, Messrs. Clyde Jacobs, Robert "Bob" Mackenzie, George Wray, Leo Stradiotti, Wayne Egelund, Nick Malysh, Al Meadows and Rob Sheret.

Friends who have assisted and encouraged in varying ways include Peter L. Wright, Ronald J. Webster and Roland Webb. Len McCann at the Vancouver Maritime Museum has always been ready to open up files. Local photographers who have contributed with many previously unpublished photos include Don Brown, Don Rose, Robert Etchell, Rod Logan, Shane Hall and Rick Garcia, all of whom opened their extensive files to me. It is a pleasure to record their photographic work along with some of my own. Access to the extensive World Ship Society collection at the Vancouver Maritime Museum has been a factor of great value without which many of the photos of the earlier ships would have been impossible.

A number of industrial concerns responded promptly to requests for information. Only two of the prominent companies involved ignored requests for confirmatory information which is a great pity as they are a part of the fabric of local maritime and industrial history.

Both are foreign owned, one from the paper section of the forest industry and one from the cement and aggregates business. Both seem to have a policy that says they have a right to be here, to extract Canada's resources and sell their end product here and overseas, but the door is closed to prying eyes and inquisitive writers seeking to place them in the history of the country. It would seem a little heavy handed to identify those companies here, but there are clues in the text.

If I have forgotten anyone I apologise. An author draws from many sources including those who have passed this way before. There is not a great deal of material available in the form of books, but where they exist I have sought to cover them in the bibliography and at the same time avoid unneeded coverage of the same ground. The pages of *Harbour & Shipping, West Coast Mariner* and the latter's successor, *Mariner Life,* have also been good sources as have the Vancouver Maritime Museum, the North Vancouver Museum and Archives and the Washington Marine Group Archives. My thanks are due to all of them.

Finally, this is not offered as a comprehensive history of an entire industry and its connections. It is a series of historical windows focussed almost entirely, but not completely, on the past and to the extent that it includes past personal involvements it becomes to a limited extent, a personal memoir and I make no apology for that.

For some quaint reason, in some publishing quarters this is regarded as trespassing on hallowed territory, a point of view I categorically reject. I have enjoyed a lifelong interest in all manner of maritime affairs and have spent two thirds of my life living at more or less close quarters with the West Coast maritime industries, the most central of which in my mind is the tugboat sector. My direct involvement in the tug and barge industry was relatively short and in my own small way I contributed to its history. The experience was heady, emotional, thrilling and at times downright exasperating, while it lasted. It will never be forgotten for as long as I live.

S.C. Heal
Vancouver, 2002

INTRODUCTION

It would be impossible to render anything near a full account of the operations of British Columbia tug and barge companies without dealing with offshore and overseas operations. In the early years some of the powerful steam tugs of their day virtually went offshore into the stormy waters off Cape Flattery to put a line on incoming sailing ships and then redeliver them fully laden once again to the open ocean where they set sail on their overseas voyages. This type of activity often well offshore and into international waters represented the first venturing of early B.C. tugboat operators away from their harbours and river estuaries. They often carried salvage pumps to pump out waterlogged vessels and from there the salvage gear became ever more sophisticated. It was the beginning of the B.C. segment of the international towing and salvage industry.

After the First World War a number of former Royal Navy, deep-sea salvage tugs ended up in B.C. waters. They came in fresh from wartime service where their duties included recovering damaged ships from the open

[1] Changing Times: Possibly the best looking coastal tanker to ever serve the British Columbia Coast, Shell Oil's **Tyee Shell,** of 2,400 dwt, was built in Canada in 1958, but was not in service for long when Shell became the first of the oil distributors serving the coast to abandon the self-propelled tanker in favour of tug and tank barge delivery when it awarded its deliveries to Vancouver Tug Boat Company.

ocean to a safe port for repair. On the B.C. coast their seakeeping abilities and relatively high power made them valuable in the towing of Davis rafts from the Queen Charlotte Islands and the handling of large railcar barges.

Before WW I Victoria became home base for the original salvage company serving the B.C. coast and it was from these roots that Harold Elworthy wetted his appetite for deep-sea towing work. Elworthy's Island Tug & Barge became the second major deep-sea salvage and towing company and successor to the first, his former employer, Pacific Salvage Company. Island Tug established a reputation for itself that was second to none. It became an efficient deep-sea tower with an early tow to Argentina which was followed by many others across the Pacific until the merger which formed Seaspan International.

Island Tug was not alone in its pursuit of transoceanic towing contracts. At one time or another Straits Towing, Vancouver Tug Boat Company, Rivtow, Gulf of Georgia Towing and Great West Towing have undertaken deep-sea tows. These have sometimes been part of a regular contract such as salt coming north from Mexico or, in other examples, have been tailored to fit in with the logistics of an employment pattern when, for example, a matching barge or rig was awaiting completion and the allocated tug needed interim employment. Occasionally there have been salvage jobs that the other companies have undertaken such as Rivtow's epic rescue of a disabled U.S. tanker and its delivery to Hawaii, but overall Island Tug and its successor, Seaspan, have been the biggest performers in this specialized branch of towing.

[2] The One That Was Not Recovered: In the post-WW II years B.C. towing and salvage operators had a high success ratio in saving stranded vessels of all types and towing in disabled ships from the open ocean. Shown here is the **Schiedijk** built in 1949, and of about 11,000 dwt, employed in Holland-Amerika Line's North Pacific service. She had loaded pulp at the Gold River mill and hit an underwater ledge off Bligh Island while outward bound in heavy fog, January 3, 1968. She capsized and fell off the ledge into deepwater where her wreck remains. It was the twilight of the cargo liners and in a previous era efforts might have been made to raise her.

After Seaspan came into being and probably influenced to some extent by Island Tug's track record in this field, the new organisation extended itself into large scale overseas and Canadian Arctic operations almost as soon as it was formed. This was though joint ventures which took it into the North Sea, Mediterranean and Red Sea. It was an exciting period driven mostly by developments in the international offshore oil industries which saw a variety of plays for exploration and development of new oil and gas fields. Other joint ventures came together in which Seaspan was a prime participant. Their purpose was to undertake long-distance delivery tows of drilling rigs and other oversize pieces of equipment using purpose-built barges built in Japan.

This was in a period in the '60s to '80s when there was a massive increase in undersea exploration. It saw the building of many offshore service and anchor handling vessels, which also did duty as tugboats. Part II of this book briefly describes the international oil scene and seeks to fit the B.C. coast into its place as an area that will brinmg much international activity in due course. It also gives a brief accounting of British Columbia's involvement in the building and ownership of rigs and service vessels. Four yards shared in the bulk of this business as did local naval architects and so far as is known little account of this activity has ever been recorded. It is hoped that this volume will usefully contribute to the record.

Smit's purchase of Rivtow Marine will change the pattern of some aspects of towing, even though much of Rivtow's business is out of character in terms of Smit's regular business. There is no doubt that Smit will leave their stamp on Rivtow, two years after the buyout. It is becoming apparent in 2003 that Smit is in the process of remoulding its acquisition into something a lot closer to its own image. Already numbers of former Rivtow tugs now sail under new management and Rivtow's reduced presence in the river where it was born has gone

[3] **Symbolic of a New Era:** The biggest single convoy of shipping to ever leave Vancouver is seen here bound for the Beaufort Sea and the Mackenzie delta in the 1960s. The activity was ongoing for about 20 years and found a great deal of gas which might be brought to market in the next several years with the proposed MacKenzie pipeline.

from the leading position to something closer to an occasional visitor, excepting the chipbarge movements which are continuous. However, it is thought likely that Smit has positioned itself to be able to take part as a domestic operator in forthcoming development of the oil or gas fields which are believed to exist in the continental shelf off the British Columbia coast.

Today transpacific towing is at a low ebb for British Columbia companies. With improved technology, larger more powerful ships and far closer scrutiny to weed out likely candidates for accidents at sea, ship casualties do not seem to occur with the frequency that pertained in the 25 years following WW II. Other than some former Seaspan barges and obsolete tugboats sold to China ostensibly for scrap as part of Seaspan's building program in Chinese yards, there is little or no sale of vessels to the Far East for shipbreaking purposes.

One development is the growth of the traffic generated by and for dockships. The self-propelled vessels of this type are not a Canadian development, although their equivalent, some submersible barges, were owned and operated by Genstar that have now passed into Norwegian ownership. These barges, dealt with as part of the story of Genstar's international commitments, can claim some degree of descent from the wartime dockships used by the Allies, but they were more directly an outgrowth of combining wartime logistical needs with the simple laws of physics. The Dutch and Belgian ships in this trade have had a very direct bearing on the B.C. maritime industries, delivering oversize container gantries built in China for our container berths, a fleet of new barges and sundry other vessels including yachts, tugs and a gambling ship, that have become a part of the B.C. scene. I admit that I have somewhat stretched my mandate, but it takes almost nothing to move from barges to self-propelled freighters engaged in the same business.

However, a new form of traffic has now taken on greater regularity. B.C. barge operators have found that China builds a suitable barge to their specifications so that fairly regular delivery voyages are now taken on by B.C. tugs and, as the need to replenish fleets increases, this traffic is also likely to increase, The current trend can be seen as a further development in the field of international competition and free trade. Unfortunately it does not bode well for British Columbia's remaining shipbuilders, despite some help in the way of a new Federal program subsidizing interest. The new place of China as a source for ship construction for B.C. marine transportation has been dealt with in Part I of this book.

The current shortages of energy are bringing about a renewed interest in offshore exploration and drilling and this in turn may create new opportunities for B.C. towing and marine construction companies even though the new conditions are not likely to be a repeat of the opportunities which high energy prices created about thirty years ago. There was a short resurgence of shipbuilding of offshore supply and service vessels in the late '60s and through the '70s when three B.C. yards participated in this surge and a similar number of local architects provided the necessary design services. It remains to be seen if some of this activity will be rekindled in the event that serious large scale exploration opens up on the British Columbian continental shelf. The historic details of this activity are covered in Part II of this book.

The last chapter is a group of realistic conclusions based on the contents of all four books in this series. How we would like things in a perfect Canadian world, but how we have to live as part of the international village. How we are affected by American protectionism on the one hand and how American economic imperialism has tended to undermine many things Canadian and give us a taste of what we might expect in the future. The suppositions set out are formed by drawing from many sources and adding the author's own observations. To the extent that they are the author's view of maritime affairs and, equally with the recognition that not everyone will agree with them, I take full responsibility for my conclusions.

Chapter One

TOWING IN FROM CAPE FLATTERY

The following is excerpted from Across Far Distant Horizons. *This book was based on the previously unpublished memoirs of the late Captain Trevor Whitla Bridges, born in Barrie, Ont., and a resident of Burnaby, B.C., for many years. Here, deck apprentice Bridges gives an account of coming to Vancouver in 1902, at the end of a towline from the steam tug* Lorne *to his own vessel, the Scottish barque* Invermay. *The Invermay hotel was a favoured watering hole for many visiting sailors to Vancouver at its location in the shipping office district on West Hastings Street, up until quite recent times. It is believed, but not proven, that the hotel took its name from the ship.*

There were a number of sailing ships in Hong Kong harbour at the time including one other British barque, *Duns Law* which arrived shortly before the departure of *Invermay*. We had been routed to Royal Roads, Esquimalt, B.C., for orders, which probably meant a lumber cargo for some unspecified destination. The prospect of seeing my native land again was quite heady for me, an emotion which was lost on any of my fellow British crew. I had read and heard a lot about Canada's West Coast port, even though the furthest place west I had ever been was Barrie, Ontario.

It took us five long weeks to beat our way out of the China Sea against a strong North East monsoon and after that we rolled for another month like a tumbling cask consoled only by the fact that by chance we overtook and spoke to a full-rigged ship,* with skysails on all three masts. She was the American *Sam P. Schofield,* bound for Puget Sound in ballast. If misery is mutually comforting, we took solace from the knowledge that she was making slower time than us.

The Pacific on this occasion had lived up to its name as we approached Vancouver Island

propelled by westerlies which had just about petered out. Slowly, we approached Cape Flattery on a glorious morning. The ship was spotless with all signs of our previous dirty coal cargo removed. The holystoned decks matched the white caps of mountains on the Olympic Peninsula. Another ship was awaiting a tug and to our astonishment it was *Duns Law* which had left Hong Kong weeks after us. By leaving later she had missed the North East monsoon and was thus able to steal a march on us.

The well-known Canadian tug *Lorne* picked us both up off Tatoosh and towed us in tandem into Royal Roads where we dropped anchor opposite to Esquimalt. The captain was soon ashore to complete the necessary clearances and pick up our orders. Sure enough we were to head into Hastings Mill in Vancouver and there load a full cargo of lumber for Melbourne, Australia.

* *As a full-rigged ship with square sails on all three masts, plus skysails which indicates a very lofty rig, the* Sam P. Schofield *should have been a faster sailer than* Invermay. *The possible reason for her slowness was perhaps a very foul bottom from a long period in tropical waters.*

[4] **Alexander:** McAllister Brothers of Victoria built this huge 180' side-wheeler tug in 1875 with the intention of towing in Nanaimo bound colliers from Cape Flattery, but her high fuel consumption and crew costs bankrupted her first owners. The paddlewheel tug never took hold on the West Coast although they were successful in Europe, particularly Britain where the last operating examples were in service into WW II. A comparison between the two suggests that **Alexander**'s wheels were too small, presenting a very small wetted surface. She ended up as an early experiment in log barging.

We were called as usual at 5:30 a.m. and with daybreak the *Lorne* came alongside to take our towline. We upped anchor to the rollicking shanty "Sally Brown, I love your daughter," and were away following in the propeller wash of the tug. Over to port and a little ahead of us was our friend *Duns Law*. We followed the route of countless other vessels before and since, threading our way through the Gulf Islands and then through Active Pass, across the Straits of Georgia, to make our landfall off Point Atkinson and then in through the First Narrows to drop anchor off North Vancouver. A few days later we towed with the aid of a harbour tug, into Evans, Coleman's

wharf to discharge ballast and then moved to Hastings Mill dock to commence loading.

We would see *Lorne* again when it came time for us, as a fully laden ship to head for the open sea again and set course for Melbourne. The good old reliable *Lorne* was to see many more years of service following this as her regular routine. Over the years she must have handled the towlines of a good many thousands of ships.

* * *

For many years *Lorne* occupied a similar position as a "hero" ship in the eyes of the public of its era as the two *Sudbury*s, half a century later. There was

[5] Lorne: Shows the classic lines of the early steam tugs. Long and narrow bodied the type were usually very fast. The long house with its many openings and low freeboard must have made them vulnerable in heavy seas, which no doubt accounts for the loss of several over the years, some by disappearance.

[6] Lorne: During her long life she never had a change of name and enjoyed a great popularity with the public in a similar way to **Sudbury** of fifty years later. **Lorne** towed everything from sailing ships to Davis rafts and at one time was owned by the Grand Trunk Pacific Railway and later by Captain Barney Johnson towing log barges. Here she is seen tending a newly launched WW I-type freighter, **Canadian Scottish,** at the GTP yard in Prince Rupert in 1921.

[7] Active: Another famous long-lived tug from the 1880s. She lived long enough to be dieselized by Coastal Towing in the 1950s, a move that was criticized by underwriters at the time on account of the vessel's great age. She did not live long after that being lost at Carrington Bay on Cortez Island.

little that *Lorne* could not do, if whoever was her capable hard driving master and strong crew set out to do. Within the context of its day, the main traffic she handled up until the opening of the Panama Canal was a succession of deep-sea, three- and four-masted barques, full-rigged ships and large ocean-going schooners up to five and even six masts. After Panama, the ocean-going steamer, which was already well known in the Pacific, multiplied in numbers and with a cargo capacity two and three times larger than the sailing ships, made its arrival increasingly on the scene. The employment of tugs like the *Lorne* for "towing in from Flattery" diminished as the numbers of sailing ships shrank.

However, *Lorne* and her big tug sisters were in increasing demand in the towing of Davis rafts from the Queen Charlottes.

Launched in June 1889 from the Laing yard at Victoria, *Lorne* came off the drawing board of George Middlemas, naval architect of San Francisco. She was ordered by James and Alex Dunsmuir, the prominent colliery owners from Victoria and Nanaimo, who had an urgent need to tow visiting coal carriers in and out from Cape Flattery. They, no doubt, also had their eyes on servicing the increasing number of vessels calling for lumber from Hastings Mill and Moodyville.

Lorne had dimensions of 151' x 26' x 18' moulded

depth with a draft of 13.2 at the stern. Her gross tonnage was 243 tons. Her registered horsepower was 114 and her steam reciprocating engine turned a propeller 12 feet in diameter. Whether this was a three- or four-bladed propeller is not noted in the available records, but a new innovation was the detachable blades which could be replaced in the event of damage, which obviated the need to replace the entire propeller as still arises to this day with a great many vessels. Both her engine weighing some fifty tons and the propeller were built by Albion Iron Works, Vancouver. This was quite an achievement for one of Vancouver's early iron foundries given that the year of *Lorne*'s construction was 1889 when Vancouver was little more than a village.

Her first master was Captain James Christensen and later his son Captain Andrew Christensen was to command her. According to Captain James Cates, one of her later masters and a member of the well-known North Vancouver family, her machinery was capable of delivering 1,200 shaft horsepower. Her free running speed was designed for 15 knots in average conditions and she had been known to exceed this on occasion. She used 1,800 feet of manila hawser with a circumferance of 16 inches which was retrieved by a steam capstan mounted on one side of her aft towing deck. Later this was replaced by a towing winch with 2,000 feet of copper-wire towline. She was capable of taking two average-sized, three-masted ships or barques in tandem from Cape Flattery inbound as happened in the case of the *Duns Law* and *Invermay*, recounted above. It's of interest to note that such ships had about the same deadweight carrying capacity as a typical average woodchip barge as presently employed in the B.C. coastal trade. Her success and

[8] **Haro:** Many of the large sawmillers built their own tugs and wooden scows in the period up to the 1930s. **Haro** was built and owned by the Hastings Mill Company and served for many years towing lumber carriers. As the bigger towing companies emerged they acquired most of the mill-owned vessels as part of the process of consolidation in the towing industry. With the purchase of the vessels, it often became part of the deal that the new owners also filled the towing needs of the mill. **Haro** passed to Straits Towing as part of this process. The last fleet owned by an independent sawmilling company was L & K's Lyttle Brothers Towing, which functioned into the 1980s.

[9] Moresby was one of two sisters built in WW II for International Towing Company for the purpose of towing Davis rafts from the Queen Charlotte Islands. The other visible funnel is that of her sister the **Masset**. Arthur Moscrop was probably the designer of what was by then a more or less standard design for local steam tugs in the larger classes.

the growing traffic of Victoria, Vancouver, Nanaimo, Union Bay, New Westminster and, by 1910, Powell River saw her being joined by others although none were quite as big or powerful. These included *Czar, Active, Sea Giant, Dola* and *William Joliffe,* the last of the generation of big steam tugs to be built and operated in B.C. waters being *Robert Preston,* built for Preston-Mann in 1923.

In 1897 she was chartered by Puget Sound Tugboat Company and in 1904 they purchased her for $30,000, half her original building cost of $60,000. She was maintained on Canadian registry and in 1916 passed to the Grand Trunk Pacific Railway and registered in Prince Rupert. Her employment was in the towing of railcar barges but she was also useful in attending newly launched freighters from GTP's shipyard at Prince Rupert which built several freighters for the British and Canadian governments around 1919–20.

In 1926 Captain Barney Johnson's Hecate Straits Towing Company bought her to handle log barges from the Queen Charlottes. Later, in the merger between Hecate, Pacific Tug & Barge, British Pacific Log Transport Company and Coyle Towing which led to the formation of Pacific (Coyle) Navigation Company, she became the big vessel of that fleet for a few years. In 1936 she passed to the firm of Shafer-Haggert Limited, a local trading company who scrapped her leaving her remains at Gambier Island, an ignoble end for one of B.C.'s historic ships. She fulfilled the early definition of a deep-sea tugboat as she had to take her station twenty miles or more from Flattery regardless of the weather, so that the awkward and sometimes hard-to-manage sailing ships did not go onto Washington's and Vancouver Island's rockbound West Coast.

* * *

The April 1993 issue of *Westcoast Mariner* carried an interesting article entitled "Early Towage Rates." No authorship is credited, so presumably it was a staff effort, but it is based on a towage card originating with Lorrie Belveal of Sointula, B.C. It covered a period when a working man with a family to support might have made just a dollar or two a day depending on his work.

The card was published by Robert Ward & Co. Limited of Victoria and Vancouver who were obviously brokers or agents. They offered British (Canadian) and American tugs, listing *Lorne, Astoria* and *Constance,* working in conjunction with the steamer *Active.* This latter vessel was the well-known tug *Active* which presumably was handled by Ward on a different basis to the other three named tugs. Ward also listed an address at 10 Basinghall Street, London, England. This was probably an agency where the London office acted for Ward and sought to have the B.C. company and its tugs nominated to tow inbound ocean vessels and redeliver outbound ships to the Cape Flattery area. Either that or Ward was an expatriate British firm, set up as commonly happened as an agency of London principals. Regardless of the arrangement, the B.C. firm and the London connection were set up to profit from the arrangement.

Up to the end of the nineteenth century, by far the greatest number of sailing ships in deep-sea trade were British, but London was also the world's largest shipping market with the Baltic Exchange which negotiated most deep-sea charters as well as Lloyds which insured a lot of them. It's a market arrangement which persists to this day, but instant communications have long since taken over from the cable services provided in those days and while Lloyds remains a key world market for marine and many other types of insurance, the Baltic has lost a lot of its importance. This is because a probable majority of cargoes shipped today are carried under contracts that have been negotiated directly between the cargo owner and the ship or tug operator.

Meeting inbound vessels was a chancy business. Without radio, there was no certainty about times or dates of arrival, which could spread over a wide time-frame of anything up to sixty days and perhaps more. A sailing ship arriving off Flattery would not want to loiter, waiting for a specifically nominated tug to show up. This might have involved a wait of days so a ship's master would probably take the towline of the first suitable tug to become available at a fair rate. It was different with outbound vessels as their departure dates were readily arrived at and would be a more certain element in Ward's business.

There were plenty of low rates posted, even as low as $45 for moving a 500/700 grt vessel from Port Gamble to Port Ludlow in Puget Sound, all the way through to $375 for towing a 2,500 grt vessel in from Cape Flattery to New Westminster, Nanaimo, Vancouver, Seattle, Port Blakeley or Bellingham Bay. Puget Sound ports almost certainly generated far more lumber cargo than B.C. ports. There was no brake on the volume of lumber that could be produced other than market demand. Environmental and ecological considerations had no real place in the parlance of the day. Mention of these two words was confined to good quality dictionaries, if at all, and American and Canadian tugs had far more freedom to compete within each other's territorial waters.

The list of whistle signals posted by Ward was also interesting. These were set out like this:

One whistle . . . . trim yards
Two whistles . . . . set fore and aft sails
Three whistles . . . . set square sails
Two short and one long . . . get anchor ready
One short and one long . . . take in sail
Four whistles . . . . let hawser go with a light
                     to be flashed when the
                     hawser is dropped.
One long and two short . . . fog signal while towing

An interesting feature of *Lorne,* which was named after the governor-general of the day, the Marquis of Lorne, is that unlike most ships she retained her original name throughout her long career of 47 years. That is always a sure sign of a famous ship and implied the respect of all her subsequent owners.

[10] Sea Lion: One of the best known of the big steamers, she had been fitted with a musical whistle which became a popular novelty to entertain the public when passing through the harbour. In this photo she is shown with another unusual feature, usually reserved for large passenger liners. Her lifeboats at that time were doubled stacked.

[11] Sea Lion: A well-known picture of the handsome **Sea Lion** following dieselization. Retaining her musical whistle, she typifies the numerous diesel convertions which took place in the towing industry up to the 1950s when new construction started to become more feasible with the creation of the Canadian Vessels Construction Act.

THE ADAPTATION OF WARTIME STANDARD DEEP-SEA SALVAGE TUGS

The two world wars of the last century were responsible for large fleets of excellent tugs built mainly in Britain in the first war and in Britain and the United States with some good units built in Canada in the Second World War. Both British and American wartime tugs found their way into Canadian ownerships and a number of vessels had very long lives with local Vancouver operators.

War seems to give everything an impetus to new levels of development. That must be because most production is for government account or is only permitted under licence where the government has a considerable say in the end product. The science of war makes demands on research, technology, design and construction facilities, usually with hard headed capital management and operating economics being far behind wartime necessity. The end result was that both wars saw huge "quantum leaps" in almost every direction.

In the First World War, the British government faced with critical losses initiated a number of emergency standard ship designs and building programs, in an effort to fill the mounting gap caused by huge losses to U-boat attacks. The war at sea created many towing opportunities in salvaging damaged or stranded ships following torpedoing and the hazards of navigation in crowded waters with the usual navigation aids such as lighthouses.

Possibly the first big class of tugs built anywhere were the excellent Saint class of steam tugs of which 17 remained in Royal Navy service when war came

[12] **St. Boswells:** The First World War did not produce the numbers of tugs that came out of WW II. However, perhaps the most successful class of WW I deep-sea tug was the British "Saint" class, shown here in wartime rig. Several came to British Columbia.

in 1939. They served with distinction until the end of the war although nine became war or marine losses. The class was far bigger when they were built in 1918–19, many finding new homes in foreign navies after the war, with others going into commercial service. Three of the group found their way to British Columbia to give many years service in towing Davis rafts and railcar barges. Another of the class, *Ocean Eagle*, ex-*St. Arvans*, went into Canadian Government service. A further vessel, *St. Giles*, is mentioned in chapter 3 in describing wartime salvage operations in Australasian waters.

The Saint class had dimensions of 135.5' x 29' x 14.5' and displaced 570 tons. Power was provided by a steam reciprocating engine of 1,250 ihp. The three examples which found their way to the West Coast were:

Canadian National No. 2, ex-*St. Catherine*, owned by Canadian National Railways, built at Hessle, Yorkshire, England in 1919. Employed by C.N. towing railcar barges until after WW II.

Kyoquot, ex-*St. Florence*, owned by Canadian Pacific Railway, built at Saltney, Cheshire, England, also in 1919. She towed railcar barges until after WW II.

S.D. Brooks, ex-*St. Faith*, owned by the Powell River Company and built at Lytham, Lancashire, England, in 1919, which was often engaged in towing Davis rafts from the Queen Charlottes.

S.D. Brooks had several changes of ownership becoming *Haida Monarch* of Kingcome Navigation and then *Le Beau* of Vancouver Tug Boat Company. When in the service of Vancouver Tug Boat Company, *Le Beau* undertook a number of tows to Hawaii delivering barge loads of steel. In 1970 she was sold to New Zealand interests who employed her as *Unit Shipper*, towing a freight barge. Eventually she went to Singapore interests and was finally broken up at Singapore in 1977, at 58 years of age, almost certainly, one of the longest lived of all the Saint-class tugs.

Texada Towing Ltd. engaged in a major rebuild of

the *Canadian National No. 2* including full dieselization, but cost overruns ruined them. After that she was purchased by Gulf of Georgia Towing Company and renamed *Gulf Freda*. They finished the conversion and retained her in their fleet until after 1977 when that company sold out to Seaspan. *Gulf Freda*, therefore, seems to have held the record for longevity in the Saint-class tugs.

Kyoquot spent almost all her life in CPR service after purchase from Britain and ended up in the old graveyard of many worthy ships in the breakwater at Royston.

A slightly smaller tug was *Canadian National No. 1*, ex-*Hopkins Brothers*, ex-*Finwhale*, also built for the British Admiralty in 1915. Jane's *Fighting Ships* described her as an Admiralty whaler, one of a class of 14 all carrying the names of different species of the whale family. They had dimensions of 140' x 25' x 6.5' and displaced 336 tons. Jane's however, does not say how these vessels were employed in naval service, although by their appearance they could have been a multi-purpose vessel, including towing duties. Their fine entrance and underwater lines made for a fast vessel and a feature that distinguished them from most tugboats was the yacht-like counter stern. C.N. acquired her from the Hopkins Brothers, an early B.C. towboat business who had built their first big tug, the *Hopkins*, on the beach at Hopkins Landing on the Sunshine Coast. The Hopkins Brothers story and a photo of *Canadian National No. 1* are to be found in *Tying the Knot*, Book 3 in this series.

The Second World War brought a much bigger crop of wartime tugs to the post-war disposal market. The British brought out two classes of large tugs. The larger size vessels consisted of seven of the Bustler class with diesels of 4,000 hp. They were very similar to Smit's last big pre-war tugs, most of which escaped the invasion of Holland and worked on the Allied side. These British tugs were the equivalent of the *Sudbury II* in size but had about 1,000 more horsepower. The smaller ships were the 21 tugs of the Assurance class of which five became war losses. They were steam propelled with an ihp of 1,350. Rivtow's *Rivtow Viking*, ex-*Hermes*, ex-*Adherant*, ex-*Tenacity*, ex-*Diligent* and *Rivtow Lion*,

[13] Kyuquot, ex-St Florence: After retirement from wartime deep-sea service, this one spent the rest of her life towing railcar barges for the Canadian Pacific Railway from Vancouver to the Vancouver Island.

[14] Le Beau, ex-S.D. Brooks, ex-St. Faith: Probably had as interesting and varied a career as any of the Saints. After service with Kingcome, she is seen here in Vancouver Tug colours being employed by them to tow barge loads of steel to Hawaii. She then passed to New Zealand owners, finally ending up in Singapore where she was broken up after a longer life than most of her sisters.

[15] **Cautious, ex-Prudent:** This ship, of the Admiralty "assurance class" of late WW II vintage, is shown here leaving Hull, England, in 1964 for her long delivery voyage to Vancouver and a date with the ship rebuilders and diesel power.

[16] **Rivtow Lion, ex-Cautious:** became the big deep-sea type tug in the fleet of Rivtow prior to the merger with Straits Towing. She was originally matched with Rivtow's first log barge, **Rivtow Carrier,** of 1965.

ex-*Cautious,* ex-*Prudent,* were both from this class, although re-engined with diesels of about 3,000 hp they became more in keeping with Rivtow's requirements in towing log barges.

THE CANADIAN WAR-BUILT TUGS

A ship type that became famous in war as a large class of British-Canadian warships was the corvette. One member of the group, *Sudbury,* became famous as the only one to be converted for deep-sea towing and salvage. She is mentioned here only for the record as greater attention is given to her and her consort, *Sudbury II,* in chapter 3 following.

Other than the above a number of tugs were built for Canadian Army service. Named after prominent military generals, some saw service on the B.C. coast as supply vessels. A smaller class was represented by

the vessels that became *Hecate Straits, Magellan Straits* and *Squamish Queen.*

Yet another group were the "Glens," some of which were built in B.C. yards, but these could hardly rank as anything bigger than coastal towers, some of which became useful on the B.C. coast after the war.

AMERICAN WAR-BUILT TUGS

The American output of coastal and ocean-going tugs during WW II was huge. Several classes of tugs were built for the U.S. Navy and the Army, which ranged from the largest U.S.N. fleet tugs with a length of over 200 ft and 3,000 hp. So far as is known none of this group were sold out of the service to find themselves in Canadian ownership.

A second large tug was the type built by the

[17] **Haida Chieftain,** ex-**N.R. Lang:** One of a wartime U.S. class termed an ATA, a fleet auxiliary tug capable of a wide range of services, built in Orange, Texas, in 1944. The high long forecastle is more usual in European practice than American. **Haida Chieftain,** after a period in layup, has now been taken over by More Marine to handle Rivtow's former freight barge run from Vancouver to North Coast ports.

[18] Johnstone Straits: The Straits Towing representative of the famous Miki (single screw) and Miki-Miki (twin screw) classes of wartime U.S. wood-built tug. Regarded by many in the B.C. towing industry as the best all round WW II-built tug for B.C. towing conditions, six in all came to B.C. fleets after the war.

[19] Lloyd B. Gore: Still in service registered as a yacht. This sturdy representative of the Miki-Mikis retained her Young & Gore colours throughout her service as a unit of the Island Tug & Barge fleet.

[20] Island Navigator: Looking long and low as she lays alongside a railcar float, **Island Navigator,** a sister of the two previously named vessels, she was acquired by IT&B immediately after the war. The grey painted railcar float, CPR's **Prospect Point** laying alongside, is almost as interesting with its overhead bridge bracing and truss-like longitudinal strengthening on deck. Without these on its wooden hull the stresses set up by a heavy load of railcars would have soon torn it apart early in its life.

[21] Gulf Joan: Although she was a bigger vessel by about 30 feet than **Seaspan Sovereign,** she has so many features that are common to both that they appear to have come from the same designer. The conversion from an ex-U.S. army tug was undertaken by Gulf of Georgia at their own facility in Vancouver. Gulf of Georgia sent her to Taiwan with a tow and also to the Canadian East coast on several occasions, but mostly she was coupled with the log barge **Swiftsure Prince,** as she is today as the **Sea Commander.**

[22] Weldwood Spirit, ex-Lady Theresa: Not an ocean-going salvage tug, but included as she came to B.C. originally from England, under her own power. Built by Cook, Welton & Gemmell at Beverley, Yorkshire, in 1963 for J. Pigott & Son of the U.K., she was acquired by the marine division of Weldwood in whose colours she is seen here in 1991 at the Hodder dock. She later became **Comox Argus** and then **Yuculta Spirit,** owned by Pacific Cachalot of Campbell River, B.C., her present owners.

Basalt Rock Company at Napa, California, two of which became *Cambrian Salvor* and *Caledonian Salvor,* later *Sudbury II.* These two vessels are dealt with in chapter 3 following.

Two other classes of deep-sea tugs, both of which did a variety of ocean long-distance tows, are represented by *Seaspan Sovereign,* ex-*Island Sovereign* and *Sea Commander,* ex-*Gulf Joan.* Pleasing in appearance both were built in the U.S. in 1944–45 and with a similar profile and common features they appear to have come off the same drawing board. However, *Sea Commander* is the bigger vessel with a length of 143' to *Seaspan Sovereign*'s 117'. Both have had a long life in the towing industry which says a lot for both their original construction and ongoing maintenance. How much longer they can be employed in their present work is a good question as few large steel tugs reach their 60-year anniversary. The smaller vessel is still employed towing limerick barges from Texada Island to U.S. cement plants and the larger tug has handled log barges for many years for Sea-Link Marine Services.

Another steel tug, midway in size between the *Seaspan Sovereign* and the *Sea Commander* and still afloat after 59 years of service, is *Haida Chieftain,* ex-*N.R. Lang,* which has a length of 137' and is of 561 grt. With a high forecastle she bears a close resemblance to the British deep-sea salvage tugs, rather than the more usual flush deckers associated with American practice. She has been paired with Kingcome's first self-loading, self-dumping log barge since that vessel, the *Haida Carrier,* came out in 1961. Both vessels have been together since then through the ownerships of Kingcome, Shields Navigation and now Blue Band Towing. Both are on the market at the time of writing, but given the state of the coastal forest industry it is difficult to see any future for this long-lived pair.*

An interesting American war-built tug was the *Seaspan Chinook,* ex-*Island Monarch,* ex-*Mogul,* ex-*Logmac,* ex-*ATR-64.* This vessel is still afloat as a ship preservation project. Designed by Alden and of wood construction, they were steam powered and designed for convoy rescue work in particular. Dimensions were 157.5' x 33.4' x 20.3' depth of hull. In war service, they ranged all over the South Pacific.

As *Logmac,* she and a sister of the same type, *Towmac,* were acquired from the U.S. war surplus by Canadian Transport Company, a subsidiary at that time of H.R. MacMillan Export Company. *Logmac* later passed to Griffiths Steamship Company of Seattle as the *Mogul* but still under the Canadian flag. When Island Tug & Barge became a part of Seaspan she was soon after converted to the company yacht.

It was in the somewhat smaller classes that B.C. owners took the greatest interest. Soon after the war ended a large number of these vessels were declared surplus and sold at knock-down prices. With currency barriers removed by the Canadian authorities, B.C. owners flocked to the U.S. and in some instances almost re-equipped their fleets with U.S. surplus vessels. Notably present in acquiring ex-U.S. government vessels were Island Tug & Barge, Straits Towing, Vancouver Tug, Young & Gore, Kingcome, Canadian Tugboat Company and even Pacific Coyle. Notably absent were Gulf of Georgia Towing, a substantial company which at that time had not made the jump into the big leagues, and River Towing, as it was becoming known. The group of small river operators that was to become Rivtow Marine was just starting to consolidate under the guidance of the Cosulichs.

Among these smaller vessels the most outstanding was probably the Miki-type boat, an excellent model based on the original tug *Miki,* built in 1929 for employment in Hawaii. Built of wood they had a length of 117' and 270 grt. The six of the type acquired by B.C. owners became *Lloyd B. Gore, Mary Mackin, Florence Filberg, Johnstone Straits, Island Navigator* and *J.S. Foley.* The vessels were built at a number of yards around the U.S. and while quality varied, the class of about 70 vessels is remembered with affection by many of the older towboatmen who served in them. The Mikis were about as small as any of the British and American deep-sea wartime tugs capable of being used in deep salvage service. Anything smaller would have been ranked as a general-purpose coastal tug.

* *At last word,* Haida Chieftain *has gone to More Marine, employed in the former Rivtow freight barge service from Vancouver to Prince Rupert and Kitimat.*

Chapter Two
WORLDWIDE INTERNATIONAL DEEP-SEA TOWING OPERATIONS

International towing takes many forms and has its own special features. For purposes of this description and in order to establish some parameters, "international" in the tugboat business usually means when a vessel or tow crosses from one national jurisdiction to another or proceeds outside what are usually taken to be national territorial waters.

Thus a tow from Vancouver, Canada, to Seattle, USA, is just as much an international voyage as one which starts in Victoria, B.C., and ends in Singapore. The objectives of this book are more focussed on the longer distance tows or rescue jobs, rather than the routine cross-border traffic such as occurs in the inside waters of the B.C. coast and Puget Sound.

International business is negotiated in a variety of ways. When arrangements lead to a firm commitment to provide a vessel to meet a charterer's requirement, this is usually termed a "fixture" in the parlance of deep-sea shipping operations. To "fix" is to "confirm a charter" in the language of the international shipping trades.

A vessel has stranded in a badly exposed position and is in danger of breaking up, or a vessel is slowly sinking following a collision. Time is of the essence and a distress call is answered by a salvage tug. The circumstances can be so dire that there is no time to bargain and await instructions from the owners or underwriters representatives who may be many thousands of miles away. The tug master and the master of the distressed ship agree on Lloyds Open Form of salvage contract, commonly called "No cure–no pay" which means what it says. Assuming a

positive outcome in dealing with the distressed ship, she is pulled off the rocks or is pumped out and towed into a port of refuge.

Under a Lloyds Open Form, payment in the event of successful salvage is usually arrived at by paying a percentage of the value of the ship and cargo saved, but in recognition of the gambling nature of ocean salvage the amount determined by the court would normally be at a considerably higher rate than the daily rate of charter hire. By way of contrast the *Chestnut Hill* case which is related in chapter 6 was arranged on a daily rate basis. The *Chestnut Hill* was exposed to danger, but was not immediately imperilled so there was no question of an emergency arrangement between the masters of the tug and the tanker. In this case as soon as the owners in agreement with the P & I underwriters learned of the casualty to their ship, they advised their London agents who put out an enquiry to the international tugboat operators to check the availability of tugs capable of towing the vessel. Most tugboat companies competing in the international market place would have London or New York agents of their own so contact would be convenient and easy between the different agents.

London was and still is the biggest market place in the world for ship chartering, ship management, marine insurance and finance and little of importance in international shipping happens without knowledge of it getting back to London sooner rather than later. Virtually any kind of insurance contract is negotiable in the London market from Total Loss Only (TLO) reinsurance by which underwriters with a potential

[23] Global Ambition: Seaspan tugs headed by **Seaspan Regent,** assisted by **Seaspan Commodore** and smaller units, bring the Korean-owned ore/oil carrier into Vancouver, following a major engine room fire which destroyed the bridge and much of the crew accommodation in August 1981.

total loss on their hands can reinsure part of their risk at, needless to say, increasingly high rates as the position of a wreck deteriorates. It represents a gamble to dilute loss and if a total loss occurs there are co-underwriters to share it. If on the other hand, the vessel is successfully salved then the high premium paid to TLO reinsuring underwriters has to be looked at as a justifiable expense in reducing the high exposure to the loss that would have occurred had the vessel been lost.

Back in the 1930s, reinsurance rates for this type of risk were sometimes quoted in the shipping press. I can remember the 1939 stranding of *Chepo*, the Panamanian steamer which had run aground in the Eastern Mediterranean and was half sunk on a submerged reef with a danger of falling off into deep water beyond the reach of salvors. Consequently, the salvage was a very delicate affair which the marine insurance market watched with considerable interest,

particularly as the reinsurance rates climbed on a more or less daily basis. After about 30 days the reinsurance rate had gone so high that it was no longer feasible to reinsure. The daily reports in the casualty list came to a sudden end with the terse report that *Chepo* had fallen off the reef into very deep water and all salvage attempts had been abandoned.

There is another gamble involved on the part of towing and salvage firms: the principle of "no cure–no pay," by which the salvor is expected to shoulder the entire risk by gambling on a successful outcome. The prospect of a large salvage award is the incentive that the contract offers, but with daily rates for large salvage tugs being measured in thousands of dollars per day, there is nothing to stop the salvage concern insuring its risk in sustaining an unsuccessful outcome. In the glory days of Island Tug & Barge and its Sudbury tugs a number of vessels were towed in from the North Pacific often under extreme

[24] **Global Ambition:** The sheer massiveness of the ship can be seen as she heads into Vancouver with a full cargo on board. **Seaspan Regent** can be seen in the lead with **Seaspan Commodore** astern. The vessel was held at Vancouver for some time while marine underwriters and the P & I clubs investigated the options for repair.

[25] **Global Ambition:** Eventually the decision was made to tow the damaged ship to Korea for repairs as even with the cost of the transpacific tow, the job would have been cheaper than dealing with it in a West Coast yard in the U.S. or Canada. There was also the advantage of being able to discharge the entire cargo to the consignees before repairs took place. Here she is seen lined up with *(l-r)* **Cates 7, Seaspan Challenger, Seaspan Sovereign** and **Cates 8** acting as drogues, while the deep-sea tug **Arctic** can be seen in the distance.

circumstances. Contracts would have been on Lloyds Open Form. To cover their potential loss in the event of a failed rescue they would have placed insurance to cover their costs.

Much of Island Tug's transpacific towing activity was of a contract nature. For instance the towing of surplus Liberty ships to Japan was arranged on the basis of a set fee per ship following delivery. To lose a ship on passage would have resulted in a total loss of fees pertaining to that vessel. In this instance Island Tug would have arranged insurance in the London market to recover its towing fees in the event of the loss of one of the towed vessels.

In later years when Genstar Marine, an associate company of Seaspan, participated in a variety of partnerships involving long-distance tows of drill rigs and production platforms on its large ocean-going barges, similar considerations applied. The cargo on deck was at the risk of its owner, but the loss of any towing fees because of a loss of the tow would have likewise been coverable by marine insurance arranged in all probability in London.

Contrary to the instances when tugs are needed in an emergency, the type of towing that Genstar Marine became involved in was usually developed by contract negotiated with great care over a period of time. Nothing has changed in that regard as companies like Smit International have been working under painstakingly negotiated contracts for a century and more and still are. In many cases this involved competition from other towing operations or today, from semi-submersible dockships, but once the transportation method was arrived at, carefully devised preparations would go ahead. Dealing with oversize heavy objects requires considerable engineering knowledge. In that there were only a few qualified companies around the world possessing the right kind of equipment for this kind of work, it is not likely to be offered into the broad international market in London or elsewhere. It would be far more likely that the few companies involved would be contacted directly and invited to bid. In the end it would get down to a very limited choice as some would automatically be disqualified by not having a vessel or vessels conveniently available and deliverable within the time-frame required.

A type of employment which was really very little different from regular contract work was the trade started in the late 1960s by Vancouver Tug Boat Company. Barge loads of salt were towed from Black Warrior Lagoon in Baja California for the B.C. chemical industry. This traffic was inherited by Seaspan after 1970 and continued for some years.

Initially this trade was handled by a self-propelled bulkcarrier, the m.v. *Argyle,* operated by National Bulk Carriers Inc. until its contract expired and the ship, worn out by the corrosion from salt cargoes, went to the scrappers and the barges took over. More recently the traffic has reverted to another self-propelled bulkcarrier. No reason was ever made public as to why the barge traffic was terminated, but it seems likely that the towing of salt cargoes on deck in open ocean conditions resulted in a reduced outturn due to saltwater erosion, while underway. In calculating cost, allowance for heavy depreciation of equipment due to corrosion would also have been an important factor. As with the *Argyle,* mentioned above, once a vessel has been taken out of long-term service in the carriage of salt, it is not fit for much else.

Whereas competition on the B.C. coast is entirely between Canadian companies, the situation internationally is global in scope. Much depends on where in the world a job is being tendered, but today the international towing business operates under many flags with some being fairly new to the field. Russian, Chinese, Japanese, Singaporean, Turkish, Polish and Croatian tugs compete against long-entrenched Dutch, Belgian and German international tugs, while Canadian, American, Australian, British, Scandinavian and French tugs are usually more prominent in specific areas of the world.

Inevitably there will be differenecs in the quality of vessels and towing gear as well as the depth of experience of managements and crews, but they are unlikely to be as radical as the differences between ocean shipping operators. Even local tows tend to be more closely monitored by surveyors working for marine underwriters. The negotiation of a major international tow involves painstaking effort on both sides, so also do the parallel insurance arrangements, which often are initiated long before a towing contract is concluded.

[26] **Arctic:** The German Bugsier Company was the successful bidder, probably against considerable international competition, including Smit and Weijsmuller. With 15,000 ihp she was more than adequate for the job. Here she is seen off West Vancouver as the tow gets under way for Korea.

[27] **Bei Hai 102:** Another large international tow involved this large Chinese tug around 1994. Two Norwegian-owned stern trawlers, **Norfisk 1** and **Norfisk 2,** registered in the Netherlands Antilles, were seized at Vancouver and put up for auction by the Federal marshal. With no satisfactory bids they were sold to China for scrap. At the same time a Chilean-owned Panamanian freighter, **Rio Mafil,** was also arrested, but she was in a deplorable condition and also went for scrap.

[28] Bei Hai 102: In this second picture **Norfisk I** is manoeuvered into position to make up a triple tow of the three ships. It is understood that one of the trawlers was lost before the tow reached its destination. The tug, which is around 200 feet in length, had about 11,000 ihp. China is now a sizeable competitor in international towing.

[29] Neftegaz 52: A large Russian offshore/supply tug owned by Sakhalin Natural Gas Enterprise is seen here in B.C. waters. She appears to have a massive funnel, but closer examination reveals twin side-by-side stacks. Some Russian vessels like oceanographic and seismic survey ships call here for fuel and supplies, but otherwise her purpose in being here is not recalled.

GULF OF GEORGIA'S EAST COAST OPERATIONS

With James S. Byrn at the head of the company, Gulf of Georgia Towing Company became one of the most aggressive tug and barge operations in the history of B.C. towing. He took over following return from wartime flying duties with the RCAF. Like Cecil Cosulich, Jim Byrne had the gambler's instincts and most times his gambles paid off.

From its founding at the end of WW I until the end of WW II it had been the leading company in providing wooden scows to the lumber industry for waterborn deliveries from the mills to other locations, particularly for shipside loadings of export lumber. So long as the wooden scow remained in vogue it was the comfortable leader by far, in this section of the towing industry. WW II changed all that. With wartime shipbuilding coming to a close there was a large contingent of capable steel shipbuilders who would be looking for post-war opportunities. These men covered many from management, experienced foremen and capable steelworkers for whom the handling of a welding torch was as easy as wielding a pen. Some of our best-known post-war shipbuilders such as John Manly and George Fryatt started by this route.

The future of wooden shipbuilding was looking very limited at this time. The last wooden tugs and

[30] Gulf Joan: In its last twenty years before its sale to Genstar in 1977, Gulf of Georgia Towing Company was one of the most aggressive in the business with a subsidiary company in Eastern Canada and another in South East Asia. In 1965, **Gulf Joan** delivered some barges to the East coast and then an interesting cross voyage was undertaken far from Vancouver. These two surplus U.S. navy destroyers were picked up at Port Arthur, Texas, for delivery to Taiwan. There was a refuelling stop in Hawaii, followed by passage through the Philippine Sea and then crossing the China Sea to arrive in Taiwan—mission accomplished. *(scanned from a much-faded photograph)*

scows were built in the early 1950s and from then on it was all steel constructiuon for the tug and barge business. Jim Byrn saw and understood these changes. After he had bought out his father Stav Byrn and uncle Ray Bicknell, he started one of the biggest transformations in local towing history. The wooden scows were disposed of as quickly as the second-hand market would absorb them. Smaller tugboats went with them as they were no longer suitable to handle the big new equipment that was coming out of the shipyards by the mid-1950s and the pace of new building was to speed up at every turn throughout the '60s and '70s.

Perhaps seeing the future, Gulf of Georgia Towing Company set up a new company in 1968 called Fluvetow Ltee, (River Towing). This was a towing company based in Montreal, P.Q., which operated as a division of Gulf of Georgia and its aim was to develop as a towing concern in the Gulf of St. Lawrence and adjacent waters. Jim Byrn was president, Henry Druce, D.S.O. of Matthews Shipping Ltd., Montreal, was vice-president and Harry Bloomfield, a Montreal lawyer, was secretary. Captain E.R. "Ed" Taylor of Gulf of Georgia, Vancouver, was the West Coast sales representative. Captain Marc Lamoreau of Prilam Transportation Ltd. of Montreal held the same post on the East Coast.

By 1970 Gulf of Georgia Towing was clearly one of the big five in the business and then came the big mergers of the 1970s as related in *Tying the Knot,* in this series. Suddenly there were three companies competing for what five had previously shared, but the new Rivtow-Straits and Seaspan combinations were so much bigger and as Byrn remarked in the book *Against Wind and Weather,* by Ken Drushka, he was feeling pretty much hemmed in by his big competitors.

Nonetheless this did not preclude Gulf of Georgia from pursuing a continuous program of aggressive expansion. It was now the loose cannon in the big end of the industry which both Seaspan and Rivtow saw themselves eventually taking over.

In 1974, Morrison & McRae Ltd. of Summerside, P.E.I., purchased the 65-foot tug *Gulf Dianne* with a 765-hp Cat diesel, plus two 3,000-tons capacity gravel barges, *G G 270* and *G G 271,* from Gulf of Georgia Towing. Limestone ballast rip-rap was loaded on the barges at Texada Island and *Gulf Dianne* was loaded on *G G 271* by crane at Centennial pier. *Gulf Joan* towed the two barges in tandem through the Panama and up to St. John, N.B., where the *Gulf Dianne* was offloaded. A new crew took the tug and accompanied *Gulf Joan* and her tandem barges to Summerside, P.E.I.

Captain Taylor assisted the staff at Mariner Towing Ltd. with their primary operation of towing gravel aggregates from the conveyor berth at Wallace, N.B. to the new barge ramp berth at Summerside. Mariner Towing was the marine subsidiary of Morrison & McRae Ltd. The company also handled aggegates from Wallace to the French islands of St. Pierre and Miquelon, as well as coal from the Prince mine at Sydney, N.S. to the Trenton generating plant at Pictou, N.S. All projects were seasonal because of the winter shutdown.

In 1977 Mr. Byrn responded to a successful offer from Seaspan and joined that company taking the post of president of Genstar Marine. Captain Taylor assisted Donal McAllister, president of McAllister Towing & Salvage Ltd. Montreal in converting Gulf of Georgia's East Coast operations into Genstar Marine. Genstar Marine, which will be featured later in this book, took a lead role in several major overseas initiatives, during the Byrn period.

For a while Gulf of Georgia also had an interest in a towing operation based in Djakarta, but this was closed down in the face of adverse business conditions including the difficulties of doing business in Indonesia.

Gulf Joan ranged over a wide area of the world while employed by Gulf of Georgia. In addition to towing to the Far East she also did at least one trip with a barge in tow to Resolute up in the far Northern Arctic around 1974–75. Her career under a later owner follows.

---

* No relation to Vancouver-based Mariner Towing.

SEA-LINK MARINE SERVICES—
A COASTAL AND INTERNATIONAL COMPANY

Founded about 12 years ago by Peter Brown who had previously been with Kingcome Navigation, the first sign of an interesting new company in the industry came when Union Tug & Barge Ltd. acquired the tug *Seaspan Commander,* ex-*Gulf Joan.* She came from Seaspan and Union Tug matched her, under the new name *Sea Commander,* with the log barge *Swiftsure Prince,* then owned by Swiftsure Towing Ltd. for the second time in the life of both vessels. Swiftsure Towing was the marine towing subsidiary of B.C. Forest Products, but it became a casualty when Fletcher Challenge (Canada) Ltd. emerged from the reorganization by which BCFP and Crown Forest Industries came together. Swiftsure's fleet of tugs was sold off about 1992 and that company was folded into Norsk Pacific Shipping as the new marine offshoot of Fletcher Challenge. Swiftsure had also operated the first of the new breed of log barges, Forest Prince, but in view of age and smaller size she was stripped down to a large flat-deck and when last noted by the writer she was carrying scrap steel. It was at about this time that Sea-Link acquired *Swiftsure Prince.*

After 1970 interest in owning self-loading, self-dumping log barges by forest product companies declined. Among the forest companies only Canadian Tugboat Company (Crown Forest and Crown Zellerbach), Swiftsure and Kingcome Navigation (MacMillan, Bloedel) had made an investment in this new technology. Canadian Tugboat Company had several large flat decks, which could self-dump but not self-load. They embraced the new technology finally in 1970 when they built *Crown Zellerbach No. 1,* but almost immediately sold the vessel to the newly created Seaspan International who renamed her *Seaspan Harvester.* Kingcome got rid of their sole self-dumper when they disposed of *Haida Carrier* in 1974 when their new self-propelled units came into the fleet.

Swiftsure was wound up around 1992, so the timing was perfect for Brown to take over the towing contract of *Swiftsure Prince* with the newly acquired *Sea Commander.* From that point on the business

grew under the second new name associated with Mr. Brown. Operating now as Sea-Link Marine Services Ltd. based in New Westminster, the fleet grew to five tugs and six barges by the beginning of the new century. This might be described as the Canadian fleet. In addition it also had one tug, *Ocean Wrestler,* and one barge, *Ocean Oregon,* registered in Barbados which could be identified as the international fleet. *Ocean Wrestler* and her barge are employed internationally carrying bulk deck cargoes between Canada and the U.S. with the ability to trade to Central American countries and the Caribbean. The tug is manned by a Canadian crew, but being on an offshore registry, operations can be kept far more flexible by not being subject to Canadian manning rules. It's an interesting innovation that has not been done in this manner by any of the other B.C. towing companies.

Peter Brown, in setting up Union Tug & Barge and Sea-Link Marine Services, brought with him established connections in the forest industries. Additional tugs and barges were acquired, including three ex-Arctic Transportation units, the tugs *Arctic Hooper* and *Arctic Taglu,* and the big barge *Arctic Tuk.* The last named had the ability to load a similar deadweight as *Swiftsure Prince* and the capability of loading large log cargoes, although she was not built as a log barge with the capability of self-dumping. Built in Japan, she still carries the evidence of having been built for pushing by two of the MacKenzie river-type, shallow-draft tugs. She also still carries a conspicuous Arctic navigation tower just aft of the bow which makes her highly recognizable.

Sea-Link has been able to acquire tugs when still in relatively good shape and without too many years under the keel. The exception is the war-built *Sea Commander,* now around 58 years in age and approaching the end of a long towing life, but like her similar and smaller sister *Seaspan Sovereign* they have both enjoyed a satisfactory and profitable life. No doubt both owners will keep them going as long as feasible. I have coupled them both together as looking at them they are very much alike, although *Sea Commander* is about 33 feet longer. As ex-Army tugs they look as though they came off the same drawing board within a year of each other.

[31] **Sea-Link Marine Services:** This New Westminster company is somewhat different to any of it competitors. It goes in for big barges and powerful tugs. Here **Arctic Tuk,** a Japanese-built barge originally a part of the Arctic sealift, is seen travelling light in Johnstone Straits. She can load about 9,000 dwt and has been used extensively to load log cargoes.

[32] **Swiftsure Prince:** A B.C. Ferry passes close astern of Swiftsure Prince and her tug, **Sea Commander,** just outside Tsawwassen Ferry Terminal. The tug is one of three American-built units in the fleet.

[33] **General Jackson:** Originally built in the States, **General Jackson,** ex-**Larain,** shows off her American origins to good effect. She tows almost anything in the fleet with the exception of **Swiftsure Prince.** After having an all light blue funnel, she now has it painted black or a very dark navy blue with a narrow white band right at the very top. The light blue stack was very impressive.

[34] Edith Lovejoy: Another good-looking product from an American shipyard. Oddly enough she sports a white funnel with a narrow black top, which begs a question. Why don't owners adopt a common smokestack and bring in an identifiable naming system? With **Neva Straits** now in the fleet and in a similar size and horse-power range, alternating on jobs for each other, it gets a little confusing for the public to follow.

[35] Neva Straits: In the disposition of ex-Rivtow vessels, **Neva Straits** is the latest addition to the Sea-Link Fleet. After considerable engine room work she has emerged with 1,500 hp. Three other fleet tugs, **Arctic Taglu** and **Arctic Hooper** are pictured in chapter 12, and **Ocean Wrestler** in the last chapter of this book.

Sea-Link prefers big tugs with high horsepower and large barges mostly handling bulk materials. An exception is the *Link 100,* a purpose-built ro-ro barge employed continuously in the Seaspan Intermodal trailer traffic to Vancouver Island.

Recent additions have accrued to the fleet as a result of reorganizations at Rivtow, which appears to be shedding parts of its fleet as it retires from some of its activities. The 87' tug *Neva Straits* has been acquired and will probably be an alternative for *Edith Lovejoy* in towing paper barges from Powell River into Fraser River Terminals in the North Arm. This appears to be another steady traffic for the company.

In addition it has also taken over two ex-Rivtow barges, *Straits Waterskidder* and *Straits Coldecker,* large flat-deck barges with a capacity of about 5,000 tons. Originally built at Burrard Dry Dock for employment in the forest industry, it seems more likely that today they would be about the right size for the aggregates industry.

Rivtow is downsizing as rapidly as it can sell off equipment, much of it of high quality, to younger and perhaps more vigorous companies who are developing strong growth trends. Leading the pack among the acquisitors is Sea-Link, with others like Hodder Tugboat and Gisbourne Marine Services also benefitting. The latter two primarily serve the logging industry, but Sea-Link has a strong interest in a broader range of business. With a substantial interest in large cargo barges it is poised for greater growth and with a reduced dependency on the depressed logging industry the downturns are likely to be less negative than with some of its competitors.

[36] **Outbound Scrap:** A triple tow of barges owned by American scrap salvage dealers in tow of **General Jackson** move several thousand tons of steel scrap south. The barges are **Con-Island 1, ZB 189** and **ZB 198. ZB** are the initials of Zidell Brothers, one of the biggest in the business. The scrap business appears to be an important element in the business of Sea-Link.

THE SEA-LINK FLEET

Tugs

Name and Former Name	Year Built	Dimensions	
Arctic Taglu	1976	110' x 34' x 17'	2,250 bhp
Arctic Hooper	1976	110' x 34' x 17'	2,250 bhp
Edith Lovejoy		68' x 24.3' x 13.3'	1,000 bhp
Blt. USA			
General Jackson	1958	100' x 27' x 12'	1,640 bhp
ex-Larain			
Blt. USA			
Sea Commander	1945	149' x 33' x 19'	3,060 bhp
ex-Seaspan Commander			
ex-Gulf Joan			
Blt. USA			
Neva Straits	1962	87' x 25' x 10'	1,500 bhp

Barges

Name and Former Name	Year Built	Dimensions	
Arctic Tuk	1980	350' x 104' x 20'	Flat-deck using mobile crane for loading 9,000 tdw approx.
Blt. Japan			
BJM No. 1	Not known	200' x 50' x 50'	Camp barge
Link 100	1957	390' x 59' x 16'	Ro-ro barge with auxiliary power 1,857 grt.
ex-Las Plumas	Reblt. 1988		
Blt. USA			Tdw not an issue for a vehicle barge of this type
Sea-Link Rigger	1963	342' x 64' x 19.5'	Sidewalled flat-deck barge 7,500 tdw approx.
ex-Crown Forest No. 4			
Sea-Link Yarder	1957	285' x 60' x 16'	Sidewalled flat-deck barge 5,000 tdw approx.
ex-Crown Forest No. 6			
Swiftsure Prince	1970	346' x 70' x 16'	Log barge, cranes on towers 9,000 tdw approx.
Straits Coldecker	1957	285' x 60' x 16'	Flat-deck barge 5,000 tdw approx.
Straits Waterskidder	1957	285' x 60' x 16'	Flat-deck barge 5,000 tdw approx.

International Fleet

Name and Former Name	Year Built	Dimensions	
Ocean Wrestler	1970	153' x 35' x 19'	4,350 bhp tug
ex-Jacqueline W			
Blt. Belgium			
Ocean Oregon	1975	398' x 80' x 25'	12,000-ton general cargo barge
Blt. USA			

Unless noted, all vessels built in British Columbia.

SALT FROM BLACK WARRIOR LAGOON

Salt from Mexico's Baja Peninsula has been a steady traffic for some forty-odd years. It has been in the hands of several carriers who have tried specialty freighters, tug and barge combinations and currently are using a conventional bulk carrier.

[37] Argyle: The traffic started around 1962 when there was a growing demand for pulp chemicals for the B.C. forest industry. Much of this chemical stock is manufactured from common salt and Hooker Chemicals of New York built a plant in North Vancouver (now Canadian Oxy Chemicals). National Bulk Carriers Inc., owned by U.S. shipping tycoon Daniel K. Ludwig, built the specialty bulk carrier **Argyle** in Japan (Bermuda registry) to commence the traffic and operated her exclusively in the salt trade on a ten-year contract. Of 53,000 tdw, a piece of nautical trivia is that she was built on the same ways at the former Kure Navy yard from which came **Yamato,** name ship of the mightiest class of battleships ever built. By the end of the contract, fully amortized with a suitable return on investment, she went to the scrappers, useless for anything else. Here she is seen discharging onto Vancouver Tug barges in Burrard Inlet.

[38] VT 200, 201 and 202: Vancouver Tug built these three large, flat-deck bulk-carrier barges at Yarrows in 1963 and the latter two in 1967 for the salt trade. At first they were used for local deliveries of salt, ex-Argyle, and as limerock carriers from Blubber Bay, Texada Island. After the Argyle contract expired they were employed in deliveries direct from Black Warrior Lagoon under a new contract which Seaspan gained. Here **VT 201,** built in 1967 with a length of 299 feet and dead weight capacity of 8,000 tons, is seen under construction at Yarrows.

[39] **VT 200** takes salt cargo off **Argyle** at Vancouver, B.C.

[40] **VT 200** delivers salt to chemical plant at Nanaimo, B.C.

[41] VT 200 loads limerock at Blubber Bay for delivery to U.S. cement plants. In the preplanning for the **Argyle,** having her load return shipments of limerock from Texada to the U.S. was actually considered, but dropped as being impractical. The ability of the Vancouver Tug barges to range as far afield as Baja and quickly clean down to load another dry bulk cargo demonstrated the versatility of the barge v. the specialty carrier, on short haul trips.

[42] Seaspan Sovereign, ex-Island Sovereign: The grand old lady of the fleet is still towing limerock barges out of Blubber Bay at almost 60 years of age. In her long life she has done everything including sustaining a sinking followed by salvage by Island Tug around the end of WWII. One of the best performers ever in local fleets her retirement cannot be far off. Here she is seen awaiting her tow at Blubber Bay, Texada Island, in 2001.

Chapter Three

TRANSPACIFIC TOWING AND SALVAGE

owing of a vessel by another vessel goes back to the earliest times and predates the advent of steam by several centuries. One of the most famous pictures of Trafalgar shows Nelson's flagship HMS *Victory,* all three masts shot away and with only a jury-rigged triangular sail aft to assist steerage, being towed into Gibraltar by another ship of the line, the similar HMS *Neptune.* Since time immemorial sailing ships becalmed in the tropics have put crews overside in the ship's boats to tow the ship until such time as a breeze was picked up. At that point, the boat crews were hurriedly recalled and everything was done on board to get the ship under way. This has been a favourite scene in Hollywood films when depicting life afloat in the days of sail.

Steam tugs grew in size and power as sailing ships became bigger, as without tugs they could not be handled in confined waters. All large ports with docking systems needed tugs to service almost all vessel movements, excepting self-powered harbour

[43] **Island Sovereign** gathered all the bouquets as flagship and achiever of towing miracles in the North Pacific, until **Sudbury** came on the scene. Later **Sudbury** was downgraded when **Sudbury II** became flagship of the IT&B fleet.

[44] Maplecove: One of the major achievements of **Island Sovereign** was recovering the broken-down Canadian Pacific cargo liner from south of the Aleutians over the New Year's holidays in 1952–3. The local public followed the progress of the diminutive tug wrestling in the towering 12,000-ton **Maplecove** seen here after safe delivery to Vancouver.

and small craft. Ports like Liverpool, Rotterdam, Montreal, New York and most others around the world had local fleets of tugboats available to help sailing and powered steamers to tow in from the sea or an outer harbour, to dock and undock or to shift berth. It was from these locally owned tugboat fleets that some owners gradually developed a presence as salvors and deep-sea towers using larger and more powerful units.

Using Liverpool as an example the process of shifting berth was a common necessity in readying ships for new voyages. In its heyday it was one of the greatest cargo liner ports of the world with huge locally based fleets. A ship might arrive in from the Orient fully laden to discharge into warehouses on the Liverpool side of the Mersey River and then, as this was often a turnaround port, move across the

river to Birkenhead to load an export cargo. The trip across the river was short and usually no greater a distance than that from North Vancouver to Vancouver.

Liverpool was a typical entrepôt port, meaning one which received imports mostly raw materials and re-exported them in the form of manufactured goods. The majority of ships calling at Liverpool until the early post-war period were coal or oil fired steamers often unloading raw materials like wool, cotton and foodstuffs which they unloaded on the Liverpool side. In port such ships would keep up steam from an auxiliary boiler to provide that needed to power winches, the anchor windlass and run the generators, but after discharge they often moved over to the Birkenhead side to load export cargoes. To make the short cross-river movement did not justify firing up the main boilers to provide sufficient steam to operate the ship's main engine. Therefore tugs would handle the ship as a virtually dead ship from one side of the river to the other, usually with only a partial crew on board. This type of movement alone required tugs of relatively high power and great manoeuvrability in tight dockland situations.

In these cases it was not much of a stretch to have harbour towers moving into seagoing and ocean-going operations. In B.C. developments took a different turn, in that most towing started with the movements of logs and scows with just a small group providing ship towing and berthing.

Between the wars, A.C. Burdick and his brother operated the Pacific Salvage Company using Victoria as their base with vessels like *Salvage King, Salvage Queen* and *Salvor* as the nucleus of their salvage fleet. The Burdick brothers also owned Pacific Dry Dock Company in North Vancouver and a part of their apparent strategy was to have the salvage tug function as an arm of their ship repair business. Maintaining tugs on standby awaiting deep-sea opportunities is a very expensive proposition unless there is other supporting business available to keep the tugs employed. What Burdicks did with their vessels is not clear at this distance in time, although some where employed in towing railcar barges. One such major salvage job stands out. This was the towing in and salvage of the new Victoria-built *Fort Camosun*, following her torpedoing and recovery off Cape Flattery in 1942.

They attended strandings on the West Coast of Vancouver Island and elsewhere until Pacific Salvage became a part of Straits Towing. A partial list of casualties attended by Pacific Salvage and its predecessor B.C. Salvage is follows in this chapter, but no notable pre-WW II transpacific tows of disabled ships are recorded. When they occurred they sometimes went to companies like Foss in Seattle until Island Tug & Barge came on the scene and offered a viable alternative.

The Burdicks sold their shipyard interests to the Wallaces at Burrard Dry Dock Company during the war and it is presumed that the sale of Pacific Salvage to the McKeen interests at Straits Towing followed as soon as it could be arranged. The

Burdick chapter closed with the death of A.C. Burdick in 1951.

Straits Towing kept a salvage tug on station from the Pacific Salvage fleet until the mid-50s, but this arm of the otherwise aggressive Vancouver-based Straits Towing appeared to fade out as Island Tug's interest in ocean towing grew.

As earlier noted, if the First World War gave ocean towing an impetus it was nothing compared to the output of new tugboats during the Second World War. Substantial numbers were built in Canadian and British yards, but a veritable flood came out of the U.S. Maritime Commission shipbuilding programs.

Island Tug's biggest acquisition in this period was the stalwart *Island Sovereign*, a larger boat again and a former U.S. Army vessel which the company had salved as a wreck in Johnstone Straits. Prior to this their flagship had been the large and powerful steam tug *Snohomish*, a former United States government vessel which in 1946 performed possibly the company's first really long-distance ocean tow when *Snohomish* and six war-surplus U.S. Government tugs mounted on a barge, the first *Island Yarder*, were delivered to Buenos Aires. Here *Snohomish* and her barge were sold in what appears to have been a smart and very profitable transaction. No record is available of how the return would have compared to a local sale of the two vessels, but with so many war-surplus diesel tugs available on the Pacific coast one presumes that the Argentinian sale brought a far better return than could have been obtained locally. It was a good example of the quick thinking and adroit moves that Island Tug & Barge demonstrated when Harold Elworthy was at the helm.

Island Tug & Barge was the one B.C. towboat fleet which, with its heroic crews, really earned its laurels as a company capable of competing with the best of the foreign fleets in deep-sea towing. Harold Elworthy had originally started work as an office boy in 1918 at the Victoria office of Pacific Salvage Company and had been fired by Mr. Burdick for making a sensible decision without authority on behalf of his employer. Despite this setback Mr. Burdick was a man who must have thought highly of young Elworthy as their subsequent business lives were to be intertwined after this up to the time that

[45] Mandoil II: Another spectacular rescue job was the recovery of this Greek-owned, New York-managed and Liberian-flagged tanker. Built in Holland in 1958 she was inbound to the Columbia River with about 37,000 tons of Sumatran crude oil on board when she was in collision in fog with another vessel. Fire raged through the ship and she was in serious difficulties when IT&B was engaged on Lloyds' Open Form "No Cure–No Pay" contract. **Sudbury II** was dispatched and *Island Monarch* assisted later in the tow which was finally, after many travails, towed into Muchalet Inlet, near Gold River. This is how she looked from the air when IT&B's crew arrived.

Harold Elworthy took overall control of Island Tug around the end of WW II. When Elworthy started Island Tug & Barge in 1925, he already had a strong interest in the potential for deep-sea towing and salvage which was to last the rest of his active business life.

Island Sovereign had been repaired and rebuilt by Island Tug at their own facility, Point Ellice Shipyard in Victoria. When completed they had the finest tug then available on the B.C. coast. Not only could she tow the largest barges then in use, but she demonstrated her capability as a deep-sea salvage tug when she towed the disabled 11,000 ton dw, Canadian Pacific Steamships *Maplecove* in from the Pacific over Christmas 1952.

The next acquisition was the *Sudbury*, ex-RCN corvette built in 1941 and one of four originally

purchased from Crown Assets Corporation by Straits Towing. From Straits she had passed to Badwater Towing Ltd. Her acquisition by Island Tug & Barge was close to perfect as it was also at about that time that the U.S. Government started the serious process of scaling down its huge fleet of laid-up Liberty ships and surplus U.S. Navy vessels, which included a number of war-built aircraft carriers.

Island Tug tendered for some of these U.S. tows and was the successful bidder for the delivery of 36 Liberty ships, plus some surplus aircraft carriers to Japanese shipbreakers. Between these tows it was also the successful salvor of the periodic disabled vessel, usually a war-built tramp. For a while Sudbury was so fully employed that two additional, more powerful diesel electric tugs were purchased from the Australian government. These two vessels

[46] **Mandoil II:** Once into Muchalet Inlet, the vessel was surrounded by a containment boom and every available tank barge was pressed into service to get her oil cargo off. It had survived the fire intact, the burning oil having come from the ruptured tanks at the point of impact. **Mandoil II** was only ten years old at the time and evidently was repaired and returned to service, for probably another ten years of life.

were originally acquired from the United States by the Australian Government. Their history and description follows later in this chapter. They were big powerful ships built in 1943 and transferred to the Royal Australian Navy. Such large modern diesel electric tugs capable of deep-sea towing and salvage were not previously available in Australia. Their need was anticipated as part of the build-up of the Australian and British war effort against Japan with whom they stood by to handle anticipated casualties to big ships. The British Pacific Fleet was based at Sydney and as the tide of war changed island hopping was to be the order of the day until the final defeat of Japan was secured.

Following the war the two tugs had few prospects and were placed on the disposal list. In 1959

Elworthy acquired *Caledonian Salvor,* which was placed on Canadian registry and renamed *Sudbury II,* and then *Cambrian Salvor,* without renaming, which was registered in the Netherlands Antilles and based in Japan. The latter vessel was actually owned by L. Smit's Internationale Sleepdienst N.V., the large Dutch tugboat company and one of the most famous names in worldwide towing. Both tugs were each owner's contribution to Transpacific Towing & Salvage Ltd., a joint-venture company which was managed by Island Tug from Victoria, B.C.

Smit was a powerful ally for a relative junior in deep-sea towing like Elworthy's Island Tug. Smit adopted its frequent pattern of buying into a joint venture with an equal interest of 50 per cent. This type of relationship was sometime defensive on the part of the smaller concern, when it was apparent that a 50/50 deal was usually better than an outright competition war as even then, back in the '60s, Smit was a powerful concern and bigger than most. Under Harold Elworthy with his well-known propensity for well-timed publicity, Island Tug & Barge actively advertised its services as a deep-sea salvage and towing concern in the worldwide shipping media and by advertising in international shipping media, such as publications published each year by Lloyd's of London, the shipping world could not help but take notice. In every way, it paid to build a strong and reliable reputation with insurance underwriters, marine surveyors, shipowners and concerns like the influential Salvage Association, London, as well as the international Lloyd's Agency system. With Island Tug's main depot being located in Victoria and with that port possessing the largest dry dock on the West

Coast at nearby Esquimalt, it was closer to the open ocean than either Vancouver or Seattle. All of these factors created obvious strategic advantages for Island Tug which it played to the maximum.

As soon as the Second World War ended British, Canadian and U.S. war-built merchant vessels were absorbed into their national privately owned fleets or sold in some instances to allied powers such as Holland, Greece, France, Norway and former enemy, Italy. The United States in a prodigious effort had built 2,700 Liberty ships alone of which about 900 had been released post-war into the American merchant marine or sold to allied powers. Most of this British-, Canadian- and American-built tonnage was to end up in Greek hands, a factor which alone

1. Today most ocean-going shipping seeks the tax-sheltered, more economical benefits of flags of convenience, including most of the most respectable shipowners of the current era.

[47] **Makedonia:** One of the toughest tows undertaken by **Sudbury** concerned the recovery of this Greek steam trampship with broken-down machinery 3,000 miles from Vancouver. Over much of the route the sea and weather conditions were extreme, but the tow reached Prince Rupert 43 days after the tow wire was connected. The press followed the entire event in a manner we seldom see today, but that was helped by Harold Elworthy's instinct for good publicity. The epic of the **Sudbury—Makedonia** tow has been well recorded. After repair she is seen leaving Vancouver with a full load of lumber. A Cates tug bunts the bow of the freighter around. The ship incidentally was the former **Empire Squire**, a British-built wartime equivalent of the Liberty and Park ships.

TRANSPACIFIC TOWING AND SALVAGE

was to create much ocean towing. Some, but not all, Greek owners were notorious for their employment of flags of convenience as tax havens,[1] registration of one-vessel companies and any device by which they could circumvent the usual obligations of ship-owning such as well-maintained ships with good, properly provisioned and qualified crews and a sense of responsibility in their obligations to both cargo owners and their own ships. Some of these flag of convenience vessels would end up in foreign ports far from their home base with crews owed back wages, inadequately fed and with their ships in a deplorable condition.[2]

2. For an account of an abandoned vessel and its auctioning at Vancouver, see the story of the Ioannis Daskalelis, *in* The Maple Leaf Afloat: Volume One, *by this author.*

International unions played their part in tightening up regulations and many countries including Canada and Britain detained ships until deficiencies had been corrected. It was notable that a majority of disabled ships towed in from the Pacific in the post-war period could trace their ownerships back to Greece.

The balance of the Liberty fleet of well over 1,000 vessels, after allowing for war losses, was laid up in several reserve fleets at places like the James River in Virginia, Suisun Bay in California and near Olympia, Washington. Some was temporarily taken out of the laid-up fleet for the Korean War, but deterioration was inevitable as lay-up procedures could not protect the entire vessel so in addition to functional obsolescence, maintaining the fabric of the

[48] **Dahlia:** When the Federal government ordered the new Vancouver dry dock in the late 1960s the construction job went to Japan. As is common with government contracts it was likely specified that the price would include delivery. The builders had the choice of the tug and the job went to Tokyo Marine Services who employed their 12,000-bhp tug *Dahlia* for the job. Here the tow *(see photo #50)* is seen working its way under the Lions Gate bridge. The local tugs in the picture are (l-r) **Lawrence L.** in Lyttle Brothers Towing colours before she went to North Arm Transportation, the first Seaspan **Venture** and **Charles H. Cates IV.**

[49] **Wave:** This Cypriot-registered bulk carrier is seen entering Vancouver harbour in 1995. She had suffered a broken tail shaft and is headed for the Vancouver dry dock. **Seaspan Commodore,** which picked up the freighter out in the North Pacific, heads the tow, while **Seaspan Hawk** takes the tail end to assist steerage of the big ship. Running alongside are **Seaspan Falcon** and an unidentified Cates vessel.

building itself into the world's second-largest economy.

Island Tug was in the right position at the right time and had already established its reputation with such activities as the successful tow to Buenos Aires. Island Tug's excellent reputation was well established by the time the tows of Maracaibo tankers took place and insurance underwriters at Lloyds readily accepted the risks. What is not commonly known is that the first Venezuelan tow of four vessels was followed by a further tow of three more tankers from Maracaibo which brought Elworthy's acquisitions from this source up to seven ships. The first of the two tows was a world record in towing history an unprecedented multiple for such a long distance.

An interim layover site was developed in Saanich Inlet by Island Tug where Liberty ships could be held and prepared for transpacific towing. In the new venture with the Dutch, the original *Sudbury* was used for towing the vessels from Suisun Bay and Olympia to Saanich Inlet. There they were readied for the big tow outwards to Japan, by one or other of the two bigger tugs.

Descriptions of some of these tows undertaken by Captains Harley Blagbourne, Hill Wilson and Frank Culbard, among others, are contained in the excellent book *High Seas, High Risk* by Pat Wastell Norris. Ms Norris successfully conveys in her writing much of the excitement and atmosphere which existed aboard the *Sudbury* and *Sudbury II.*

Island Tug had the ability to fully employ its two deep-sea salvage vessels between ocean towing assignments. They were in the lead at that time with log barges and developed the first self-dumpers from some of the tanker hulls they had towed up from

laid-up ships represented millions of dollars in annual costs. A program of fleet reduction was commenced in the mid-fifties and while many vessels went to breakup yards on the U.S. East and Gulf coasts, the West Coast fleets were to a great extent denuded by sales to Japan, by now recovering rapidly from its Second World War defeat and

Venezuela. The two tugs could be kept moving in paying work, a very important factor in tugboat economics, and apparently this was the case right up to the merger with Vancouver Tug Boat Company out of which grew Seaspan.

None of the other B.C.-based tugboat companies developed anything like the same presence in deep-sea or international towing, although they did own some powerful tugs and were fully capable of taking on extensive tows. Vancouver Tug Boat's involvement in major tows of rocksalt from Black Warrior Lagoon in Mexico and deliveries of steel to Hawaii were two such examples and Straits Towing's acquisition of *Superior Straits* and her delivery to Vancouver towing a second-hand ferry was another. But these were in the nature of regular towing or the cheapest way in which the operator could get a newly acquired second-hand tug on station. Gulf of Georgia Towing Co. towed some U.S. Navy surplus vessels from the Gulf of Mexico to the Orient for scrapping using their newly refurbished *Gulf Joan* while awaiting another assignment for which they had contracted. Another example was Great West Towing's delivery trip of its new tug *Ocean Master* from its Dutch building yard. The company needed a deep-sea master so engaged Captain Art Gallant, a well-known wartime captain in Park Steamship Company vessels, who took his new charge on a voyage to Japan towing war surplus vessels. Many of these "odd job" tows were arranged through brokers in the London and New York charter markets.

There was a period in the 1960s and 1970s when North Sea oil exploration was at its most active. As a result a pronounced shortage of anchor handling and supply vessels developed on a worldwide basis, but

[50] Since installation of the new Vancouver Dry Dock, a great many vessels have used its facility. Here **Wave** is manoeuvered in the vicinity of the dry dock seen in the upper part of the photo. **Seaspan Chinook**, now retired from the fleet, can be seen alongside the wharf. **Seaspan Falcon** tends the bow, while **Seaspan Hawk** can be seen tending the stern as they swing the big ship.

particularly in the North Sea with its need for more rugged vessels than many of those on offer which had been built for tropical service in any event. Straits Towing took advantage of this and sent their new *Gibraltar Straits* over there for employment and others followed.

PACIFIC SALVAGE COMPANY AND ITS ACHIEVEMENTS

The author is indebted to Captain R.A. Fulton for the use of his notes on Pacific Salvage Co. Ltd. and its predecessor, British Columbia Salvage Company Ltd. While not to any great extent a participant in "Offshore and Overseas Operations," the work area did extend to the Washington coast and even to California on occasion. The corporate history and salvage record is included here as it was effectively the predecessor of Island Tug & Barge Ltd. whose deep-sea towing and salvage feats are very legitimately a part of this book.

Arthur Charleton Burdick was one of five children born in Ontario in 1875. He died in Victoria in 1951 at age 76 as one of the giants of the first half of the 20th century in the B.C. marine industries.

The Burdick family moved west to Calgary around 1885. Young "A.C." as he became generally known, worked in the local Hudson's Bay Company store for some six years and then moved to Kaslo, B.C., where he opened a clothing store to serve the Kootenay Lake country which was then the centre of much mining activity.

In 1905 he and his brother Newton Burdick moved to Victoria, B.C., where they set up a real estate and financial management company with a Mr. Green, under the name Green & Burdick Brothers. Captain Fulton does not confirm this, but it is suggested that Mr. Green might have been Morris Green who founded Capital City Iron, a ship breaking and scrap business that is still active in modern form at its original site in Victoria's inner harbour.

The marine activities of the Burdick brothers started soon after 1905 by participation in a number of companies including B.C. Salvage Company, a firm connected to the Bullen brothers who operated the shipyard and government graving dock in Esquimalt which later became Yarrows Ltd. The company became Pacific Salvage Company Ltd. in 1916 probably after the Burdicks assumed full control. Harold Elworthy joined Pacific Salvage as office boy later rising to office manager. In 1925 Elworthy struck out for himself, founding Island Tug & Barge Ltd. with one vessel in each category of the corporate name. While Elworthy is reputed to have been fired by A.C. Burdick for taking a sensible decision without proper authority it is also noted in Fulton's notes that Elworthy was assisted by Burdick in starting up his own company. Elworthy was able to buy out the far larger Gardner Towing in 1926 and it follows that

Burdick might have been the source of financial backing although this has never been so stated.

All along Burdick also owned Dominion Tug & Barge Ltd. which he operated as a general towing business. The connection between the Burdick brothers and Harold Elworthy remained strong over the years, although what is not generally remembered is that A.C. Burdick maintained what amounted to a controlling interest in Island Tug until Elworthy left to join Senator S.S. McKeen in setting up Straits Towing. What might have brought about the separation of Elworthy from Burdick could have arisen because Burdick from being a backer of Elworthy, probably became an obstacle to Elworthy's further growth. As is generally known, when the opportunity came in the mid-1940s for Elworthy to acquire control of Island Tug & Barge, he seized it and moved back to Victoria to make Island Tug a household name with an international reputation.

A.C. Burdick eventually moved his main business to North Vancouver to a site a little to the west of the Burrard Dry Dock Company and the foot of Lonsdale Avenue. When WW II came and the Canadian Government instituted its plans for building North Sands freighters, this site was expanded and a full-blown shipyard, building 10,000 ton ships of this type, commenced business as Pacific Dry Dock Company. PDD was sold soon after to Burrard Dry Dock Company and its name changed to North Van Ship Repairs Ltd. Its production was coordinated with Burrard and its two yards and Burrard's interest in Yarrows, Victoria, to make the largest block of wartime shipbuilding capacity in Canadian history.

In 1948 Pacific Salvage was sold to the McKeen interests at Straits Towing Ltd. and continued operations as a division of Straits, but its new owners gradually wound it down as a viable salvage entity as

Elworthy's Island Tug grew in prominence as the Victoria-based salvage and deep-sea tower serving the North Pacific. Straits however, had an efficient salvage division for many years, headed by George Unwin, which was closely geared to its own needs as a coastal towing company. Unwin enjoyed a reputation as a salvor that was second to none with the marine insurance underwriters and to know that Unwin was in charge of a salvage operation generated confidence.

The list of the bigger, successful and unsuccessful salvage operations undertaken by Pacific Salvage and its predecessor, B.C. Salvage, as assembled by Captain Fulton, is as follows:

1906: *Valencia,* American steam passenger ship on passage from San Francisco for Seattle, missed the entrance to the Strait of Juan de Fuca in bitterly cold January fog and rain and hit the rocks, 10 miles east of Cape Beale. The vessel started to break up immediately. Some 24 men made it ashore and left the wreck site. 124 people took to the rigging and died of exposure overnight. Rescue vessels including the tug *Czar* and the steamships *Queen* and *City of Topeka* could not approach on account of the heavy breakers and could only stand by waiting for an improvement in the weather. The next day with a moderation in the weather, the whaler *Orion* was able to go alongside the wreck and reported no survivors.

1907: *Indravelli,* 5806/1897, owned by Indra Line Ltd. (T.B. Royden & Co., Managers), Liverpool, England, struck Kellet Bluff, Haro Strait, in fog, November 13, while travelling at speed. Refloated by tug *Pioneer* and B.C. Salvage steamer *Salvor.* Removed to Vancouver and repaired there.

1909: *Princess May,* Canadian Pacific passenger steamer, August 5, struck Sentinel Island in fog. Vessel carried onto the reef with such force that at low tide she was high and dry. American wrecking steamer *Santa Cruz,* with B.C. Salvage tug *William Joliffe,* refloated the stranded vessel a month later with heavy hull damage. She was repaired and returned to C.P. service.

1911: *Sechelt,* March 21, a small excursion passenger ship owned by H. Whittaker of Sechelt, was wrecked at Beecher Bay, Vancouver Island. B.C. Salvage tug *William Joliffe* stood by but could do nothing. Twenty passengers lost.

1911: *Iroquois,* April 10. Passenger vessel in a virtual repeat of the *Sechelt* was lost off Sidney, Vancouver Island. *William Joliffe* stood by helpless.

1911: *Tees,* November, Canadian Pacific coastal steamer struck rock in Kyuquot Sound and feared a total loss. Refloated by B.C. Salvage vessels and U.S. tug *Tahoma.*

1912: *Cottage City,* January 26, American passenger ship ashore near Cape Mudge, opposite Campbell River. Passengers removed to Campbell River. Ship became a total loss after mail and baggage returned to Seattle in U.S. government tug *Snohomish.*

1912: *Tees,* Canadian Pacific coastal passenger freighter, stranded at Gowland Island, Toquart Bay, Barclay Sound. B.C. Salvage Company's *William Joliffe,* U.S. cutter *Tahoma* and Canadian tug *Lorne* refloated the stranded vessel the next day.

1912: *Carrier Dove,* U.S. fishing schooner stranded at Cinque Islands, Discovery Pass. Salvaged by *Salvor,* but off Nanaimo while the schooner was under tow they were caught in bad weather. *Carrier Dove* broke away and sank with much salvage gear on board.

In 1916, B.C. Salvage went into liquidation and was reorganized as Pacific Salvage Company with A.C. Burdick as managing director. The other directors were H.F. and W.F. Bullen, G.G. Bushby and Captain J.W. Troup.

1916: *Bear:* U.S. passenger steamer enroute from Portland, Ore., to San Francisco, struck rock near Cape Mendocino, Cal. There was some loss of life but most people were taken off. *Salvor* attempted salvage without success and the *Bear* became a total loss.

1916: *Congress:* U.S. passenger steamer caught fire off Crescent City, Cal. Passengers taken off. *Salvor* approached but could do nothing in face of the intense heat. Fire in upperworks burned itself out and *Congress* made for Seattle under own power with tug escort.

1917: *Prince Rupert*: Sept 28. The Canadian National coastal passenger liner struck a rock at Swanson Bay and sank. In what was one of Pacific Salvage Company's most memorable salvage jobs, divers George Unwin and Albert Smith over a period of several weeks constructed a coffer dam over the vessel. *Prince Rupert* was pumped out, raised, removed to Victoria, repaired and returned to service.

1918: *Canada Maru*: Japanese steamer, aground on reef near Cape Flattery, successfully refloated by *Salvor*. After this *Salvor* sold by Pacific Salvage. As temporary replacement took *Tees,* on charter from Canadian Pacific. Renamed *Salvage Queen*.

1921: *Canadian Exporter*: Grounded in Willapa Bay, Wash. U.S. tug *Wallula* and Pacific Salvage *Algerine* attended, but the freighter broke her back and became a total loss.

1923: *Czar:* Vancouver-based tug struck rock in Smith Inlet. After being raised and pumped out by unnamed steam tug, the rescuer developed boiler problems and became disabled. *Czar* was able to restart her engine and in an unusual reversal of roles, towed her rescuer back to Vancouver.

1924: *Tatjana:* 5329/1920, owned by A/S Den Norske Rusland Linje, Winge & Co., Mgrs. Oslo, Norway. Vessel struck Village Island, Barclay Sound, crew of 24 rescued, total loss, abandoned following unsuccessful salvage attempts by Pacific Salvage vessels *Salvage Chief* and *Burrard Chief.*

1925: *William Joliffe:* while attempting to help tug *Cape Scott* recover two Davis rafts after the latter's towline broke, *William Joliffe* drifted onto reef near Merry Island, Sunshine Coast. Impaled on a rock she eventually broke her back after salvage and all other gear had been removed.

1925: *Eemdyk:* Holland-Amerika line freighter stranded near Race Rocks, tug *Hope* conveying 28 longshoremen collided with *Salvage Queen* and seven men were lost.

1926: *Tex:* ex-U.S. submarine chaser, employed as a tug sank in Howe Sound in 600 feet of water. Captain E.B. Clarke, chief surveyor at the Vancouver office of the Board of Marine Underwriters of San Francisco, representing marine underwriters, was suspicious of the circumstances. Pacific Salvage derrick scow *Skookum Two,* raised the vessel and found everything intact with seacocks open.

1927: *Catala:* Union Steamship coastal passenger ship, crashed into Sparrowhawk Reef near Port Simpson in fog. *Lorne, Salvage Princess* and *Cape Scott* tried to free her without success. A total loss was feared, but weather remained moderate and she was freed a month later and returned to service after repair.

1929: *Empress of Canada:* Canadian Pacific transpacific liner, went aground in fog near Race Rocks. *Salvage King* and other vessels freed her with damage sustained to the liner.

1931: *Guldborg:* Danish freighter owned by D/S A/S Dannebrog, C.K. Hansen, managers, Copenhagen, ran aground outside Nanoose Bay when proceeding inwards to load lumber at the Straits Lumber Company dock. She was freed by *Salvage King* with considerable bottom damage, repaired and returned to service as *Hoegh Trader.*

1942: *Fort Camosun:* June 20, this Canadian-built, British-flagged freighter was torpedoed outside Cape Flattery by a Japanese submarine, but remained afloat saved by her full lumber cargo. *Salvage King* and other vessels managed to get her into Esquimalt where she was repaired and returned to sea.

Through the thirties the volume of distressed vessels reduced with better technology and navigational aids. Mr. Burdick continued to operate his Dominion Tug & Barge though the war as a general towing company with some salvage capability.

In 1948, Pacific Salvage was sold to Straits Towing, Burdick having by then sold off everything that was of a marine nature. Among vessels he had sold *Dola* to Captain Ted Wilson and thus Dola Towing Ltd. came in being.

Arthur Burdick died in 1951 at 79 and the Burdick empire was no more.

[53] **Salvor:** Seen at Victoria in 1953 when Pacific Salvage still had a station there although owned by Straits Towing. By that time, Island Tug & Barge was making a name for itself and Straits eventually retired its Victoria-based salvage arm. **Salvor** was a sister of **Seaspan Chinook.**

[51] A famous old ship, the former H.M.S. **Algerine,** rests at the Pacific Salvage dock in Victoria Harbour. Acquired from the Royal Navy by B.C. Salvage, Pacific Salvage's predecessor, when she had already had years of service on the coast, she combined the charm of old sailing ships with her clipper stem, her warship past with her plated-in gun ports and the salvage steamer with her heavy-duty derricks aft.

[52] One of **Algerine**'s biggest jobs was raising the C.N. coastal liner **Prince Rupert** from the bottom of Swanson Bay. This was the site of one of the coast's earliest pulp mills and was a port of call for shipping. The Canadian National ship hit a rock and sank. In the picture her forward funnel and part of her upper works can be seen. B.C. Salvage built a cofferdam around the ship to raise her.

HMCS SUDBURY

*In memory of the fighting corvette
that became a famous tug*

Winston Churchill, the foremost Briton of the twentieth century, had a great sense of history. He had a habit of naming some of the most successful weapons or military formations of the Second World War. The well-known British assault troops, the Commandos, took their name from Churchill's brush with Boer Kommandos during the Boer War. The Kommandos were Dutch farmers who operated in quasi-military formations carrying on a guerilla war against the British.

Being also a great romanticist, he conjured up the names frigate and corvette from vessel types of the sailing navy era, even though there was no connection between the modern vessel and its predecessor of the same name.

Churchill gave the name "corvette" to this new class of escort/anti-submarine vessel when it first came out and joined the Royal Navy in April 1940. It was based on a design for a whalecatcher, the *Southern Pride* of 1935, which was completed in

Middlesborough at Smith's Dock Company. The plan of the corvette had dimensions of 205' x 33' by a draught of 15'. She displaced 1,200 tons, and was driven by a quadruple expansion reciprocating engine delivering 2,750 hp. She had a range of 4,000 miles at her economical speed of 12 knots but could reach 16 knots when required. The corvette had great manoeuvrability and the U-boat commanders quickly learned that they were escort vessels to be respected.

The whalecatcher design selected early in the war, anticipated the need for more anti-submarine vessels as German U-boat strength increased dramatically. The navy had been building a vessel type it called the sloop, a light escort vessel similar to some types of minesweepers and relatively more expensive and sophisticated than the corvette design. The corvette was to be a vessel that could be quickly built in lesser merchant shipbuilding yards that were not already engaged in naval work. It was deemed a better emergency proposition compared to the sloop.

The whalecatcher was a tough little ship designed to operate in all weathers. The type was not unknown on the B.C. coast having first made its appearance in

[54] Sudbury: There was a great affection for this former corvette, which had already put thousands of miles in war service under her keel before becoming flagship of Island Tug & Barge for a few brief years. The photo shows her soon after coming into service.

[55] Sudbury. In this shot **Sudbury** is getting into position to add her strength to that of **Sudbury II** in assisting this fully loaded, but grounded, Greek Liberty ship off the mud. From what can be faintly seen the grounding appears to have taken place in the region of the Sandheads.

the local whaling industry around the end of the nineteenth century. The operations of Consolidated Whaling Corporation and its predecessors through to the last operator, Western Canada Whaling, were described in some detail in the book *Boomsticks & Towlines* in this series. All whalecatchers were built with considerable towing capability as they had to be capable of towing dead whales alongside at a fair speed and over considerable distances in order to deliver their catch to the whaling mother ship. Some years after the *Sudbury* came to this coast as a working tugboat, some of the more powerful former whalecatchers were also converted to tugs with excellent results. (see *Pacific Challenge* and *Samarinda*)

Sudbury was built by Kingston Shipbuilding Company at Kingston, Ontario, being launched May 31, 1941. She was in commission as an RCN unit from October 15, 1941, until May 28, 1945, but did not become a tugboat until 1949. Immediately

following the war, there was little further work for the 300 corvettes built in more or less equal numbers in British and Canadian shipyards. Of these 34 became war losses and a few passed to foreign navies after the war, but the vast majority went to the scrapyard. *Sudbury* was acquired from Crown Assets Disposal Corporation by Straits Towing, but after minimal conversion work, Straits and *Sudbury* soon parted company. The vessel was turned over to Badwater Towing, a subsidiary of Pacific Mills Company, employed in towing Davis rafts from the Queen Charlottes destined for the Ocean Falls mill.

By the 1950s, log barging was coming into vogue with Powell River, Straits, Crown Zellerbach and Island Tug all employing earlier versions of the post-WW II log barge. They lacked the self-loading and -dumping feature which was still about a full ten years away. Gradually the Davis rafts were phased out and *Sudbury* became surplus to her owner's

[56] **Sudbury** brings in the disabled Greek Liberty ship **Andros Legend.**

needs. Harold Elworthy acquired the vessel and further converted and adapted her to become a deep-sea salvage tug. She thus became a consort of *Island Sovereign*, the slightly smaller flagship of the Island Tug fleet.

Notable vessels often make their way through multiple ownerships and a long life without change of name. In the history of B.C. tugboats, *Lorne, Sea Lion, Active, Georgia Transporter* and *Sudbury* are examples and there are others. If there is a reason for this, considering the many name changes of other vessels, it may be that they have some claim to being unique either in the minds of their owners or in the

esteem in which they are held by the public. Certainly a number of the older tugs became public icons in their own right and were held to be able to do almost anything in the popular press of the day.

Sudbury was acquired by Island Tug & Barge, and after a major refit at the Point Ellice shipyard, emerged fully fitted for ocean service, but still propelled by her original steam reciprocating machinery and boilers. Great tugboat that she turned out to be, she was the only vessel in the entire fleet of wartime corvettes to be converted to this purpose, although some were converted to whalecatchers under foreign flags. *Sudbury* became the flagship ocean tug for Island Tug, undertaking a number of rescues and transpacific tows. She was the major tower in bringing the seven Maracaibo tankers up from Venezuela to Victoria. *Island Sovereign* generally reverted to the secondary position when the two were working together.

As Island Tug became more involved in the removal of surplus American hulls to Japan, the company acquired the vessel that became *Sudbury II* and entered into a joint venture with Smit International. Their story follows, but the net effect of this was to reduce the original *Sudbury* to a secondary role in which she delivered surplus U.S. Liberty Ships from Suisun Bay in California and the Olympia, Washington, reserve fleets to Saanich Inlet where a temporary anchorage was laid out by Island Tug and tows made up, ready for the two transpacific tugs.

Eventually her usefulness came to an end. Natural deterioration, her steam power, higher manning costs and the increasing expense of her bunker fuel hastened the end and she was disposed of for scrap at Victoria in 1967 after a good life of 26 years. Her career had been a notable one, serving originally on the East Coast–Guantanamo Bay convoy run. She was never credited with killing any enemy submarines, unlike a number of her sisters that were mostly engaged in the transatlantic run. As the biggest unit for some years in Victoria-based Island Tug & Barge, she built up her own following of admirers and media functionaries who followed her career knowing that every so often she would add drama to the news.

Her name will always be associated with Captain Harley Blagbourne who was her principal master when not otherwise relieved and under him her feats became legendary. Like any great vessel her memory lives on and will continue for a longer period than she saw active service.

[57] **Glafkos:** The former Canadian-built Park ship **Algonquin Park** was succesfully refloated by **Sudbury** in 1962 after running on rocks near Amphitrite Point, Vancouver Island. Island Tug took the damaged freighter into Victoria's Inner Harbour for stripping by Capital City Iron and then towed the hull to Seattle for final scrapping.

CALEDONIAN SALVOR AND CAMBRIAN SALVOR
—AMERICAN-BUILT, AUSTRALIAN-OWNED TUGS—
AND THE B.C. CONNECTION

The War in the Far East and South East Asia hit the Allies with near lighting speed. The attack on Pearl Harbor took place December 7, 1941. Three days later on December 10, Japanese torpedo planes sank the new British battleship *Prince of Wales,* and the older, more lightly armoured battlecruiser *Repulse,* off the east coast of Malaya, a huge distance from Hawaii. The Japanese invasion spread like the tentacles of an octopus. Hong Kong surrendered, December 25, 1941; the Japanese captured Rabaul in the Solomons, January 23, 1942. Manila fell and Singapore finally surrendered, February 15, 1942. The first Japanese air raids on Port Moresby occured February 3, and on Port Darwin February 19, 1942. Going against the trend of rapid collapse, Corregidor surrendered as late as May 6, 1942.

As the ramparts of old empires collapsed, the myths of the invincibility of Singapore and Corregidor were shattered and the Japanese Empire's advance finally came to rest at the gates of India, in the Aleutians, outside Port Moresby in New Guinea and at Guadalcanal Island in the Solomons. These were the broad extremities of the Japanese advances, reached despite the fact that Japanese lines of supply and communication had been stretched to their maximum. During 1942 they stretched to the furthest extent of their penetration when Japanese carrier planes bombed Colombo and Trincomalee, Ceylon and sank merchant shipping and Allied warships alike in the Bay of Bengal.

The process of hammering back the prongs of the attack started almost immediately and certainly as soon as defensive forces had the strength to go over to the attack. The battle of Guadalcanal was a bloody affair, which proved that U.S. forces could fight a successful amphibious offensive war. The turning back of the Japanese by the Australians in the Owen Stanley range of New Guinea was a relentless campaign against natural conditions, as much as the enemy. It was much the same in Burma and Northwest India which was fought by British and Indian units using guerilla tactics supported by

relentless air support to get at Japanese targets. In Burma, the Japanese did not have the support of their naval carriers, as they did elsewhere, and were forced to fight along similar lines to the British, guerilla style with only skimpy air support. They became a prime target of the RAF who soon had command of the skies.

It was with all this as a background that the Commonwealth Marine Salvage Board came into being in March 1942. Australia had tugboats for both towing and salvage purposes but they were geared to peacetime needs. They were therefore wholly inadequate for the needs of a war. Already there had been some shipping casualties within the broad spectrum of Australian and New Zealand waters because of the attacks of commerce raiders. The only two vessels it had available for salvage purposes were *St. Giles,* a WW I Saint-class Admiralty tug that had several sisters in British Columbia and *Tambar,* a small former coastal steamer.

As the Japanese worked their way south, intensified attacks on shipping were expected, but there was also another consideration which showed signs of taking effect early in 1942. With General Douglas McArthur out of the Philippines and with his appointment as Allied Commander-in-Chief, there was every expectation that the roll-back of Japan would soon start in earnest. The Commonwealth Marine Salvage Board saw an increasing role for itself as previously occupied areas were recovered and this was born out by the events that took place to the north of Australia.

To rectify the shortage of tugs, Australia turned to the United States, which was already building several classes of deep-sea salvage tugs. Australia was still at that time a self-governing dominion and like Canada its ships were all carried on the register as British ships. Five vessels allocated to Britain under Lend-Lease were diverted to Australia. These were in two groups, two larger tugs, designated ARS-class salvage tugs and three smaller tugs, designated ATA-class tugs, by the Americans. With the two existing vessels named above this gave the Commonwealth Marine Salvage Board a fleet of seven vessels for its purposes.

The three ATA tugs were named *Reserve,*

[58] Sudbury II, ex-Caledonian Salvor: The second of a busy and successful trio. Judging by the white band on the red and black funnel this photo was taken soon after the merger that became Seaspan in 1970.

Sprightly and *Tancred* and were of the same class as *Haida Chieftain*, ex-*N.R. Lang*. However, they do not need to concern us further as it was the two larger tugs that are at the centre of this story. Designated *BARS. 1* and *BARS. 2* in accordance with the US Navy standard classification system, by which ARS indicated a salvage vessel and the B indicated allocation to Britain under Lend-Lease. The two ships were completed as *Caledonian Salvor* and *Cambrian Salvor*. The name "Salvor" was a British system of nomenclature used for its Admiralty salvage tugs and the choice of name in each case was to honour the Scottish and Welsh backgrounds of the first chair of the salvage board, Judge Clyne and the head of salvage operations, Captain John Williams.

The two tugs were part of a group of 24 sister vessels built by the Basalt Rock Company shipyard at Crescent City, California. For their day they were among the biggest and most powerful tugs. They had a length overall of 213' 9" and beam of 39'. They were of 1,750 gross tons and were powered by a diesel electric combination, consisting of four Cooper-Bessemer, 4-stroke, single-acting diesels of 900 hp each. These were coupled to four 610-Kw, 300-volt generators supplying power to four, 760-shp electro-motors, two to a shaft to give a total horsepower of 3,000 shp. They have been described in other writings as being British designed, but it is virtually certain that this was not true. Everything

about them was typically American and was to a superior specification throughout.

As operated by the USN this class was manned by seven officers and 86 men, The Australians got by with a total crew of 45. However, when taking delivery of the vessels, the negative reputation of Australian maritime unions came to the fore. Despite the peril presented by the Japanese forces on their country's doorstep, there was trouble with crews sent to take delivery of the ships. Three men went missing on arrival in the U.S. and were returned as distressed British seamen and there was trouble with a large part of a crew when one of the vessels reached Tahiti.

Despite breaking in new vessels and crews, the Commonwealth Marine Salvage Board operated with considerable success. Tugs attended on a wide range of vessels from simple strandings to some complex raising jobs of sunken and capsized vessels. About 140 incidents representing 600,000 gross tons of merchant shipping were dealt with in addition to some 60 incidents involving naval vessels.

The war ended in August 1945 and a return to normality followed at a surprising pace, once the Japanese forces had surrendered or withdrawn. The first vessel to go into lay-up was *Caledonian Salvor*, at Sydney, NSW, in September 1945. *Cambrian Salvor* joined her in 1946.

In 1948 they evidently passed to the Royal Australian Navy, but were placed on the disposal list in the late 1950s. Apparently some sort of a deal was made, but never actually completed to sell the two tugs to an Indonesian named Kimodo. This man was fronting for a Philippine/Hong Kong company called Pacific Tug & Salvage Ltd., but its arrangements appeared shaky. The Hong Kong firm of Anderson & Ashe Ltd. appeared to be the focal point of a consortium which had managed to gain some support from the two major Hong Kong towing and salvage concerns, operated by John Manners & Co. and Moller's Hong Kong Towage & Salvage Co. Ltd. and the Bradman Corporation of Manila. These were the backers of Pacific Tug & Salvage Ltd. but some sort of disagreement seems to have developed after Pacific Tug advertised its two acquisitions as being stationed at Yokohama and Manila to service their respective areas, which effectively meant that they would be competing with Manners and Moller. The consortium fell apart and the purchases were cancelled before completion.

In 1958, Harold Elworthy at Island Tug & Barge in Victoria made an offer for the two ships, which was accepted. *Caledonian Salvor* was renamed *Sudbury II* and registered at Suva, Fiji. Without change of name, *Cambrian Salvor* was transferred to the Costa Rican flag, but remained on station at Yokohama. It appears that Island Tug's strategy was that by having tugs of equal capability on both side of the Pacific they would be able to develop a strong hold on transpacific tows as well as to Alaska and down into the States.

This strategy was born out in the Eastern Pacific in that the Victoria location was excellently sited to be the kick-off point when towing redundant warships and Liberties to Japan, although there was no return traffic of any consequence. There were some pipe-laden barge tows from Japan to the North slope and the memorable delivery of the Chilean battleship *Almirante Latorre* to Japan, which *Cambrian Salvor* handled, but generallty she was underemployed. The Hong Kong and Manila competition resented her presence and it might have been an error on the part of Island Tug to appoint as their Japanese agents, the same company that represented Smit International. The agents probably saw to it that with Smit being their most important principal, they

got first choice of any plum jobs that came along.

Island Tug had no infill work for *Cambrian Salvor,* which because of its foreign flag could not be employed on the B.C. coast. At least in Victoria it had its big barges moving logs and limerock to which its Canadian tugs could turn for employment when needed. As noted in the previous section, the original *Sudbury* reverted to handling tows on the coast, including the movement of surplus Liberties up to the anchorage at Saanich Inlet where they were prepared for the delivery trip to Japan. Smit wanted to get in on this traffic and Island Tug needed to contain them as they were even then a formidable potential foe and also a strong ally where one was needed.

The end result was that Island Tug and L. Smit International formed a joint venture in 1961, in the name of Transpacific Towing & Salvage with each providing $90,000 for working capital. Smit acquired the *Cambrian Salvor,* which became their contribution to the joint venture. In 1962 she was transferred to the Netherlands Antilles register, the Dutch flag of convenience for Dutch shipping, and was renamed *Caribische Sea,* following a major refit.

Joint ventures often tend to make for uneasy bedfellows. They are a little like a marriage when one partner wonders what the other is up to. The best of transpacific towing was likely coming to an end by then. In 1963 Smit sold their tug to Collins Submarine Pipelines of London, England, and the joint venture was effectively over. After several changes of ownership she was hulked at Abadan and at final report was laid up at Khorramshahr, Iran.

In 1965 Island Tug moved the registry of *Sudbury II* to Victoria and in 1970 she became a unit of the joint fleet, without renaming, when Island Tug and Vancouver Tug merged to become Seaspan International. In 1979 she went into layup and was placed on the market for disposal. She was acquired in that year by Doug Logan of Seattle for conversion to a fish processing vessel, Soon after, she caught fire and became a total loss.

I am indebted to Allan D. Cornes of Williamstown, Victoria, Australia, for supplying notes that enabled me to complete this section. The original notes are indexed in the bibliography.

[59] **Cambrian Salvor** does not appear to have been as often photographed as her Canadian sister. Here she sports the Island Tug colours, but other photos show her with a yellow funnel.

[60] **Cambrian Salvor** is seen here with the Chilean battleship **Almirante Latorre, ex-HMS Canada.** Naval historians will remember that Canada was present at the battle of Jutland in 1916, when the massed British and German fleets locked horns in what is recognized as the greatest naval battle in history in terms of the huge fleets that were ranged against each other. It was the last major naval battle before the advent of the aircraft carrier as the prime ship of war. At 11,000 miles this was the longest tow ever undertaken by Island Tug in its great years of transpacific towing.

[61] Surplus Liberty Ships: A tow is readied for Japan. Here the s.s. **Henderson Luelling** (*right hand vessel*) and another unidentified Liberty are positioned for the tow by one of the two sisters.

[62] Triton: A nasty collision occurred outside Nanaimo harbour between the Greek Liberty ship **Triton** and the passing Alaska-bound passenger ship **Baranoff** in heavy fog. The Alaska vessel was owned by Alaska Steamship Lines and was assisted by local tugs into Vancouver with a massive gash in her side ahead of the bridge. **Island Sovereign** and **Lloyd B. Gore** assisted **Triton** into Esquimalt for drydocking.

[63] Clearton: Minor strandings and mishaps occurred of which there is now little record. Here **Sudbury II** stands by this British steamer after a mishap while another IT&B tug heads the tow.

[64] Salvaging One's Own: Bulkcarrier barge **Seaspan 240,** ex-**Island Importer,** was raised after a capsize and placed back in service. She is usually employed in the limerock service from Blubber Bay.

[65] Queen of Alberni: After an unfortunate grounding and partial sinking in the west end of Active Pass. One life only was lost and that was an unfortunate horse in a trailer that was crushed. The ship was refloated, repaired and to some extent was remodelled.

[66] Sundancer: One of the more spectacular strandings was that of the former Baltic ferry after her partial conversion to a cruise liner by Seattle interests. She hit a rock near Campbell River in 1989 and was taken into the Elk Falls mill dock where she sank by the stern, but all passengers and crew were saved. Here she sits at the mill dock a considerable embarrassment to the owners of the mill.

[67] Sundancer: Eventually raised after some weeks, she was taken to Vancouver by Seaspan tugs and is seen here coming through the First Narrows with **Seaspan Monarch** leading the way, heading for the Vancouver Shipyards floating dock.

[68] Sundancer: She made a strange sight with her oil-stained flanks visible from a distance. Her owners disposed of her on an "as is" basis to Greek owners. After doing only what was needed to make her safe for towing, the Greeks had her towed to Greece for repairs and rebuilding.

LOG OF ISLAND TUG & BARGE DEEP-SEA TOWS

Some readers will be familiar with the publications mentioned as follows, but it was felt important to set this out for the record. The best available public record of the earlier post-war transpacific rescues and tows is contained in the Island Tug & Barge publication Ocean Highway. *It covers the tows from 1956–66. The book* High Seas, High Risk *records the details of some later tows. Likewise some additional information has come from the Seaspan Archives. However, the record set out below is far from complete and additional information would be welcome.*

Date	Vessel	Owners	Tug	From/to	Remarks
1952	**Maplecove** ex-**Beavercove**	Canadian Pacific Steamships	**Island Sovereign**	North Pacific —Vancouver	
1956					
Sept.	**Straits Maru**	Japanese s/breakers	**Sudbury**	Vancouver —Osaka	32d 9hrs
1958	**Andros Legend**	Orion Shipping & Trading (Goulandris Brothers)	**Sudbury**	1,970 miles west of Osaka —Japan	
1959	**Almirante Latorre** ex-HMS **Canada**	ex-Chilean Navy	**Cambrian Salvor**	Conception —Tokyo	11,000 mi
Nov.	**Cape Esperance**	ex-USN carrier	**Sudbury II**	Honolulu —Osaka	23d 12hrs
Dec.	**Guadalcanal**	ex-USN carrier	**Sudbury II**	Open Pacific —Hirao	14d
1960					
Feb.	**Fanshaw Bay**	ex-USN carrier	**Sudbury II**	Victoria, BC —Osaka	40d 15hrs
June	Two unnamed Liberty ships	ex-Reserve fleet	**Sudbury II**	San Francisco —Hirao	37d 15hrs
Aug.	**Lone Star State** *(U.S. flag Liberty ship escorted because of a distressed condition)*	States Marine Corp.	**Sudbury II**	Yokohama —Portland, OR	16d 18hrs

Date	Vessel	Owners	Tug	From/to	Remarks
1960 *(cont)*					
Sept.	One unnamed Liberty ship & a/carrier **Munda**	ex-Reserve fleet ex-USN	**Sudbury II**	Los Angeles —Osaka	47d 12hrs
Oct.	Two tankers, midbodies	U.S. oil companies	**Sudbury II**	Yokohama —San Francisco	47d 19hrs
1961					
Jan.	Two unnamed Liberty ships	ex-Reserve fleet	**Sudbury II**	Victoria, BC —Hirao	50d
March	One tanker, midbody	U.S. oil company	**Sudbury II**	Yokohama —San Francisco	29d 18hrs
Sept.	**Offshore 55**	U.S. oil drill rig	**Sudbury II**	Port of Spain —Unknown destination	
1964	**Olympic Palm**	A.S. Onassis	**Island Mariner Island Monarch**	Orcas Island	Vessel ashore Refloated
Aug.	**Atlantic Sun**	S.G. Embiricos	**Sudbury II**	2,300 mi due west of Vancouver —Vancouver	
Dec.	**Elli**	Greek owners	**Sudbury II**	3,000 mi NW of Victoria —Seattle	Dropped prop
1965					
Dec.	**Tainan**	Taiwan Navig. Co., Taipeh, Taiwan	**Sudbury II**	South of Adak, Aleut. Is. —Vancouver	Broken tailshaft
1966	**Lefkipos**	Skarasteel Shpg. Co., Panama Greek flag	**Sudbury II**	30 mi off Barkley Sound —Vancouver	Blown boiler

Chapter Four

MULTIPLE TOWS FROM VENEZUELA

It was an audacious move for which Harold Elworthy was well known. Like his development of transpacific towing, his imagination and capability for turning the wildest flight of fancy into a realistic, soundly based concept became legendary and no one, before or since, in the British Columbia towing industry has exceeded his record for pulling such rabbits out of the hat.

The story of the Maracaibo tankers and how they came to Canada was a classic Elworthy story. These ships had been engaged in working the shallow waters of oil rich Lago de Maracaibo and its surrounding basin. The lake, which was actually an arm of the sea, was a balloon-shaped area into which drained a number of rivers which flowed from two arms of the Northern Andes. The two mountain ranges, one east of the lake and the other to the west, joined across the south and thus encompassed the lake and its surrounding flat lands to form the Maracaibo basin. It was the sort of natural formation that immediately caught the attention of oil geologists probably going back into the 19th century. When developed it was to make Venezuela a world class oil producer, fifth on a world scale, and the only OPEC member in the Americas, a position it still adheres to.

The two biggest concessionaires in developing the Maracaibo oilfields were, as so often was the case, the Royal Dutch Shell group followed by Standard Oil of New Jersey (Esso). To service the shallow inland sea and the coastal shelf which was similarly shallow both Shell and Esso developed fleets of small shallow draft tankers with a deadweight capacity of around 5–6000 tons. These ships transported the oil from the production points to offshore terminals, in the case of Shell to Aruba, for transhipment to deep-sea tankers which would take the oil to world markets. By the time such vessels as these lake tankers exceeded 24 years they were becoming overage and went on the disposal list. With this type of ship the scrapyard was usually the final destination.

In 1954 the first group of four ships had been advertised for disposal by Shell and Esso, probably with the idea that they would go for scrap, but certainly without any thought that they were fit for further service elsewhere as self-propelled tankers. Classification society rules such as those of Lloyds and American Bureau of Shipping would have probably ruled that out.

We do not know exactly how they came to the attention of Elworthy, but ship sale brokers around the world, particularly London and New York, would let any likely prospect know of possible purchases if they fitted a buyer's specification. Aside from obtaining plans of the vessels and sending one of more of his experienced executives down there to view the ships, it was probably seen that with the vessels internal subdivision of tanks they were adaptable as log or tank barges.

Full details of the seven ships involved are set out in the accompanying fleet list for there were two tows. The first, consisting of the Shell tankers *Chepita, Conchita, Carlota* and the Esso tanker *Icotea* took place in late 1954. By the time they reached Victoria it was February 15, 1955, when they were registered as Canadian vessels. The Ship Registry documents clearly show the original name of all four vessels so their identity is certain.

There was evidently a legal factor to do with

registry that had a bearing on their import into Canada. The Esso ships had been under Venezuelan registry, but to bring them into Canada they had to be reregistered in London where they had been registered from their original construction until before World War II.

The second tow took place nearly two years after the first when three former Esso tankers reached Victoria and were registered as Canadian vessels. By some strange process of faulty registration, their former names were not noted on the registration documents, but the three vessels are known to have been *Tamare, Surinam and Ule.* They were owned by a Venezuelan subsidiary of Standard Oil and likely came on the market in exactly the same way as the first four, being condemned for further trading as self-propelled tankers on account of age.

The story of the first tow has been well told in Pat Wastell Norris's book *High Seas, High Risk. Sudbury* was dispatched to Venezuela to undertake the tow.

Island Tug superintending chief engineer Norman Turner was in charge of the operation and supervised the making up of the tows. As a first move the tankers were flooded forward, sufficiently to expose the twin bronze propellers which were removed and rudders fixed to follow the centreline of the ships. What happened to the valuable bronze propellers is not recalled, but they were likely secured on deck for disposal in Canada where they would probably fetch a better price. *Sudbury* evidently handled two tankers in two tandem tows from Maracaibo or Aruba to Limon Bay at the east end of the canal. Panama Canal company tugs assisted and crews supplied by the canal company handled the tankers through to the western end of the canal. The Pacific tow was made up in the Bay of Panama from which they left as a quadruple tow off *Sudbury*'s towline, each ship, except the last in line, was secured by pennants to the towline.

In the meantime *Island Sovereign* left Victoria,

[69] The First Tow: The first Maracaibo tow of four tankers follows **Sudbury** in a memorable tow. Triple ocean tows have been fairly common, but quadruple tows are unusual. The engineering of a tow like this involves a considerable amount of heavy-duty gear and a lot of preparation, not only in putting the tow together, but also in support services. Keeping the tugs refuelled and crews supplied usually involves much prior preparation. The three ex-Shell tankers led and ex-Esso **Icotea** brought up the stern.

proceeding south to meet *Sudbury* off Manzanillo, Mexico. *Island Sovereign* placed her towline on to the lead tanker and when it came time to relieve *Sudbury* to allow the bigger vessel time to go into port for refuelling this was easily accomplished by simply shackling her line onto the main towline and taking over the tow. When *Sudbury* returned the process was reversed as the bigger boat retrieved the main towline and the smaller tug resumed towing off the lead tanker. Aside from providing additional power, *Island Sovereign* could more handily attend to any needs that any of the unmanned tankers might require in an emergency, which fortunately never arose.

In the famous picture of the first tow, the smaller vessel to the right is *Island Sovereign.* She is not quite in line with the towed vessels, being somewhat ahead of *Sudbury,* probably applying a slight amount of starboard rudder to hold herself and her towline clear of *Sudbury* which would be consistent with her not having her towline out beyond the leading tanker.

The organization of a tow like this would call for considerable support from shoreside management. The appointment of agents to handle such matters as fuel bunkering and seeing to all the paperwork in clearing port and handling through the Panama Canal would have been set up before the tugs left Victoria. Both had considerable fuel and water capacity as they had undertaken long-distance transpacific tows before. However, it is part of ship economics to rebunker at the cheapest bunkering port no matter what the ship's fuel needs might be. Oil burning or diesel ships on these routes usually make for Long Beach and Aruba for the cheapest oil bunkers as both practically pump oil out of the ground on which they stand. Either that or it's very close by.

The two tugs probably topped up at Long Beach when southbound and in the case of *Sudbury* also at Aruba as the turn around point. When there was a need to refuel *Sudbury* northbound, *Island Sovereign* was standing by at Manzanillo as that was where they met. Off Long Beach it is understood that first one then the other tug cast off from the tow to make for port to top up her tanks and take in any other needed supplies.

For the second tow two years later, *Sudbury*

picked up a large dredger in Puget Sound and delivered her to Venezuela, a revenue job which more than covered her costs, to put her in position for the second tow of the three slightly larger vessels that were sisters to *Icotea,* namely the aforementioned *Surinam, Tamare* and *Ule. Island Sovereign* also contributed to this tow in the same manner as described for the first tow. It made sense to hold back *Island Sovereign* as there was plenty of work for her in local waters and it was in the final half of the voyage when her additional muscle was needed.

The second group of vessels entered Canadian registry on November 12, 1957, which meant that the tow left Panama probably in the early summer of that year. They were probably granted an interim certificate of Canadian registry to enable import duties to be paid on arrival while the ships had their lowest value at net purchase cost in Venezuela from Shell and Esso. The considerable costs involved in the tows represented a higher value "on arrival" at Victoria, which would not have been subject to tax as the entire tows were done by Canadian vessels.

Work went ahead on their conversion as soon as possible after arrival and then the vessels would have been permanently registered as towed barges without power on the dates indicated. Both tows were completed without mishap and all seven vessels were successfully converted at Point Ellice Shipyard, Island Tug's own yard in Victoria Harbour. Only the three ex-Shell tankers entered the Seaspan fleet and one, the former *Seaspan 922,* ex-*Island Hemlock,* ex-*Conchita* is still in service in 2000 at the venerable age of 76 years as *WD 205,* a dredge support barge with Westview Dredging.

The two tows were completed without mishap, except that the third vessel on the second tow took in water and was down by the stern when approaching Cape Flattery. The cause is not recalled but a leaking stern gland from one of her two propeller shafts might have been at fault. The company tug, *Lloyd B. Gore,* met and stood by the second tow from Destruction Island until the, by now six ships, reached Victoria. Once in Esquimalt Roads, *Island Sovereign* and *Lloyd B. Gore,* likely released the two leading tankers from their pennants and then handled them into Victoria harbour to tie-up berths.

The loss record of this group of vessels was not good. The ex-Shell ships fared reasonably well, but the former Esso ships were particularly unfortunate with two of them breaking their backs while under tow, within eight days of each other during a period of very bad weather. This marred the record of a good, well-managed fleet which happily avoided major loss over most of its period as Island Tug & Barge. The remark of Bob Rolston of Dale & Company who brokered the fleet in the marine insurance market is well remembered. He lamented the fact that these vessels were breaking up too readily and that his company had advised, if not beseeched Harold Elworthy to get rid of them as soon as he could in the interests of maintaining insurance rates that could be lived with. It follows that an adverse loss record forces rates up and makes the job of the insurance broker that much more difficult in presenting a case to marine underwriters and seeking to maintain an economic rate structure.

In any event the former Esso ships had either been lost or disposed of before the merger.

The important feature of these vessels is that they gave Island Tug & Barge a strategic lead by creating the largest fleet of self-dumpers, quickly and cheaper than building new. It also gave the company a considerable head start and experience in developing the largest fleet of self-loading, self-dumping, purpose-built log barges, up to the time of the two big mergers of 1970 detailed in *Tying the Knot,* Book 3 in this series. These included *Island Forester,* the biggest ever built, and when the merger which brought about Seaspan International was finalized one of Island Tug's contributions was two up-to-date log barges as well as the three ex-Shell ships with their capability of being loaded with logs.

Details of the towing arrangements have been confirmed by Captain Alan Gray, a retired tugboat master with Island Tug and Seaspan International. Captain Gray was second mate aboard Sudbury *for both tows. The author's thanks are due to him.*

[70] The Second Tow: Consisted of three ex-Esso tankers and came two years after the first. In this aerial shot the ships look like toy boats. The lead vessel is **Island Sovereign** with her towline to the lead tanker. The second vessel in the procession is **Sudbury,** with the first two tankers attached by pennants to her line which goes to the third tanker. **Lloyd B. Gore** runs alongside the tankers ready to assist as the tow reaches Esquimalt Roads. When the tow was broken up, **Island Sovereign** would have peeled off the first tanker, **Lloyd B. Gore** would have taken the second, leaving **Sudbury** with the last. Both tows arrived without mishap, beyond some water ingress into one ship due likely to a leaking sterngland.

FLEET LIST OF THE MARACAIBO TANKERS PURCHASED BY ISLAND TUG & BARGE

The First Tow

Island Cedar
,

Blt. U.K. in 1927 by Harland & Wolff, Belfast, ex-*Icotea*. First owner Lago Shipping Co., London (mngd. by Andrew Weir & Co.). Transferred in 1939 to Cia de Petroleo Lago, Caracas, Venezuela, at time of purchase. Managed by Creole Petroleum Corp., both subsidiaries of Standard Oil Company of New Jersey.
Dimensions: 325' x 55.2' x 15.2', 2370 gt.
Sold to other owners December 14, 1961.

Island Fir

Blt. U.K. in 1925 by Wm. Beardmore & Co., Glasgow, ex-*Chepita*.
Registered owner Curacaosche Scheeps, Maats. Emmastad, Curacao, Netherlands Antilles, at time of purchase. This was a subsidiary of Royal Dutch Shell Company.
Dimensions: 305' x 50.2' x 14.9'. Registered net tonnage 1,885.
Estimated deadweight 5,000 tons, plus or minus.
Passed to Seaspan in 1970. Renamed *Seaspan 921*. Disposed of in 1980.

Island Hemlock

Blt. U.K. in 1924 by Wm. Beardmore & Co., Glasgow, ex-*Conchita*.
Registered owner and dimensions as above with *Island Fir*. Renamed *Seaspan 922* following the merger of 1970.
Disposed of to Trident Foreshore Lands Ltd., North Vancouver, B.C., in 1979. Later transferred to Westview Dredging Ltd., Delta, B.C. and still afloat in 2000 as *WD 205*.

Island Spruce

Blt. U.K. in 1924 by Wm. Beardmore & Co., Glasgow, ex-*Carlota*.
Registered owner and dimensions as above with *Island Fir*. Renamed *Seaspan 920* following the merger of 1970. Disposed of in 1979.

The Second Tow

Island Balsam

Blt. U.K. in 1929 by Harland & Wolff, Belfast, ex-*Ule*.
Registered owner as above with *Icotea*.
Dimensions: 325' x 55.2' x 15.2', registered net tonnage 2,293.
Estimated deadweight over 5,000 tons.
Sold in August 1969 to R. Goodwin Johnson.
Sunk as breakwater at Naden Harbour, B.C., Oct. 1970

Island Cypress

Blt. U.K. in 1929, by Harland & Wolff, Belfast, ex-*Surinam*.
Registered owner as above with *Icotea*.
Dimensions: as with *Island Balsam* above.
T.L. Oct 14, 1963. Broke in two near Destruction Island, Wash.

Island Maple

Blt. U.K. in 1929 by Harland & Wolff, Belfast, ex-*Tamare*.
Registered owner as above with *Icotea*.
Dimensions: as with *Island Balsam* above.
T.L. Oct. 22, 1963. Broke in two in Straits of Juan de Fuca, while on passage from Woodfibre, B.C., to Hoquiam, Wash., with a cargo of black liquor, a biproduct of the wood pulping process.

[71] **Safe Arrival:** One of the vessels from the first tow, the **Conchita,** awaits the shipyard crew who will soon strip off every vestige of her upperworks and fittings to make her ready for employment as a log barge.

[72] **Completed Project:** Here **Island Monarch** has loaded log barges in tandem tow. **Island Balsam,** ex-**Ule,** leads and **Island Maple,** ex-**Tamare,** follows.

[73] **Last Survivor:** Seen here in the Fraser River with the Lafarge plant as a background in the year 2000. **WD 205** was operated as a barge by Westview Dredging. Previously she was **Seaspan 922,** ex-**Island Fir,** ex-**Conchita.**

Chapter Five

THE DEVELOPMENT OF TOWING GEAR, RECOVERY GEAR AND CHAIN PENNANTS

Composed from extensive notes prepared by Captain J.P. Brown, retired senior marine surveyor at Vancouver.

In a covering letter to the author, Captain Brown stated:

I was perhaps fortunate to have been in charge of the Marine Surveyors office through the late '50s and '60s when great changes were taking place. I lived through the transition from wood to steel in the construction of barges and tugs during that period. When the Federal Government introduced the subsidy program covering building costs for marine equipment, the main towing fleets together with their barges were more or less completely renewed over a relatively short period of time.

Confronted with new tugs of greater size and horsepower and also with a big increase in the size of barges and a broad extension of the areas in which they were towed, we at the surveyors office were faced with making recommendations regarding towing gear, taking into account the above factors.

As there was little background to fall back on, much had to be devised from scratch, so to speak. As I mentioned in my notes we were able to gain valuable information from the experience of the towing industry in Puget Sound who had been towing to Alaska throughout World War II and from much of that was developed the systems used in British Columbia. Upgrading took place as experience dictated and presumably is still taking place.

I was very fortunate to have good working relationships with the managements of all the main towing companies and this helped considerably in accomplishing a great deal often over a simple lunch. At the time of my retirement I had the satisfaction of knowing that tug and barge operational arrangements on the British Columbia coast were second to none and that losses were minimal.

During Captain Brown's tenure at Marine Surveyors of Western Canada and its predecessor office, it should also be remembered that in addition to witnessing and advising as the transition was made from wood to steel, a big locally owned barge around 1950 would have been something with a capacity of around 2,000 tons. The exception would have been certain railcar units and one or two early post-war log carriers converted from wartime landing ship hulls. Within the next 20 years the largest log barges had deadweight capacities up to ten times bigger culminating in the *Seaspan*

Forester, at 20,000 tons deadweight. Captain Brown's comments are therefore particularly valuable as they cover this historic period of greatest growth in local tug and barge designs.

A further point which bears repeating is the role of the marine surveyor and just why such details as are set out here are so vital. Every tug and barge owner, large and small, negotiates marine insurance cover on his vessels, with underwriters, through his broker. Likewise the commodities, or merchandise carried are usually insured as a separate contract for the benefit of the cargo interests. In a similar way to the manner in which the vessel owners engage a surveyor for an "on hire" survey, by which the parties rely on the surveyor for approval of the vessel with all faults noted, so also will the surveyor be called upon to perform a similar "off hire" survey to determine what damage has been incurred beyond ordinary wear and tear while on charter. The surveyor will recommend a basis for settlement of any adjustments which might be the responsibility of the charterer or underwriters.

In a similar way underwriters rely heavily on that same surveyor in making recommendations to improve or correct shortcoming in vessels or cargoes, or as the marine insurance industry terms it "the risk." Usually in consultation with the owner he will also agree a value for the vessel which becomes the basis of insurance. The surveyor is a specialist expert in his field and is often fully involved in developing new techniques such as those described here. Taking all these factor of condition, detail and valuation, one might say that the surveyor's report is the essential lubricant in persuading the underwriter to accept the risk and assess its merits to arrive at a premium.

DEEP-SEA TOWING GEAR FOR LARGE BARGES

A bridle is that part of the towing gear which couples the end of the tug's towline to the barge under tow. The bridle is shaped like a V and extends to each bow of the barge being looped over bollards on the barge's deck and thus transmits the strain of the tow to the barge. The bridle is also a spring or cushion between the tug and barge and the heavier it is the better is its ability to act as a spring. In a similar way a long towline also acts as a spring or cushion but as it is shortened up it loses this advantage. On smaller vessels the bridle is usually made of wire if engaged in shorter coastal tows and can be quickly assembled when making up a tow, but on bigger barges engaged in long-distance ocean tows chain is the better material. Strength and chaffing are the major factors governing this choice and the setting up of the towing arrangements are much more sophisticated engaging a good many hours of crew time. Here also the chain bridle also doubled as a surge chain which allowed some

freedom of movement on the part of the barge when buffeted by heavy seas.

A more sophisticated adaptation was introduced on two of MacMillan, Bloedel's large covered newsprint barges towing to Long Beach, Cal., from Port Alberni. Here the technique was developed for using two towlines by welding a heavy round bar into the hull structure at centre line at about main deck level and a second bar of similar dimensions again at centre line just above the load waterline of the vessel. The hull plating in way of these bars was recessed to provide room to fit the heavy towing shackles and to give room for some sideways movement of the chain pennants. Each chain pennant was connected to a towline, the length of chain being adjusted to provide adequate surge effect.

It is of interest to note that a third barge was built for MB somewhat later. Fully laden with newsprint this vessel was towed from Port Alberni, through the Panama Canal and on to New Brunswick where it then went into service delivering newsprint from the Rothesay mill to Miami.

Today some of the large log barges are towed with two towlines in a similar arrangement to the above. Some of the earlier strandings in large barges were the result of reliance on one towline which had parted, as in the cases of the *Straits Logger* and *Rivtow Norseman,* referred to elsewhere in this series. Recently *Seaspan Rigger* nearly came to grief of the Oregon coast when its single towline parted.

The chains used are very heavy, mostly originating from anchor chains from scrapped wartime merchant ships. They necessitated much heavy work on the part of crews when connecting up for a tow or disconnecting following a tow. Wear and tear was watched for at every opportunity and particularly at any point when connections were made or chain passed through fairleads where friction could develop.

When the two-towline method was first introduced, in the manner previously described, there was little experience in regard to this method. In order to observe the action of the two chains under tow, with the barge fully loaded and proceeding down the Alberni Canal, observations made from a small vessel running alongside confirmed that the system would work well.

SKETCH ILLUSTRATING A DEEP-SEA TANDEM TOW

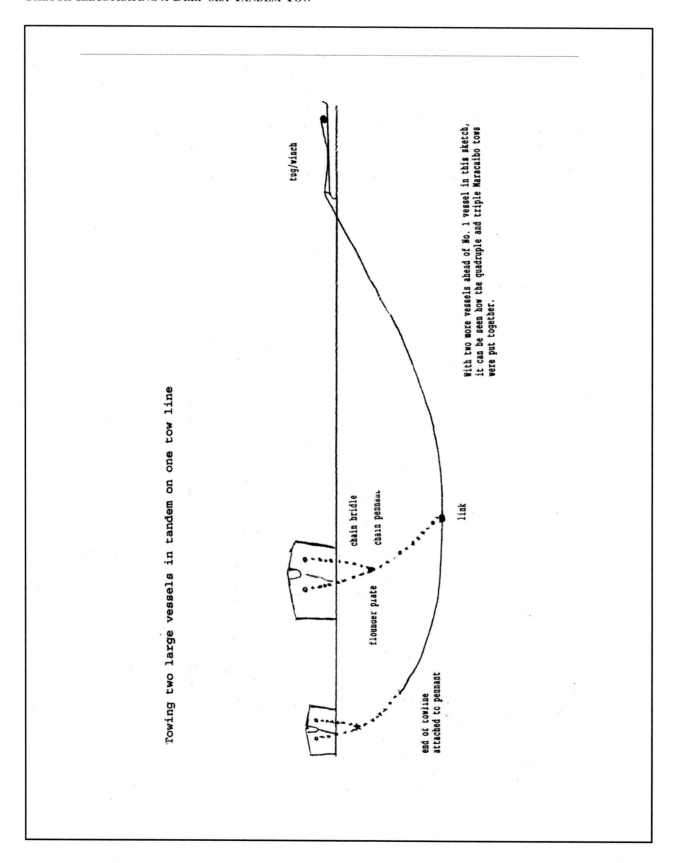

RECOVERY GEAR

This describes a system developed whereby a barge, broken adrift from the towing vessel, could be recovered without loss. Captain Brown's office obtained particulars of a recovery system which had been in use by the towing industry in Seattle and was used extensively on tugs on the Puget Sound-Alaska run. The senior surveyor for the Board of Marine Underwriters in Seattle was Captain "Doc" Stream who had spent a good many years as master on tugs on this run and had been instrumental in the development of this system.

Briefly, the system consisted of fitting a spare emergency towline on the barge which could be recovered in open water without putting a crew member on board. This spare line was attached to a towing bitt at the bow and then led aft along one deck edge then across the stern and forward on the opposite side of the vessel. At the bow it was turned around and again led aft where the balance of the line was flaked down. The line was secured in place by means of lightly welded straps. A floating line was attached to the end of the towline and this line was thrown overboard at the beginning of the tow and allowed to trail astern. The emergency procedure consisted of the tug picking up the floating line, securing it on board and then steaming up one side breaking off the towline, turning around at the bow, returning aft and up the opposite side at which time the towline would have all been pulled free and the barge reattached in a towing condition. However, despite "the best laid plans of mice and men," a recent case when a large barge had broken away proved that nothing is foolproof. The emergency or insurance line aft had become fouled on the barge and could not be released or picked up. Only the personal courage of one crewman in going aboard

[74] California Bound: Fully laden with Doman lumber out of Cowichan Bay, **Seaspan 270** and **Seaspan 271** follow **Seaspan Commodore.** The tow was made up using the methods described in this chapter. *(see also #132)*

the barge in extreme conditions saved the vessel from disaster.

This procedure was modified to suit barges with insufficient deck space outboard of the box where an emergency towline could be secured and initially concentrated on fitting the line across the aft deck. The first trial was on board a barge owned by Straits Towing which was heading out on a voyage from Vancouver to San Francisco with a full load of reinforcing steel. The late Captain Jim Foster of Straits Towing was very supportive of this safety feature.

Vancouver Tug Boat Company then took up the procedure. The late Captain Charles Plester, their barge superintendent, was particularly keen and over a period of time improved the method of stowing this spare line, eventually moving it below deck at the aft end of the barge where a watertight valve was fitted keeping water out, but allowing the line to be pulled free. It did not matter to the surveyors that the barge would be reattached with the line made fast at the stern, as its function was to get hold of the barge and prevent loss, and when weather permitted attach a towline to the head end of the barge in the conventional manner. This system was used extensively by Vancouver Tug in their offshore tows to Hawaii and Central America.

From this simple beginning, as barges increased in size modifications were continually made until eventually, in the large barges, this spare towline was carried on a drum below deck under the fo'c'sle, the line being led out through a suitable valve on the bow at which point a lighter line was shackled on and led aft with sufficient length to suit and the floating line attached. The drum holding the spare line was fitted with brakes to prevent overrunning should the line be hauled out and the end of the line on the drum was fitted with a "stopper" which would come into contact with the valve and at this location the structure was strengthened to permit a safe towing connection.

At one point Captain Brown came across a report which suggested that these "pickup" lines were redundant. "This upset me," he said, "as at that particular time I was aware of seven barges, over a period of one year, which had been picked up by this method." These instances were not given any publicity, it being only the owner's concern and of interest to underwriters as the elimination of potential loss was of primary interest to them. Media publicity only takes an interest, raising speculative expectations, when disaster strikes.

TOWLINE DIMENSIONS AND BREAKING STRAINS

With the rapid increase in size and horsepower of towing vessels, particularly those matched to the large log barges and newsprint carriers, a corresponding increase in size and breaking strain of wire towlines had to be considered.

At one time size was often determined by bollard pull and in this regard the one official gauge for this purpose was owned by Burrard Iron Works Ltd. The gauge would be attached to a bollard at the North end of Ballantyne Pier, Vancouver, the towline attached and as the pull took place a record would be made of the gauge reading together with certain engine readings and a certificate issued.

Underwriters' rule for towline size was the formula:

$$30 \times BHP + 1/3rd \ displacement \ weight \ of \ hull \\ = breaking \ strain \ of \ towline \ in \ pounds.$$

This formula was found to be satisfactory for the greater horsepower now encountered. Larger towlines meant larger towing winches as there is a limit to the dimension of the drum over which a wire can be wound, for example, a 6 x 26 wire rope requires a drum 16 times the diameter of the rope. Considerable care also had to be applied to the diameter of the stern roller. The term 6 x 26 when applied to wire rope means six strands with 26 wires to each strand.

During the period described the larger tugs were fitted with a towline consisting of 2500 feet of 2 1/8th inch wire with I.W.R.C. (Independent Wire Rope Core) with a breaking strain of almost 200 tons. The use of Wire Rope Core as compared to Fibre Core produced a slightly stronger but heavier wire and one less likely to crush.

At about this time there was a small machine shop located in Georgia Street at Coal Harbour,

Vancouver, managed by the late Howard Leeming. This gentleman took a great interest in developing equipment advantageous to the towing industry. Many of his patents originated as a pencil drawing on a paper napkin in the local coffee shop. Leeming was encouraged in his work by the late Captain Wm. Dolmage, amongst others, and was successful in developing hydraulically operated towing pins using the three-pin pattern.

Leeming also developed a hydraulically operated holding down gear for the towline. Such improvements enable the master of the tug to handle this work from a remote location on the after end of the boat deck where he had a commanding view of the towing gear one deck below and no crew member had to be put in the way of the towline. These pins were fitted on many of the newer tugs and the holding down gear installed, for example, on the *Rivtow Lion*, the former Navy salvage tug that Rivtow brought out from the U.K.

CHAIN BRIDLES AND SURGE CHAINS

Captain Brown prefaced his notes in this section with this explanation of size and length of chain on ships of approximately 10,000 tons in the years of which he wrote:

For many years merchant ships had been fitted with about eight cable lengths of stud link chain on port and starboard anchors, the links being of about two inch diameter steel. A cable length was 15 fathoms or 90 feet (as opposed to the Royal Navy where a cable length was 12 1/2 fathoms.) This length should not be confused with the measurement of distance used in navigation called a cable, which refers to one tenth of a nautical mile or six hundred feet. Each length of cable was marked adjacent to the joining shackle by using seizing wire. At the first shackle it would be placed one link ahead of the shackle, at the second two links ahead, etc., in order that the officer in charge of anchoring would know just how much cable had been paid out. It was normal practice to pay out about six or eight times the depth of water depending on the holding ground in the anchorage. I myself would try to anchor in about eight fathoms of water and would give the order to "put four shackles" in the water.

In U.S. ships and later Canadian vessels the use of the word "shackle" gave way to the "shot," which is really more descriptive and therefore when referring to surge chain we would specify "one shot" (90 feet) or "one-and-a-half shots" (135 feet).

Once again information gained from experience in the use of chain, particularly surge chain, on Miki-Miki-type tugs on runs to Alaska, was a guideline and it was considered advisable to use heavy studlink chain for bridles on each of the large specialized barges. The chain used was of the size fitted as anchor chains on American Liberty and Victory ships. As quite a number of these ships were at that time being scrapped there was a good supply of this chain available.

These studlink chain towing bridles were attached to the fittings on the barge's bow by means of approved towing shackles, i.e., full floating pins with double nuts and cottered. The outer ends of bridles were similarly attached to a flounder plate.* The surge chain which led ahead of the flounder plate was also attached in this manner.

The idea of the surge chain was to act as a spring in that the catenary of the chain was such that the towing vessel could not bring it all up taught.

As the size of tugs and barges progressed it became normal for some tugs to be fitted with double winches and in such cases two towlines would be attached to the barge, sometimes one above the other but always in a manner whereby they would not foul each other. Sometimes one would be left lazy to act as a backup should one fail, at other times, where

* *Flounder Plate: So named for its resemblance to the common species of flatfish. This is a triangular-shaped steel plate with two holes cut through the base of the plate and one hole at the apex. The outer ends of the chain bridle would be shackled through the two holes at the base, while a surge chain is shackled at the apex and connects with the towline. Flounder plates are tested to a breaking strain similar to the towline.*

71

[75] Seaspan 270 returns to the Fraser River to load another lumber cargo. She is tended by Westminster Towing Company's ship berthing tugs. The heavy chain bridle can be seen attached low down to both bows of the barge and coming to a flounder plate joining it to the chain pennant extension of the towline which flows over **Seaspan Commodore**'s stern apron. Barely visible is a recovery wire also attached to the head of the bridle which enables it to be picked up for working purposes by the barge or when not in use.

tugs were fitted with tension gauges then each line would take equal loads. Up until the time of Captain Brown's retirement this system worked out very well and a great many successful ocean tows were carried out without problems.

The use of specialized barges, particularly in the logging industry, made these barges a vital link in the supply of logs from distant coastal areas to mills in the lower mainland area. If by chance a barge became lost or very heavily damaged then the supply "pipeline" from logging camps to manufacturing mills broke down as it was not possible to charter or rent a similar barge to fulfil its function. Realizing this, the owners and operator of log barges, fully appreciated the necessity of doing everything possible to ensure the safety of towing gear and its attachment to both barge and tug which called for safety maintenance of all gear at all times.

Another note of historical interest relates to the use of nylon towing pennants. For the unitiated a pennant was a chain or wire connecting an individual barge in a multiple tow to the main towing line which stretched under water to the last vessel in the tow *(see sketch p.68)*. The main towline, always controlled from the towing tug's own winch, was the strongest member in the towing gear making up a multiple tow. Experience had shown long ago that this was a superior method to joining say three barges in a tow by way of individual towlines from one barge to the next.

Reportedly nylon pennants were being used on the east coast of the U.S., but certainly not here in the west. Dupont engineers, in discussion with local towing companies, were advised that any use of nylon would have to be tested by the Marine Surveyor's office and approved by Captain Brown. Much information was forthcoming regarding breaking strains, elasticity of nylon, length of time required for nylon to regain its normal length after being strained and also the limit of elasticity. Dupont manufactured, at their expense, two very large nylon pennants of suitable size to be used in towing a flat deck barge and a section was supplied for testing purposes.

The only approved testing equipment at the time was in the Canada Chain & Forge shop on Granville Island, Vancouver. It was interesting to stand there and watch this large test section of nylon pennant being pulled to destruction and to watch the gauges as this took place. Vancouver Tug Boat Company was willing to try these pennants out on a tow from Vancouver to San Francisco and Captain Brown approved on condition that a chain pennant was also fitted from the flounder plate to a towing attachment on the bow of the barge. The chain pennant was to be such a length that it would remain lazy and act as a preventer only. The tow proceeded in relatively normal weather but when passing under Golden Gate Bridge it was noted that the chain pennant was taking the strain as the nylon apparently had stretched considerably. Vancouver Tug tried other local tows using nylon pennants but as this material will not stand friction or chafing it proved just too difficult to police and so was abandoned.

RADIO-CONTROLLED ANCHORING DEVICES

At about the same time that many of the above noted devices were evolving, a radio controlled anchoring unit was also developed. The name of the inventor is not now recalled by Captain Brown, but it is believed that he had been employed in the logging industry and had been instrumental in designing a radio controlled carriage operating on a sky wire.

Apparently the gentleman concerned was asked by the superintendent of Island Tug & Barge in Victoria if he could adapt this principle to control an anchor windlass and that was the start. Once again the windlasses used in the original installations were taken from Liberty ships then being scrapped. These windlasses were cut in two as only one anchor was required. Once mounted on a barge the system was controlled from a unit on the towing vessel from which signals could be sent. These signals in turn, started up the hydraulic motor, lifted off the cable brake and started the motor for paying out the anchor. Safety features were incorporated in the radio control unit and, all in all, the device worked in a very satisfactory manner.

On one occasion Captain Brown was contacted when a barge had broken away from a tug while crossing Hecate Straits. During the hours of darkness and in poor weather the tug lost sight of the barge, but was able to follow it on radar. It was decided not to lower the anchor at that time due to the depth of water and so the tug continued to track it on radar while Brown was kept advised of the location having a chart spread out on his desk. Eventually when the barge had entered an area where the depth of water was favourable it was recommended that the tug should start paying out the anchor using its radio command system. All worked as intended and the barge was brought up to the anchor and safely reconnected to the towing vessel.

[76] **Recovery Line:** A recovery line lies coiled on the deck of a barge awaiting tow by **Seaspan Regent.**

Chapter Six

RIVTOW TO THE RESCUE

January 17, 1997, opened like any other day when Captain Don Rose anticipated another call back from time off, ashore, for a routine tow by his command, the Rivtow flagship, *Rivtow Captain Bob*. He expected a call to tow Rivtow's largest log barge, *Rivtow Hercules*. Instead it was a call to go to the assistance of a disabled American oil tanker, adrift out in the Pacific with a seized tailshaft. Captain Rose tells it in his own words:

[77] Rivtow Captain Bob: Seen here running free and as she looked when dispatched to help the U.S. tanker **Chestnut Hill** in distress in the North Pacific. A feature of this tug which distinguishes her from all others on the B.C. coast is the sheer massiveness of her wheelhouse, which is a virtual operations room for all purposes.

Rivtow's personnel office said that a deep-sea ship, the *Chestnut Hill,* was broken down and we were asked to report to the dock as soon as possible to prepare *Rivtow Captain Bob* for sea. By mid-afternoon we were ready for sea and departed.

After three days steaming we met the stricken tanker 685 miles west of Cape Flattery. The wind was NNW 25/30 with a rough sea. All hands turned to and proceeded with the task of getting the ship hooked to our towline. A rocket line was fired across the ship's bows, then a series of messenger lines were used with the ship's capstan employed to pull the towline up on to her deck. At that point the towline was joined into the ship's anchor chain. Four shots1 were then fed out through the ship's bullnose (a closed fairlead mounted on the stem and much favoured in American practice as a useful aid when taking a towline). Due to the weather, water was washing across the aft deck of the tug making the situation, to say the least, unpleasant. At times the crew were up to their shoulders in water, but the job was completed in two hours and five minutes.

At this time we were advised that our destination was Honolulu. From where we picked up *Chestnut Hill,* this meant 1,910.8 miles of deep-sea towing. During this leg of the voyage we encountered a great variety of wind and sea conditions that varied from light winds with low swells, to winds of 55 miles an hour and higher with swells 40–50 feet high. The temperatures varied from near freezing with snow and rain and of course hot sun tanning weather as we neared Hawaii. Towing speed ranged from 7.8 knots to less than 3 knots.

Throughout the voyage, even with the worst of sea conditions the crew gave 500 per cent and made me proud to sail with them. Not only that, during all this time, good and bad weather, we never missed a meal.

We arrived at Honolulu on the morning of February 5, 1997. There we anchored the ship and ourselves. Because *Chestnut Hill* was disabled we had to stand by her. After five days, a Chinese tug, the 12,000-bhp *De Yi,* arrived and continued with the tow to Bangledash to discharge her 80,000-ton cargo of grain. Following unloading, the ship was then to be towed to the shipbreakers at Alang, India for scrapping.

Five days anchored off Honolulu in February sure beats the Gulf of Alaska. After the Chinese tug took over the ship, *Rivtow Captain Bob* went into Honolulu for fuel, grub and some R & R. Our trip back to Vancouver took us 8 days. The total time from leaving Vancouver to return Vancouver was 34 days, during which we logged a round trip total of 5,170 nautical miles.

Captain Rose explained that it was only after reaching Hawaii that the two crews met face to face. All contact to that point had been by radio, but in a sense they got to know each other quite well.

The *Chestnut Hill* was commanded by Captain Charles Ebersole and operated by Keystone Shipping of Philadelphia, Pa., a large independent tanker company. Built in 1976 at National Steel Shipbuilding Corporation, Los Angeles, she was part of a program by which a substantial fleet of new, large tankers were built in the United States to coincide with developments on the North Slope of Alaska. She had a deadweight capacity of 89,700 tons and dimensions of 272.5 m x 32.29 m x 14.955 m. The ship operated under a subsidy agreement which ran out in the allotted 20 years typical of this type of arrangement, both charter and subsidy being

calculated to fully amortize the vessel and show her investment owners a reasonable profit. At the end of the twenty years, fully written down to scrap value, the only thing remaining was to send her to the scrap yard. She was actually owned by Girard Trust Bank of New York in a typical fully secured sale and leaseback arrangement which sees an increasing volume of Western world shipping owned by banks and leasing companies. She was about the maximum size for transitting the Panama Canal but had been employed in carrying Alaskan oil to the lower 48 as well as bringing Venezuelan oil from Maracaibo through the Canal to the West Coast markets.

Twenty years was the usual life span for large tankers and today few survive much beyond this period and a good many have been scrapped at age 15, more because of premature obsolescence caused by rapidly escalating size economics, than the fact that they were physically worn out.

The circumstances and type of arrangement under which *Rivtow Captain Bob* was engaged for this

1. For an explanation of "shot v. shackle" and how they measure, see Captain J.P. Brown's explanation in the previous chapter under subheading "Chain Bridles and Surge Chains," p. 71.

[78] **Chestnut Hill,** as she looked wallowing in big North Pacific swells 700 miles out from Cape Flattery when **Rivtow Captain Bob** came up to her. Although her dead-weight capacity was 89,000 tons for oil cargoes, the differing stowage factor permitted her to load 80,000 tons of grain destined for Bangladesh.

[79] **Now Connected:** The disabled tanker obediently follows the tug.

[80] Massive Swells sometimes almost hid the big tanker as she went down into a trough. From the tanker there were moments when **Rivtow Captain Bob** disappeared in those same watery valleys. For those who have sailed deep-sea, many will remember the strange sight when only the smoke from another vessel could be seen magically rising out of the water!

[81] Quieter Seas: After days of mountainous seas, it was a relief for both crews to hit calmer waters as the two vessels made a good towing speed of about seven knots.

[82] On Arrival at Honolulu: Captain Don Rose *(centre in the striped shirt),* master of **Rivtow Captain Bob,** goes aboard **Chestnut Hill** to meet his opposite number, Captain Charles Ebersole *(second from left).* Previous to that they had only known each other as voices on the radiophone.

major tow are of interest. First *Chestnut Hill* was about six times the deadweight of the largest barge in the Rivtow fleet, *Rivtow Hercules,* to which *Rivtow Captain Bob* was normally coupled.

Towing in North Pacific winter conditions was no mean achievement when considering the relative sizes of the two vessels and the fact that Rivtow was not known as a deep-sea salvage company, plus the fact that the tug's horsepower of 6,100 made her a relative lightweight compared to the 12,000 hp of the Chinese tug that took over the tow at Honolulu for the longer, but likely easier, conditions of the tow to Bangladesh.

Chestnut Hill was deeply laden but not down to her fully laden loading mark as her capacity for oil still left an unutilized 10,000 tons of deadweight capacity when laden with grain. However, it should

be remembered that the density of grain is less than oil, so she was no doubt full to her tank tops and therefore had used her volumetric capacity to its fullest extent.

How did Rivtow come to obtain the tow job, bearing in mind that there are higher horsepower tugs out of Seattle and San Francisco? First, the *Chestnut Hill* was in no immediate danger although she was wallowing in uncomfortable sea conditions while awaiting rescue. When the P & I club got the first news of her predicament their first act on behalf of the owners would have been to advise their London agents, who would have put a call out to all potential tug and salvage companies to enquire as to what tugs with sufficient horsepower and experience might be available. London is still the world's main centre for all matters pertaining to marine insurance

[83] **Mission Accomplished:** The Canadian tug had to await the arrival of the 12,000-h.p. Chinese tug **De Yi,** seen here circling the American tanker. After a short rest in Honolulu, **Rivtow Captain Bob** returned light, having been away from home base for 34 days.

with Lloyds, the company market and the Protection and Indemnity (P & I) clubs. Most foreign marine insurance companies, P & I clubs and a great many international shipping and salvage companies of any stature maintained branch offices or were represented there through agencies. As noted the ship was not in danger of going ashore, but she was in peril of suffering structural failure from the constant stressing of the hull due to racking and bucking while she was in gale force seas. A dead ship is more prone to damage in these circumstances than a ship under power and underway.

Then there was the question of availability. Tugs, particularly in the high horsepower range, are not always available on demand. Often they are working on other assignments and every tugboat company seeks to keeps its equipment employed and moving. The luxury of having large deep-sea salvage tugs on standby awaiting a casualty can only be justified in high density traffic areas such as the English Channel/North Sea, Cape of Good Hope, Straits of Malacca or at Aden to cover the Red Sea approaches.

Another factor would be the matter of daily rate plus available horsepower. With up to 9,000 hp installed in some of the units of the Crowley fleet out of San Francisco, *Rivtow Captain Bob* would have rated as a modestly powered vessel, probably drawing down a lower daily rate compared to the bigger vessels but, as noted, availability would have been the first factor to take into account.

It will be seen that there would have been many complex considerations involved in reaching some quick decisions. Rivtow itself would have had to allow for their biggest vessel being unavailable, as it turned out for over a month, until her return to home base. Fortunately they had other units that could be substituted on log barge duties or they could charter from another company.

The situation from the point of view of the owners and charterers of the *Chestnut Hill* was also interesting. For the tailshaft to seize must have involved some special engineering problems leading to a lack of adequate lubrication. One option would have been to tow her back to Puget Sound or Esquimalt for attention, declaring a general average to cover the cost of salvage, but a fully laden tanker would not normally be drydocked without first removing the cargo so that would have needed attention first and then where would one store it in the interim? West Coast grain terminals are built to load ships and are not designed to handle this kind of traffic where grain is unloaded from a ship. Then removing and replacing a seized tailshaft would have been an expensive and difficult job involving special techniques not readily available in every shipyard. As the vessel only had a limited life ahead of it, having been sold for delivery to an Indian scrapyard and, after crediting earned freight for delivery of the 80,000 tons of grain on board, the presumption is that when everything was added up it was still cheaper in the long run to tow the ship the many thousands of miles from Hawaii to Bangladesh.

How would the costs of towing the tanker by *Rivtow Captain Bob* to the agreed port of refuge at Hawaii been covered? Possibly by way of salvage charges under a general average by which the underwriters on the cargo, the freight money and the hull and machinery underwriters, all three of whom could have been quite separate groups of insurers would have paid out their rateable proportions based on the declared value of the cargo, the freight money and the hull and machinery of the ship. The ship was worth no more than scrap value delivered in India, so the most valuable interest might have been the grain cargo. In any event the cost of fixing the tail shaft, had it been attended to, would have been settled as a particular average (or partial loss) on the hull and machinery policies and would not have fallen on the other interests as in a general average. In view of the ship's intended disposal this was clearly not an option.

However, in view of the complexity of the loss, where, in addition to the costs of the Rivtow tug which was called in, in an emergency situation, there was the considerable extra cost of using the Chinese tug *De Yi* to complete the tow to Alang, India. This was probably covered by the ship's Mutual P & I Club, a combination of shipowners who pool their resources to meet members losses. The members meet calls (or make contributions) at so much per ton based on the tonnage of the vessels they have entered into the club and, as the clubs usually cover vast fleets for risks that are not placed at Lloyds or in the company market, the loss per member becomes relatively small.

In the settlement that followed, no doubt Rivtow did well enough out of the episode. They would have earned their vessel's daily rate, plus a probable additional bonus for successful completion of their leg of the last voyage of the *Chestnut Hill*. To offset this they would have had to take into account their own time and inconvenience in arranging a substitute tug, either from their own pool of vessels, but quite likely from Seaspan. I have seen a photopgrah of *Rivtow Hercules* when under tow by *Seaspan King*, so such an arrangement is not unknown.

Incidentally the entire rescue operation was capably filmed from *Rivtow Captain Bob* by deckhand Murray Haines and put together as a video incorporating footage taken by Captain Ebersole aboard the tanker. The end result was an interesting production which gave an excellent view of the sea and towing conditions and views of each ship in operational mode taken from the other. There is something very impressive about the sight of a 90,000-ton tanker deep in the trough of a sea with only the funnel and wheelhouse visible, particularly when viewed from the comfort of one's own living room! Just as impressive is the sight of the relatively small tug bouncing around on massive ocean swells, always moving forward while its massive tow follows obligingly.

Chapter Seven
INSURING THE TRANSPACIFIC TOWS

Of all the people I have ever known in a lifetime's business career, Peter Leckie Wright must rank as one of my most valued colleagues. This relationship dates back to 1952, a watershed year in my life when I first came to Vancouver and sat for the first time opposite Peter at my first weekly meeting of the Association of Marine Underwriters. I was a stranger among strangers, not helped by my first meeting with Peter's then boss, Bob Rolston, a rough diamond at any time, with a strange way of breaking the ice with a newcomer. In the thrust and shove of the marine insurance market, Rolston could be as tough as anyone, but I never knew his honesty to be held in doubt.

Rolston and Wright sat next to each other, it was Mutt and Jeff all over again, or Laurel and Hardy or some such fanciful duo. Bob Rolston took a little knowing, but once known he was another friend for whom I developed a profound respect, but in his case it took time.

Not so with Wright, a diplomat supreme, urbane and possessed of an easy charm that puts people instantly at their ease. We are both retired now, but are alike in more ways than one. We both enjoy a very busy productive life, but for Peter it has led to an extraordinary post-retirement career as an international marine insurance consultant, which has taken him to many foreign parts from London to Moscow, from Kuala Lumpur to Oslo, entrusted with handling complex assignments to do with international insurance matters. In between, he still manages to provide his services as a teacher to students undertaking insurance studies and as a mediator and arbitrator in resolving commercial insurance disputes.

It was because of these qualities, a good many years ago, that he was entrusted by his employer, Dale & Company, to handle one of their most prized accounts, Island Tug & Barge Ltd., then of Victoria, headed at that time by Harold Elworthy. One of the great names in B.C. towboat history, Elworthy was a man who took pride in surrounding himself with the best men at sea and ashore and this extended to his assessment of those who in other ways served the company. Elworthy insisted on the same high standards with his fleet of tugs and barges which is one of the reasons their loss record was so good, except for the brief period of the former Maracaibo tankers.

This formula showed up to advantage. One of Wright's early experiences with Elworthy was the occasion when he was asked for an opinion on an insurance claim which had been rejected by underwriters for reasons that did not appear to be legitimate in Elworthy's view. The risk had been placed by another broker and in Elworthy's estimation the broker had failed in his duty to his client to represent his best interests. At that point, Dale only had the marine account and Elworthy only wanted an honest opinion and Wright gave it to him. To Wright's surprise Mr. Elworthy pulled a great batch of policies out of his drawer and handed the entire non-marine account to his visitor. Premiums on these other interests involved around $70,000 per year, which was a considerable sum in those days.

"Here, Peter, I want you to handle all our other insurances from now on. I don't want anything to do with an underwriter who doesn't respond to a legitimate claim," said Elworthy. The truth was that the other broker had unfortunately placed the insurance with an underwriter whose first principle of doing business was to automatically reject any claim and then, in effect, require the insured to fight for his recovery. That was not Mr. Elworthy's way of doing business. For him it was a matter of honour to meet obligations without quibbling and he expected others to do likewise.

Some of the most exacting responsibilities undertaken by Wright were in placing the marine insurance on the many transpacific tows undertaken by Island Tug. Making all the arrangements for a major multiple tow involves a lot of preparation and heavy work in rigging the gear, which could take days. It was easier that way compared to rigging a tow when in the open ocean under often stressful and adverse conditions. In rigging for a multiple ocean tow, bridles of heavy chain are rigged from each ship in the tow, shackled to pennants which are linked to the towline which will be riding deep in the water under each of the vessels in the tow.

The two multiple tows from Venezuela were detailed earlier in this chapter. A quadruple tow of this nature had seldom, if ever, been undertaken before and would normally have been ringed around with a variety of warranties governing safety factors and towing arrangements. Remarkably, the London underwriters had such confidence in Island Tug and its superintending engineer, Norman Turner, that they never questioned the towing arrangements he set up. Having two tugs on the tow meant that when refuelling was needed the tugs could take turns in detaching themselves to slip into port while the remaining tug could keep the tow moving forward.

Remarkably, Island Tug never lost a single vessel in the many transpacific tows that it undertook from a port to port. The longest single tow was the 11,000-mile tow of the Chilean battleship *Almirante Latorre*, ex-HMS *Canada*, to Japan. She was a veteran of the First World War battle of Jutland and her tow was successfully handled by the *Cambrian Salvor*.

To insure the risk one needed to determine a value. The value of obsolete vessels being towed to Japan would be based on their scrap value at so much per ton of estimated recoverable steel which was probably the responsibility of the Japanese purchaser and was likely insured in Japan. The insurance of the

cost of the tow would have been for Island Tug's account and its contract no doubt called for safe delivery in order for the towing company to collect its completion fees at destination which was a different arrangement to that applying to the Maracaibo tankers. To arrive at a value for the Maracaibo tankers purchased by Island Tug, at or close to scrap value, "as lies" at Lake Maracaibo, one would have to add the cost of delivery to Victoria, B.C. This would be the "value of the tow," as the ships were already the property of Island Tug. After safe arrival they would have developed an increasingly higher value as work proceeded to fit them for their new careers as log barges, but that is another story after arrival at Victoria.

At first the insurance rates for "Total Loss Only" coverage, to the best of Wright's recollection, started at four per cent of the value of the tow in the case of the Maracaibo ships, or the cost of the tow in the case of the Japanese-bound Liberty ships, but gradually these came down to around two per cent, as underwriters in effect built up a reserve fund from premiums on earlier tows, as their favourable experience grew.

On one occasion a vessel called the *Gambler* was in serious trouble in mid-Pacific. Island Tug was hired to bring her in on Lloyds' Open Form, usually referred to as the "No Cure–No Pay" salvage form which meant what it said—there would be no towing or salvage fee if the vessel was not successfully recovered. The *Gambler* was a Greek-owned, Panamanian-registered freighter managed from New York in a typical arrangement involving flag-of-convenience shipping. Of 5,700 gross tons and built in the United States in 1919, the ship was on its way from Baltimore to Kobe, Japan, when her engine broke down and she developed a sinking condition - without power her pumps would not work. A towline was put aboard her on January 10, 1960, but by the 14th it was obvious she could not be saved, so the crew was removed and *Gambler* was abandoned.

Mr. Elworthy had previously asked Wright to place insurance to cover the expenses of a lengthy ocean trip for his tug, in the event that the salvage attempt was unsuccessful. Wright was successful in quickly placing the needed insurance, as he put it, "so the gamble was taken out of the *Gambler,*" so far as Island Tug was concerned. To have saved the *Gambler* would have been a matter of pure luck on top of towing skill. The incident serves to illustrate the nature of ocean salvage. It was and is a speculative business best left to those equipped to take the risk. The loss of the vessel could in no way be laid at Island Tug's door, the ship was already destined, barring a miracle, for the bottom of the sea. This was one of the very rare occasions when Island Tug went to the rescue of a distressed ship at sea and had not succeeded in bringing her in.

It was common enough for ocean salvage and towing companies to insure their fees for unsuccessful salvage attempts. In fact ocean towing contracts had been developing since large tugs had developed, mostly in Europe, by firms such as Smit. They had made a specialty of towing large floating dry docks and oversize dredgers to faraway destinations as the needs of international shipping grew. This traffic had started about 1875 and a small group of specialist marine underwriters had grown with the business, building up experience and reserves to enable them to offer a highly specialized market. What is not usually understood by laypeople, is the nature of specialization in insurance and the fact that markets for handling it are usually only to be found in such organizations as Lloyds. There are also a few specialist companies usually centred on London, New York and certain offshore centres such as Bermuda. If an insurance market for this highly specialized class of risk had not been available at Lloyds, it is doubtful that there would have been many, if any salvage companies willing to gamble their all on hazardous undertakings such as ocean towing and salvage.

Chapter Eight

THE HAZARDS OF THE OCEAN PASSAGE

Quoted with the permission of Captain James E. "Ted" Wilson from his book Full Line, Full Away.

TORPEDOED BY A LIMEROCK BARGE

To the layman the entire concept of "risk" can be a jungle to understand. For the moment it is sufficient to say that danger, hazard, jeopardy and peril are all embraced within the word "risk," as these are the exposures leading to loss. The avoidance of loss, or at least its minimization, is the objective of risk management. Risk management carries with it the responsibility of avoiding or at least containing danger, hazard, jeopardy and peril.

The following incident occurred in the 1970s, probably at a time before Seaspan had its own risk manager. At the time Captain Wilson was acting as port captain at Seaspan, a role he filled until his retirement in 1983. In those days he became involved in a number of international "incidents" involving marine accidents at sea which required him to undertake coordination duties involving pilotage authorities, the U.S. and Canadian coastguard safety requirements and liaison with both coast guards as well as Seaspan's legal counsel and insurance broker. In fact, many of the duties now picked up by a regular risk manager.

However, no amount of risk management is able to guard against the wholly fortuitous. In this instance it was the navigational error or misjudgement of a third party many miles away, whose action transformed the wrongdoing vessel into the other party in an international legal wrangle as blame was fixed or apportioned.

In the case now cited, *Sudbury II* was towing the barge *Seaspan 270*. Laden with about 12,000 tons of limerock from Texada Island destined for the Columbia River. The tug and tow had made the critical turn past the traffic separation buoy at the entrance to the Straits of Juan de Fuca so that both vessels were now on a southerly course paralleling the Washington outer coast. Traffic was moderately heavy in the area as ships came out of Juan de Fuca Strait and came in from the open ocean to make a landfall.

As *Sudbury II* and its barge proceeded, a vessel was perceived on the radar screen rounding Cape Flattery which was travelling at a greater speed than the tug and tow and would pass between the Washington coast and *Sudbury II*. With no vessels ahead the mate went into the chartroom and a little later felt a distinct jar or jerk, followed immediately by an increase in engine revolutions. He observed by radar that the image of the *Seaspan 270* had merged with another.

It was self-evident that the towline had been cut as *Sudbury II* took in her remaining towline, 1,600 feet of the 2,400 feet that had been paid out. By now a vessel named *Japan Maple* was sending out a mayday to the effect that she had been hit by an unknown vessel and was making water. Arriving back at her tow, *Sudbury II* found the bow of *Seaspan 270* deeply embedded in the hull of the Japanese bulk-carrier, *Japan Maple*. With all accommodation and machinery aft, the barge had hit the Japanese ship almost like a torpedo, just ahead of her navigating bridge and the two were now locked in place. Both U.S. and Canadian Coast Guard vessels were on the scene. The Seaspan barge's collision bulkhead was holding and while her stem had penetrated almost to the Japanese ship's centreline, it was determined that they could be safely parted.

Japan Maple was taken into Victoria where she was joined by *Sudbury II* and her barge. Damage to the Japanese ship required considerable shipyard attention and then she was allowed to proceed after posting the usual guarantee bonds. Other than a broken towline damage to the tug and barge was confined to the actual collision damage sustained by the barge, but because of her ship-shaped bow even that was not too serious and she could complete her voyage. *Japan Maple* was held wholly responsible when the case came before the Federal Court as there was clear failure to understand the nature of the tug and tow and the hazard of crossing a towline, despite the fact that all lights of the Seaspan tow were in good order and correctly displayed. This meant that in the final settlement Japan Line's hull and P & I underwriters would have paid Seaspan's account for damage sustained as well as the consequences of delay. For them, it was a relatively small bill compared to the damage sustained by the freighter.

ASHORE AT LONG BEACH

This account is composed from notes and photographs supplied by Captain J.P. Brown, senior marine surveyor at Marine Surveyors of Western Canada, who attended the wreck and advised on salvage on behalf of underwriters.

Anyone familiar with Vancouver Island's West Coast will know that Long Beach is famous for the beach that gives it its name. Long, flat and shallow for a long way out it is not a good place for a ship to go ashore. It's a favourite haunt for wind surfers and ski boarders on account of the usual surf conditions and high winds. From a ship operational point of view, in the event of a stranding, the only good thing that can be said of it is that the sand is packed very hard and is not prone to tidal scouring under the extremities of a stranded vessel, such as happens at the Goodwin Sands in the English Channel. There, tidal scouring is a certainty and few vessels that go ashore ever come off. Their usual fate is to quickly break their backs with the two halves sinking in the sands never to be recovered.

Forest Prince was built at Yarrows, Esquimalt, in

[84] **The First of a New Breed:** The **Forest Prince** was the first of a revolutionary new design for a self-loading, self-dumping log barge. As the forest industry was in an expansionary mode, she was also the smallest of the twin-craned version and succeeding barges increased in size.

[85] Superior Straits was her usual towing partner, but on the occasion of this mishap another tug was doing the job. In those days lighter lifts of a few logs at a time were the standard. Today they pick up bundles equivalent to a logging-truck load weighing up to 60 tons.

1960. She was the first of a new generation of self-loading, self-dumping log barges to be followed by 14 similar ships, including two self-propelled units owned by Kingcome. They were built with the maximum of technical efficiency for heavy-duty log handling and the hard usage to which they were put quickly showed up in fore and aft bulkheads or bunkers and along the cargo deck. *(see chapter 5 in Boomsticks & Towlines, Book 1 in this series)*

With an overall length of 305.77 ft, breadth of 60.0 ft, depth of hull of 17.03 ft and draft of 11.58 ft, she had a gross tonnage of 2,724 and an estimated deadweight carrying capacity of about 7,000 tons. The Straits Towing tug *Superior Straits* was usually matched to her and on this occasion she had loaded a full cargo of red cedar for account of her owners, B.C. Forest Products Ltd. On the way south the towline broke and the barge drifted ashore before

much could be done to avert the accident. She came to rest in the surf of Long Beach, like a massive, helpless beached whale, burdened with a capacity load of red cedar logs.

On the occasion of the accident in 1969, she was in the charge of a tug owned by another company when the towline broke. They were in a gale out in the open ocean. The barge was cast ashore before anything could be done to reconnect tug and tow. An examination of the barge indicated that there was no discernable twisting, hogging or sagging in the hull as it rested on a firm sand bed. The usual flurry of activity followed between the owners of the barge, the insurance underwriters and the marine surveyors. A "No Cure-No Pay" salvage contract was negotiated with Island Tug & Barge in Victoria in the amount of $100,000. A special clause in the contract covered the salvage company for expenses incurred

[86] Grey skies watch over a rough sea as it buffets **Forest Prince** as she lies broadside to the waves.

[87] Here a helicopter borrowed from the Shell Oil exploration effort in Hecate Straits carried the specially made floatable towline from **Sudbury II,** laying beyond the surf line, to the stranded barge.

if the operation was cancelled before the special equipment laid on for the job could be readied. Obviously in a period of severe weather the vessel could have been destroyed, before salvage could be started, so it was very much a race against time before storm weather intervened.

Salvage operations could not be started immediately. There are two surflines on this beach, one just outside the low water mark and the other about a mile offshore. *Sudbury II* had to lay outside the offshore surfline, clearly too far for any standard towing line to reach the beached barge. An extended steel towline would have been an impossibility on account of weight. Instead, a three-inch diameter towline made up of nylon and polypropylene fibres, with a length of 6,500 feet was specially manufactured. This was estimated to have the requisite

strength and it would also float, thus avoiding the additional friction of dragging along the bottom which would be a deterrent to successful towing.

While awaiting delivery of the new towline a careful watch was kept on the barge to detect any distortion or unusual strain on the hull. Also a few logs were thrown off to follow where they might drift with each tide. As it turned out they were simply cast ashore over a relatively short distance. A large helicopter was borrowed from the Sedco drill rig working for Shell Oil Company in Hecate Straits. This machine had a pulling capacity of about 5,000 lb. On arrival at the beach the helicopter landed to allow Captain Brown and people from B.C. Forest Products including Captain Jack Bruno to confer with the pilots so that they understood what was planned.

In the meantime an assist tug stood by *Sudbury II*

[88] With the towline connected, a strenuous effort started on the falling tide to lighten **Forest Prince.** Here the crane operators pile logs on the beach to lighten the barge ready for the big pull on the next high tide. The lightened barge came off on the next tide and the jettisoned logs were recovered later from the high tide mark with an 80 per cent recovery. Still afloat in 2003, **Forest Prince** now functions as a flat-deck barge.

to help keep her head to sea while the actual towing operation got under way. The towline was coiled on the working deck of the big tug and from her it was lifted inshore by the helicopter for attachment to the barge while the tug paid out the line. As the tide receded the previous day two crane operators had been placed on board to jettison logs as far as possible to lighten the vessel so that she would lift more readily on the next flood tide which came during the night.

Sudbury II exerted her pulling power while the assist tug helped keep her on course. The log barge, with buoyancy now under her, eased off the sandy beach which had been her resting place and was towed into deep water and then into Ucluelet where an examination of the interior took place. The exam-ination showed some internal buckling and distor-tion, but she was otherwise found fit for removal to Victoria. The few remaining logs on board were removed and held in a bag boom pending future col-lection.

Later BCFP arranged with the owner of a nearby waterfront property to upgrade an access road to the beach to remove the jettisoned logs which had spread over a distance of about a mile with each change of tide. The final recovery of logs was over 80 per cent.

Forest Prince is still in service at the age of 43 years. Her cranes and the twin towers have been removed and when last seen by the author in 2002, she was in use as a flat deck barge. She had been fitted with conventional sidewalls and was loading a large cargo of scrap from the Mitchell Island facility.

A COLLISION WITH A CURIOUS PASSER-BY AND A BROKEN TOWLINE

Reprinted from the April 2000 issue of Wheelwash, *a Washington Marine Group employee publication, with permission of Corporate Communications, Seaspan International Ltd.*

The adventure of *Seaspan Commodore*'s crew began on January 13th, as the *Seaspan Rigger* was loaded with hemlock bundles and departed in tow of the *Seaspan Commodore,* destined for Coos Bay, Oregon. At around 0600 on January 14th, while outbound in Juan de Fuca Strait just west of Victoria, the deep-sea vessel, Philippino-owned *Cynthia Harmony,* struck the *Seaspan Rigger* while overtaking the two Washington Marine Group (WMG) vessels.

The collision occurred in the wide-open reaches of the strait where it is approximately 20 miles wide between Vancouver Island and the Olympic Peninsula. This was outside the B.C. Pilotage area so there were no local pilots on board at the time. International collision regulations require that a ship overtak-ing another is responsible to do so without causing the other vessel(s) to change course or speed to avoid collision. As a result, the *Seaspan Commodore, Seaspan Rigger* and *Cynthia Harmony* were required to return to Victoria for inspection by both Coast Guard and WMG engineering and operations personnel. After inspection and a 14-hour delay the unscathed log barge was released and proceeded to sea.

Coast Guard on the other hand detained *Cynthia Harmony* for a couple of days pending a complete inspection and repairs to the vessel. The ship actually sideswiped the *Seaspan Rigger* and, because the bundled logs overhung the barge, slight damage was restricted only to the cargo itself while the *Cynthia Harmony* had significant damage to its lifeboat and davits which were scraped by the logs.

[89] The Philippino bulk carrier **Cynthia Harmony,** seen here on a later voyage, was the ship that came too close to **Seaspan Rigger** when in the Straits of Juan de Fuca. The projecting logs on the barge scraped the upperworks of the bulk carrier which sustained damage to its porthand lifeboat.

Saved by a Hairsbreadth

Two days later and running about 100 miles behind schedule, the tug and her log barge encountered what was reported to be the worst storm of the winter.

"It was flat calm," said Captain Cam Hutchinson. "You'd think we were in Lost Lagoon. The storm came out of nowhere."

The shore-based weather station near Cascade Head on the Oregon Coast reported the wind at 116 knots. The *Seaspan Commodore* was 50 miles west of this headland and in the bight of the storm, running at reduced power heading into the wind or "heaved to." Shortly after daybreak, under the strain of the relentless seas, a wheelhouse window was pushed in, flooding the bridge and moments later the towline parted. This disastrous set of circumstances posed a great danger to the crew, tug and the barge.

First things first. The wheelhouse window had to be secured and the water damaged electronic navigation equipment assessed. After installing the storm cover on the window and mopping up the water it was determined that one radar and one VHF radio were damaged. Fortunately *Seaspan Commodore* carries secondary radar and radios. Once back on

their feet, the crew were faced with the extremely difficult and often impossible task of reattaching a towline to a barge in heavy seas. The drift rate of the barge set the rules—reattach a towline by 01.30 the next morning or the barge would be aground at Falcon Rocks on the Oregon Coast.

"Our number-one concern was making sure that no one got hurt." said Captain Hutchinson.

Weather conditions at the time were so severe that putting *Seaspan Commodore* near the barge would be too risky for an attempt to pick up the emergency towline. From the float line at the stern of the barge any contact between the *Seaspan Rigger* and the *Seaspan Commodore* would certainly hole one or both vessels. Complicating the situation, log bundles were being tossed off the barge as it rolled broadside in the 35-foot seas. The tug had to stay clear of the "propeller inspectors" until the top load of logs shed into the sea and the barge drifted well clear of its cargo. A log in one or both of the propellers had to be avoided. As the barge dispersed its cargo, the remote ballast system was activated to ballast the barge and slow its rolling and pitching. The situation became one of complete helplessness unless the weather conditions improved.

As the seas battered the *Seaspan Rigger,* water

found its way into the machinery space and shorted-out needed electrical components, which can be used remotely from the tug to drop the barge's anchor. The crew recognized this problem when the barges lights went out during the ballasting operations. This event ruled out dropping the anchor, which had been in the rescue plan once the barge drifted over the 100-fathom mark on its course for the rocks. This was another major setback and only one small glimmer of hope remained. Forecasters were cautiously predicting a slight improvement in the weather later that night. However, they were unable to make any rescue attempts until daylight hours.

Once the barge had finally shed better than half its cargo the *Seaspan Commodore* was able to come in for a closer look. A disappointed crew saw the floating trailing line, which was attached to the emergency towline washed up and fouled on the stern of the barge. Someone would have to transfer onto the barge and rig another trailing line. The weather was persisting and plans were well under way for the worst—a grounded barge.

As darkness fell response for a salvage of the *Seaspan Rigger* grounding at Falcon Rocks was set up, with a WMG team on site at Tillamook coast guard station, just south of Falcon Rocks. A coordinated team from North Vancouver resources was also being mobilized.

Meanwhile *Seaspan Commodore* and crew were vigilantly shadowing the barge in an effort to take advantage of the right moment when the sea might blink and allow a light-footed sailor to spring onto the barge. Several attempts were made throughout the night and miraculously the mate, Ray Nicol, jumped on the barge after a unique opportunity of timing, athletics, seamanship and boat handling. With great difficulty in the prevailing conditions a new trailing line was rigged by Nicol, the connection to the emergency towline was made and the *Seaspan Commodore* gently nursed the barge away from the shore which was now visible only one and a quarter miles from the barge.

Throughout the rest of the night *Seaspan Commodore* with *Seaspan Rigger* in tow, with Mr. Nicol still aboard the barge, proceeded north and into the Columbia River where anchors were put down at

Astoria and an exhausted crew were able to rest. Temporary repairs were made to the towing gear at Astoria and the voyage recommenced the following day to Coos Bay to deliver the remainder of the log load.

Author's notes:

No reason has been advanced as to why the Cynthia Harmony *sailed so close to the log barge, but it was probably for some mundane reason such as curiosity as to the unusual sight of a loaded log barge at sea. B.C. log barges are unique and have no exact equivalent anywhere else in the world except for two barges in the Baltic. It seems possible that someone in authority on board wanted to get close enough to shoot a video or take photos. In this instance they came too close!*

It is worth noting that the practice at Rivtow differs from Seaspan. After the first major stranding of Rivtow Carrier *when she was still relatively new, Captain J.P. Brown of the Marine Surveyors of Western Canada, Vancouver office, recommended the doubling up of the single towline by rigging the emergency towline as a second towline. The proposal met with resistance from the towing industry, but after the loss of* Rivtow Norseman *in similar conditions, Rivtow adopted the double towline policy, particularly for its new combination of* Rivtow Captain Bob *and* Rivtow Hercules. *Depending on the service the same requirement is sometimes applied to lesser units in the fleet. In retrospect, it is difficult to understand why underwriters did not insist on this practice at all times.*

Seaspan Rigger *might be regarded by those who are superstitious as being an "unlucky" ship. Although she survived the ordeals described above, she was very nearly a total loss when still a relatively young vessel. She ran aground while towing light on the West Coast of Vancouver Island. She broke her back, the two halves being recovered and rejoined in Esquimalt dry dock. Photos of this event are set out in* Boomsticks & Towlines, Book 1 *in this series.*

More recently, in October 2002, while dumping her load of logs in Howe Sound, the barge flipped over completely and remained there, keel up and with cranes resting in the mud. This was a perplexing matter as such an event was regarded as being outside the realm of possibility. Equally challenging was the matter of salvage, which necessitated the cutting away of the cranes underwater. In November 2002, a contract for salvage has been awarded to Smit International to right the barge. This was successfully done and after a period in the shipyhard for repairs, the Seaspan Rigger *re-emerged as* Seaspan Phoenix.

In the same winter Rivtow also had a large barge overturn while under tow with a full load of a coal product on board. This was Powell Carrier *which Smit also righted.*

Chapter Nine

RESTOCKING A FLEET: SHIP AND BARGE BUILDING OVERSEAS

From time to time in this series, reference has been made to the looming problem of replenishment of the British Columbia fleet of tugs and barges, particularly with a view to replacing the many vessels built in the period of the 1950s, through to the 1970s. These were the boom years for post-war shipbuilding as the industry, with the aid of a steadily reducing shipbuilding subsidy, strove to keep up with both expansion and replenishment of a fleet which at that time was phrasing out wooden equipment at the same time as it kept up with the expanding demands of its customers, particularly those in the forest industries.

Vessels wear out or become functionally obsolescent, which was the position faced by Rivtow when Harmac, one of its prime customers, in the interests of its own efficiency, changed its method of unloading woodchips at the plant. Theoretically Rivtow could have rebuilt the boxes on a number of its barges to accommodate the new method, which required a gate at the front end of the barge instead of at the stern, the previous method of allowing access to the inside of the box when unloading with wheeled equipment. In practice the existing woodchip barge inventory had a lot of older units which were facing a date with the shipbreakers, so that even in the ordinary course of business a replacement program was looming up.

The need to replace was a matter that could not be put off as the customer's reasonable demands had to be dealt with if the towing company wished to retain its account. It was a shot in the arm which would have done wonders for the two remaining locally owned yards—Allied and McKenzie—which were capable of building the latest advance in size required by the tug and barge industry. However, B.C. shipyard rates of pay and benefits had increased more substantially over the years and union contracts, while beneficial to workers, had contributed to pricing our shipbuilders out of the market. Added to these woes, the former Minister of Industry, Hon. John Manley in Ottawa, in correspondence with the author, advanced the suggestion that a program was in place with the additional bait that the fast write-off program was still available. Manley confirmed in writing that "programs were in place" to help Canadian shipbuilding and implied that his government felt that it was doing enough to help builders already. He avoided the question of wholesale obsolescence.

The last federal election resulted in a change in the ministry, with Manley being replaced by Hon. Brian Tobin, the former premier of Newfoundland. Tobin had been nicknamed "Captain Canada" for his aggressive stance in the fisheries "war" with foreign fleets in the matter of fishing the Grand Banks in the early '90s. Following his appointment to succeed Manley, Tobin released a major review of Canadian shipbuilding policy, which might bring some answers that could help West Coast yards. What Tobin has recommended for adoption is $150 million of preferred low-rate financing, which it is claimed will enable Canadian shipyards to compete with foreign builders. Presumably the theory is that when low financing costs are factored in, these will offset the higher price paid to a Canadian shipyard by comparison with a foreign yard. That proposition overlooks the "first-cost factor" which represents "a bird in the hand" by comparison with lower future interest charges which still have to accrue over time and may be said to be like "a bird in the bush." Time will tell as to how beneficial this new package will be to the West Coast yards, but to the time of writing only one West Coast owner, Gemini Marine Services, has seen its way to taking advantage of the scheme.

Shields Navigation, now operating as Island Tug & Barge Ltd., was the first to go to China to have a new oil products barge built there. Price and delivery were attractive and with proper supervision, quality met the requirements of the major oil company whose mixed products are distributed from the barge. Going to China could be taken in part as a response to Federal inactivity, but was mostly a result of a hard-headed business decision. Shields was bidding for a major oil distribution account in a competitive situation and had no real choice if it wanted new equipment, custom designed for the needs of its customer.

The oil barge could have been built in Vancouver, but Chinese prices indicated that woodchip barges could also be built there and still landed in Vancouver at about a 30-per cent saving including import taxes and delivery charges. Presumably a similar measure applied with the oil barge.

In any event both Rivtow and Seaspan, each faced with the same basic problem of replacement in many older units of each of their fleets, no doubt exhausted all other alternatives and then settled on Chinese yards near Shanghai. China is not a newcomer to shipbuilding as even as long ago as WW I steel freighters were built in yards around Shanghai for the British and American governments, but in more recent years it has undergone a massive expansion as the needs of the Chinese nation have grown. During the past 20 years or so, it has competed with other Far Eastern nations and has succeeded in obtaining contracts for large bulk carriers up to about 50,000 tons. On the other hand when Chinese owners have needed something more technically advanced, such as the new generation of container ships they have gone to foreign yards, an example being the

container ship contracts placed by Seaspan Shipbrokers on behalf of China Shipping Container Lines with South Korean yards.

Building chip barges is relatively simple being mainly a matter of the quality of the steel and the welding employed and both are understood to be fully adequate. Design was entirely Canadian with Marc Mulligan, then with Seaspan, designing the units built for his company.

Getting the barges delivered is a more challenging problem, which both companies handled differently. Seaspan detached its flagship tug *Seaspan Commodore* from its log barge towing duties and sent it to China towing a number of obsolete barges ostensibly sold for scrap. The tug returned to Vancouver with four woodchip barge hulls, two stacked on two with a fifth barge hull for Fraser Terminals making up the third vessel in the tow. In each case the woodchip box or covered barge house was completed at Vancouver.

Rivtow brought eight barges over on the deck of a dockship, the Belgian-flag submersible freighter *Swift*, which normally was employed in carrying heavy drill-rig platforms and similar large volume objects. For purposes of loading, the eight Rivtow barges were rafted abreast of each other being wired very tightly together so that they floated like one unit. The dockship was then submerged deeply enough that the rafted barges could be floated over the cargo deck of the dockship, which was then pumped out. Having regained its seagoing trim, the barges were secured to the ship by welding small steel plates, called bendplates from the bottom of each barge to the deck of the ship thus making ship and deckload integral to each other for the transpacific voyage. On arrival at Vancouver the bendplates were burned away, *Swift* submerged and the raft of eight barges floated off ready to be fed into the traffic movement from lower mainland mills to Harmac and Crofton.

Since this initial order to China, Seaspan has gone back to Shanghai for a large push-pull trailer barge, *Coastal Express*, which was delivered in 2000 with two further chip barges loaded as deck cargo for their maiden voyage to Vancouver, and further orders from B.C. owners are understood to be in the works.

Unfortunately *Coastal Express* became a total loss following a marine mishap in 2001. She has since been replaced by *Coastal Spirit,* a similar but somewhat larger barge. Island Tug & Barge has also been back to China for a two more large petroleum product barges to meet its delivery commitments.

ORIENTAL SHIPYARDS

Steel shipbuilding has been an important industry in Japan since the late nineteenth century. Lacking technical proficiency at the beginning of the 20th century it went to Britain for its warship needs and at least one battleship, the *Kongo,* built in Britain in 1912 survived to fight as a major unit on the Japanese side in World War Two. Japan sent technicians to Britain for training and engaged British managers to help set up its own shipyards up to 1914. Since then it has relied on its own resources and after WW II exported some of them to neighbouring countries

The Japanese became so proficient in building merchant ships, that the First World War brought it big orders from Britain and the United States for cargo liners and trampships. Delivery of these ships proved conclusively that anything in the way of ship-building that could be done in the west could also be done in Japan. Japan did however have difficulty in bringing shipbuilding costs down to international levels of competitivenes partly because it had to rely on foreign sources for technical equipment and machinery for both shipyards and ship outfittings. It was so busy building up its own navy and merchant marine between the wars that it was not a factor in the competitive aspects of international shipbuilding. It was not until after World War Two when its ship-building industry became the first major export industry to help turn around the country's prostrate economy that the world started to take note of Japan as a serious competitive factor in world shipbuilding.

The Philippinos and Greeks were the first to go to Japan for new ships after the war, but very soon international oil companies found that the Japanese yards could do highly acceptable enlargement jobs on U.S. war-built T2 tankers, replacing midbodies and increasing deadweight capacity in the process. Very soon orders for new tankers followed until by 1956 the Japanese shipbuilding industry had become the world leader eclipsing Britain as the world's largest post-war shipbuilder.

Inevitably as the standard of living of the average Japanese increased so also did many of its industrial costs. While it remained competitive on complex more highly technical ship types such as container ships and liquified gas carriers, the orders for more mundane types of shipping where labour costs were much more of a factor swung in favour of Japan's Oriental neighbours, most particularly Korea and then China. Singapore and to a far lesser extent, Hong Kong and Thailand, also had thriving ship-building industries, but they tended to rely on smaller craft and a great deal of repair and outfitting work which focussed on the oil industry. In fact they also tended to benefit from Japanese investment in Singapore and Thailand which for political reasons was not going to go into Korea and China. The latter two countries, in particular became Japan's out and out competitors. In fact Korea became a major builder of Very Large Crude Carriers (VLCC) and Ultra-Large Crude Carriers (ULCC), two classes of outsize tankers and is now in first place as the leading builder of container ships.

Although there are many issues to be taken into account in costing shipbuilding, the core factors affecting shipbuilding costs are the ready availability of low-cost shipbuilding steel and low labour costs. When these are combined with skilled labour and technical proficiency, it all adds up to an unbeatable combination. Barges, for example, are nothing more than a combination of low-cost steel and moderately skilled labour and the technical supervision involved can be provided by the foreign buyer's representative. That, of course, is exactly what happened when B.C. tug and barge companies went shopping in China. It's a process which now seems set to continue until Chinese shipbuilding loses its cost advantage which will happen at some time in the future while shipbuilding, particularly that which is simplified, swings to a new low-cost economy in another country.

DEALING WITH THE SINGAPORE SHIPYARDS

In the early '70s, Singapore was a thriving centre in total contrast to an earlier visit immediately after the war. The naval dockyard at Johore, located on the north shore of Singapore Island where it faced the mainland across a narrow strait over which the Japanese had attacked when they captured the city in early 1942, was the only really visible sign of shipyard activity. Most of the rest of the shoreline bordering Johore Straits as it swept in from the sea at its eastern entrance was lined with mangrove swamps, rubber plantations and a few small villages. By the time I retraced my steps 25 years later much of this land and its shoreline had given way to industrial activity, with large new shipyards like Keppel (not in Johore Straits), Jurong, Sembawang and Westbank, in addition to the former navy yard now known as Johore Dockyard, as well as a variety of minor concerns.

I had the opportunity of visiting several including one which intrigued me greatly as it was solely engaged in barge building. They called them pontoons there, following European practice, but they were Singapore versions of barges that might otherwise have been built on the Canadian or U.S. west coasts, but there were differences.

The barges built in Singapore at that time paid little attention to sophisticated hull forms. The rakes at either end were virtually identical without any semi-circular profile at the bow end. Aft they lacked skegs so that towing on any sort of a long towline or in tandem must have presented problems as without skegs they would not track well. All angles were sharp except where the top or brow plate at bow and stern was faired around to join the side shell plating. The bilges were constructed by using a relatively small diameter pipe to which bottom plating and side shell plating was welded to form a severe 90-degree join unrelieved by preformed quarter round or twin chine bilge plates. Rubbing strakes of split half-pipe were welded all around at deck level and in some instances the sides were protected by a strake placed at the mid-depth point.

[90] Singapore was one of the hot new places for foreign shipping interests to have ships built in the smaller size range back in the 1970s. Several shipyards built offshore supply vessels, anchor-handling tugs and a range of barges. Skills initially were limited, but with technical help from Japan, Europe and North America rapid strides were made. Oil exploration gave the shipyard business a huge impetus and here can be seen a Singapore-built jackup rig with an assortment of barges at a Johore Strait shipyard.

Perhaps the most surprising feature of everything I saw was the location of this Singapore barge builder. It was hidden away in a jungle thicket of dense mangrove trees into which a muddy tidal creek threaded its way. The creek had several branches in which barges were moored drying out at low tide. The building berths were nothing more or less than mud berths on which sat low level wood piles made up of dunnage type lumber arranged criss-cross. When the barge was ready for launching at a high tide it would take little power to push the barge with a bulldozer and as it was moved the piles would collapse, the barge with partial flotation would then be towed or pushed across the mud into the creek. Here it would sit haphazardly among other barges while work proceeded above the waterline to finish her. By comparison with B.C.-built barges, the vessels coming out of this yard, which were probably mostly meant as harbour craft were very lightly built, but compared with our costs, they were likewise very cheap.

This jungle yard was owned by a local Chinese businessman. The bigger yards were mostly owned or certainly heavily influenced by foreign ownerships, particularly such companies as IHI of Japan. An odd exception was the Westbank yard owned in those days by a group of Israeli Jews who controlled a larger conglomerate type company called Pan Electric. Among other interests Pan also controlled the locally based deep-sea salvage and towing concern which operated a former British Admiralty salvage ship. It had undertaken the usual range of building jobs mostly for the oil industry, but a big part of the industry down there was also given over to conversions, typically wartime LCTs which were augmented with derricks for use in carrying baled rubber and logs. Westbank did its share of all this work and, as I relate later in chapter 15, I came into contact with them over the proposed matter of building some pipe-laying barges.

In this instance these vessels had been designed in the States to standards laid down by the American Bureau of Shipping. This was a different proposition to the flimsy barges built without classification society supervision in the jungle yard mentioned above. Like Canada there were no Singaporean rules requiring classification society involvement on locally owned unmanned vessels. That was entirely a matter of owner's choice.

The naval architect at Westbank was very interested in the B.C. use of skegs on barges when I first met him in 1970, but at that time they were not properly understood in Singapore, perhaps because at that time local tows seemed to be undertaken on short towlines. I was able to help him out by sending a set of plans for a B.C.-designed and -built barge, so that when I went back in 1972, the use of skegs was becoming more widespread in that area. Apart from my small contribution in this regard, the projected American designed pipe-laying barges had skegs of adequate design and dimension.

The small steel shipyard I visited in the same period in Hong Kong was situated on the ocean side of the island at Aberdeen. This yard specialized in building self-propelled lighters and landing craft type vessels. It was owned and run by expatriate owners from Denmark and the United States as I recollect. In contrast to the sprawling jungle yard at Singapore, this little yard occupied a very small patch of waterfront, sandwiched between neighbouring buildings. Every square inch of land was therefore very important and reflected the high land values prevailing in Hong Kong even then.

Thirty years later, in fact very recently, I have been able to witness at first hand similar dealings with Chinese builders. In this instance dealings were negotiated through a non-Chinese supervisory firm specializing in handling contracts on behalf of clients. They were also used to working in close concert with the classification societies. Negotiations were handled expertly and with great promptness by the Chinese yards and the facilitators, but great emphasis was placed on the necessity for continuous supervision by genuine arms-length supervisors. This was to ensure that work was done to required standards and classification rules. Mistakes were not simply glossed over.

Supervision was not cheap and was factored into the overall cost of the vessel. The classification societies do not provide building supervision in detail, but they can be expected to reject classification when they find that work is not to specification, if it has any bearing on their rules.

[91] Jungle Shipyard: Situated in a mangrove swamp on Singapore island, this Chinese-owned shipyard built a variety of steel barges to very simple specifications. With identical rakes fore and aft, they did not have skegs. The chines were a hard right angle welded to a steel pipe or shape set internally.

[92] Jungle Shipyard: Two new refu-elling tank barges built for Esso lay on the mud awaiting a high tide. In the fore-ground miscellaneous barges, including an open hatch lighter, will shift their position with every tide.

[93] Jungle Shipyard: Three barges under construction on a mudflat sur-rounded by palm trees. When ready for launching, bulldozers were brought in to do the honours shoving the barges on rollers into the water.

Chinese-built barges delivered to Vancouver have been found to be fully satisfactory and are standing up to usage requirements without any specific problems. The jury will be out for many years on matter of longevity and what they will be like after forty years or so of hard service on the coast.

LOSSES ON DELIVERY TOWS OF BARGES TO VANCOUVER

The several owners who have had barges built in China have used differing ways of getting their vessels to British Columbia. As noted Rivtow took its only delivery of chipbarges on the deck of a semi-submersible freighter, Seaspan has towed both ways with redundant equipment deemed only fit for scrap, from Vancouver to Shanghai, returning with a multiple tow usually with part of it piggy-backing as deck cargo. *Seaspan Commodore* is the vessel normally nominated for these transpacific tows.

Island Tug & Barge, through its more recent years under the leadership of Captain Bob Shields were the pioneers in this trend. They first went to China for a fuel barge in 1999 and since then a succession have followed involving IT&B, Seaspan, Rivtow and Fraser River Terminals. International Maritime Organisation (IMO) rules now require double hulls for all new tanker tonnage around the world and in accordance with this requirement Island Tug was the first on the coast to place a double hull barge in service.

At least one delivery had a bad experience with a tow, which has been noted. This became a Federal Court of Canada case, *Island Tug & Barge v. the ship Haedong Star 99, et al (2002)*. The plaintiff, Island Tug & Barge, successfully presented its case based on the facts which stated that the newly completed tank barge *ITB Provider* was in tow of the delivery tug *Haedong Star 99* when the barge sustained damage through the fault of the tug and both had to put into the Russian Siberian port of Nakhodka. The barge had to be returned to its builders to make good the damage, but as she was deemed unseaworthy for the tow back to Shanghai she was lifted and removed by a semi-submersible vessel to Shanghai. With the cost of delivery, repairs, cost in part of delivery voyage, loss of use and earnings, the claim added up to 1.76 million dollars. The Federal Court found for Island Tug although it should be noted that this type of loss often takes years to settle finally, as marine

[94] The revived **Island Tug & Barge** under Shields management can fairly claim to be the first to "discover" the potential of the Chinese shipbuilding industry. Here is the 15,000-barrel **ITB Provider,** built at Jinling Shipyard near Shanghai, in 2001, proceeding down Vancouver harbour. Built to a high IMO specification with a double hull and ten cargo tanks, the barge was delivered via a transpacific tow direct from China. IT&B has two tugs capable of transpacific ocean towing, **Island Monarch** and **Island Tugger.**

underwriters have the right of subrogation. They can and do litigate for and against each other in the names of the original contracting parties who might have been fully compensated years earlier.

Island Tug has two vessels in its fleet, *Island Tugger* and *Island Monarch,* both capable of undertaking delivery voyages, although it is usually the former vessel that would do such jobs. The third delivery of an oil barge is expected in September 2003.

The trend to offshore construction in China is now well established and for at least the bigger companies it will likely be expanded. Already tugboat hulls are coming over as deck cargo on a new barge to be fitted and finished in Vancouver. The first of these, *Seaspan Tempest* and *Seaspan Venture* are now in service and look like attractive and efficient additions to the fleet.

[95] **Old Ships for New:** When Seaspan dispatched **Seaspan Commodore** to China to bring back five barges in a transpacific tow, the opportunity was taken to dispose of old equipment. Here **Seaspan 200,** a limerock and salt barge, is towed out past West Vancouver on June 3, 1998, with tank barge **Seaspan 823,** ex-**G G700,** loaded on deck, bound for a Chinese scrapyard. When they arrived there the Chinese found further employment for them. Note also the heavy ocean towing gear rigged as described in chapter 5.

[96] The latest addition to the Island Tug & Barge fleet left China in September 2003 in tow of **Island Monarch.** Named **ITB Trader,** it will be an ocean-going tanker capable of world-wide trading including the Arctic. She will carrying 65,000 barrels, which represents a dead-weight of close to 10,000 tons. **Island Monarch** has been refitted with an Intercon coupler system to facilitate push towing in open ocean conditions.

Chapter Ten

THE SUPPORTIVE SERVICES: SHIP FINANCE AND KINDRED ISSUES

Since time immemorial, man has needed help to launch or maintain marine ventures. Thus in modern times financial services have been provided from sectors of the financial markets which over time have developed very sophisticated working methods that are supportive of the needs of traders and vessel owners alike.

For many centuries the only way in which a vessel could be financed was through equity investment or the process known as bottomry. In the first instance equity in the vessel was sold off to investors in fractions. Thus the practice grew up when eventually a vessel was recognized in law as being divisable into 64 shares, the simple process of division by two, so that the two halves become four quarters and four quarters become eight/eighths and so on. Why it was halted at 64 is not known, but presumably 64/64ths, the fraction into which a British vessel can be legally divisible was recognized as being sufficient to ensure an adequate spread of participation and, therefore, distribution of the risk over a wide number of individuals. It also had the advantage that a wide number of people could own the vessel without incurring too much personal risk or having to outlay a larger amount of investment money.

Up until repatriation of our constitution from Britain, a Canadian vessel was always a British ship by nationality. After repatriation ships owned and registered at a Canadian port of registry became Canadian legally, as well as in fact. In that Canada acquired almost every facet of its maritime laws and shipping practices from Britain, it follows equally that the principle of divisibility into 64th interests

applied to Canadian vessels also.

Who started the division into 64ths is not known, but the practice probably started with the early Phoenician traders of the Eastern Mediterranean who were also credited with devising the security instrument known as bottomry. This was a method whereby a loan could be arranged against the security of the vessel, a form of mortgage, but raised for a somewhat different purpose. It was a temporary way of raising funds to enable a voyage to be completed. A bottomry bond could be arranged by the master of the vessel without reference to the owner who might be hundreds or thousands of miles away and totally out of touch as would inevitably apply in ancient times. The practice of bottomry was used until comparatively modern times up to the period when availability of cable and telegraph services enabled masters to contact owners.

A rate of interest was charged for advancing the bottomry loan, but it was at a higher rate of interest, perhaps twice that charged for ordinary loans. It was a way of recognizing risk by way of what amounted to a premium as the loan was automatically extinguished in the event of the loss of the vessel before arrival. It might be said to be the forerunner of the policy of insurance, generally credited to the same Phoenicians. A bottomry bond was without conditions save only for repayment upon safe arrival whereas the marine policy was something more specific carrying conditions and making exceptions. These gradually became more sophisticated with time until we reached the stage of the modern marine policy.

Many Phoenician insurance and other commercial practices spread throughout other Mediterranean trading communities, such as those of Greece, Venice and Carthage. It was probably such groups as the Hanseatic merchants of what became North Germany and the Lombards of Italy, the latter among the first recognizable bankers, who formed powerful asociations and greatly influenced the development of trade. It was the English who first codified a great deal of this to give us banking, shipping, insurance and commercial laws which provide the basis for much of today's modern commerce. English law (Scottish law differed) was so widely respected that provision was, and still is, made in many foreign insurance and other contracts such as bills of lading, charters and contracts of affreightment for disputes to be settled in accordance with British law and practice, even in some instances naming the City of London as the place where contractual issues were to be resolved and settled.

Selling of 64th shares was common until late in the nineteenth century. An example where the ship manager distributed risk was set out in the book *Evan Thomas, Radcliffe: A Cardiff Shipowning Company*, by Geraint Jenkins. In it the full details of the financing of the steamship *Gwenllian Thomas* of 1882 are laid out. Nine individuals held 2/64ths each and the remaining 46 shares were held by 46 named individuals. Many were tradesmen who hoped to profit in their specialty beyond their proportionate share of profits. Almost all were from South Wales or vicinity but two shares were held by a marine insurance broker at Lloyds, who would profit from insurance commissions and one each by ship agents at Malta and Palermo, Sicily. As the ship was to be used in the Mediterranean trade, these agents stood to gain by way of fees and commissions on freight. It was a time-honoured way of building a business based on controlled connections.

In any event, the process of selling 64th shares still exists, although selling off of 64th interests to a variety of people is relatively uncommon as a great many vessels are registered to the ownership of limited liability companies whose title is registered to show that the company owns all 64 shares in the vessel...but there are always exceptions to every rule.

The author's own company, Georgia Shipping Ltd., financed a number of its barges during the period 1963–65 through the sale of 64th shares, each of which were shown on a common contract signed by all participants as being owned by an individual registered owner who in most instances owned more than one share. By this agreement between the various 1/64th vessel shareholders, one shareholder was shown as managing owner, in these instances it being Georgia Shipping, as it took care to be the holder of one or more shares registered in its name, and the entire group agreed in the same common contract to raise a mortgage on the vessel. The mortgagee did all its dealings with Georgia Shipping. Georgia was empowered by the common contract to encumber the vessel with a preagreed mortgage. It was an arrangement very similar to a limited partnership in real estate. The Germans have handy legislation covering marine partnerships of this nature, which they call "partenrederei." We have no such convenient arrangement in Canada, it being up to the entrepreneur to create his own limited partnership as he is best able within the existing legal framework. Some real legislation governing strata properties was found to be a good starting reference point and was useful in formulating an arrangement comparable to the German partnership company. Incidentally it should be noted that Germany has one of the most vigorous post-war merchant navies and it is due in no small part to widespread use of these partnership companies which are also understood to create tax shelters for the participants.

The common contract between the syndicate owners, which was not a registered document in the ship's registry, specified that Georgia would operate the vessel. It would also collect its earnings, pay the mortgage and cover the vessel's other expenses such as periodic maintenance, provide a vessel name in keeping with its system of naming and paint it in Georgia's colours and do all other things in the best interests of the vessel, as if it was Georgia's own property. This included placing suitable insurance on the hull as well as P & I (legal liability) insurance.

While there was nothing illegal about the arrangement, the process of winding up Georgia Shipping some years later led to an interesting legal case which demonstrated the flaws in the Georgia arrangement. What we could have done is file the partnership contract, ancillary to the bill of sale, with the Registrar of Shipping even if it meant putting him to the trouble of repeating all the participants names on the register and, of course, making our business open to all and sundry. Better still, we should have used another third party or corporate entity as the ship's husband or managing owner, virtually a trustee, which would have obviated the need to set out all the participants names where they would then have become common knowledge to others who had no business accessing this information. Georgia could have maintained its position as a management company at the same time as it could have maintained an arms length relationship with the vessel owning syndicate.

In any event the case which was brought by the late Timothy Cameron of the law firm McMaster Boyles & Parkes, acting for a number of creditors of Georgia from among the towing fraternity, failed. It was alleged that Georgia by painting its name on the barges had sought to mislead, if not defraud, in obtaining credit by misrepresenting that it was stronger by virtue of its presumed ownership of three barges beneficially owned by the investors to whom it had sold 64th interests. We went through the usual Examination for Discovery and presented our documents dealing with ownership and denied any intent to mislead, citing numerous examples where shipping and local tugboat companies like VanTug painted their name on their barges without having actual ownership.

In an effort to split hairs during the examination, it was alleged by the plaintiffs that there was a difference between painting the company's name on the hull, which implied ownership, and painting the name on the sidewalls or the woodchip containment box which was by way of an advertisement. We maintained that the sidewalls or woodchip box was an integral part of the entire vessel, making it suitable for its particular employment and it made no difference as to where the name was painted.

It was alledged that by not filing the contract with the Registrar of Shipping we had sought to perpetrate a fraud on our creditors. The able defender was W.J. "Bae" Wallace of Bull, Housser & Company who acted for the receiver of Georgia Shipping in the matter and the judgement when handed down fully vindicated our action in painting our name on the barges in accordance with common custom and, when the contract between Georgia and its investors was produced, the argument as to intent to defraud was demolished. As with "the pot calling the kettle black," the very people who sought to upset our beneficial owners and claim title as creditors, were never known to release details of their own financing arrangements beyond what went on the ship's registers.

There was an attractive feature from the investor's point of view in raising a mortgage. In the first instance, the investment was made by the individual to gain the advantage of the fast write-offs allowed under the Income Tax Act, by which vessels that qualified for construction under the Canadian Vessels Construction Assistance Act of 1949 (CVCA) could be depreciated at the rate of 100 per cent over three years and the depreciation used as an offset against other income, a provision which still applies under the Income Tax Act. The other beneficial provision of the CVCA was the shipbuilding subsidy which was paid directly to the shipyard. When it was first made available, it was set at 40 per cent of gross building cost and then over the years of its existence gradually reduced until, at about 12 per cent, it was ended. The first reduction was from 40 to 33.33 per cent followed later to 25 per cent and then by successive reductions until it was phased out in the 1970s.

The availability of investments in vessels had appeal to people in higher income brackets as the depreciation could be taken against the gross value of the investment and was not confined to the net value. Using values that might have been typical in the '50s and early '60s, a man with a $50,000 cash investment against which a back-to-back mortgage had been raised of a further $50,000 could depreciate against the gross value of $100,000, effectively doubling the value of his tax shelter. It became even better when say a one-third shipbuilding subsidy was awardable under the CVCA Act so that equity of $50,000 could be matched to a subsidy of $50,000 (at 33.33 per cent of gross building cost) and a mortgage of say $50,000 by which the investor would depreciate against a total gross of $150,000. These were typical values of the barges we built in the 1960s. Today that amount would be several times greater.

The ability to write off 100 per cent of the gross investment, in this example, of $150,000 was a tax shelter few who could lay out the initial funds, could refuse and it was used extensively to finance many of the barges employed in the woodchip trade. To increase flexibility several investors could club together to own the vessel using 64ths as the convenient divisible method, but single holdings by wealthy individuals were very common as the raising of $50,000 in cash was easily attainable by a surprising number of investors. An examination of the ship's registry documents revealed where substantial pockets of wealth existed in Victoria and Vancouver, although this was also cloaked in many instances by registering ownership to a nominee, most commonly a trust company. This was the usual practice at Straits Towing, probably influenced by Fred B. Brown who had close connections with the trust industry. Vancouver Tug and Island Tug did not ever seem to share the concern of Straits, registering in the name of the beneficial owner.

To be able to participate in this type of tax-sheltered investment usually required access to an intermediary individual who understood the business. It was a logical business to be handled by chartered accountants who could not only be the introducer of their investor client to a proposal, but could also work out all the tax implications. Georgia Shipping built one such vessel, the *Cement Transporter,* which incorporated all the needed ingredients to attract a large investor anxious to develop a tax shelter exclusive to himself. The intermediary was a well-known chartered accountant from one of the large accounting firms and the long-term charterer was Lafarge.

Unfortunately, in the case of the *Cement Transporter,* Georgia was learning the sophisticated ways of ship finance with great alacrity, but it was still sufficiently of a neophyte concern as to allow the matter of towing to be covered by a gentleman's handshake, rather than a firmly set up contractual arrangement. The large corporation in this instance was not a gentleman! In the end result we only tied our towline to the barge, which we had brought into existence as the potential operator, on one occasion, although we did make the difference between what we paid the investor and what we received by way of charter hire payable as a fixed amount monthly. It was not a bad deal but it could have been a lot more beneficial to Georgia than events turned out.

Specialist activity on the part of some accountancy firms was big business. One retired chartered accountant friend confirmed that his firm put together over an estimated thousand ship financing contracts in one form or another during the period while the shipbuilding subsidy lasted. The scope of his firm was national and the contracts included lakers and some deep-sea ships as well as B.C. tugs, barges and fishing vessels.

Probably the most successful intermediary of all those operating in the Vancouver marine market was the late Douglas Maitland of the well-known, long-established and much-respected real estate and insurance brokering firm of MacAulay, Nicolls, Maitland Ltd. This company dated back to the late '90s of the last century and had occupied a strongly visible place in the growth of Vancouver since relatively early times. Maitland had come out of the navy following the Second World War as something of a war hero. His association with Cornelius Burke, towboater and later a leading travel agent, and Graham Ladner of the equally well-known law firm of Ladner, Downs & Company, while on naval service has been well told in a memorable book, *The Champagne Navy.*

Doug Maitland had an array of powerful connections from the beginning and he used these effectively as a tool to build his insurance portfolio. The late Harold Jones and associates at Vancouver Tug Boat Company and the Cosulich brothers at River Towing and its various subsidiary towing companies, rated Maitland as a "best friend" and with good reason. Maitland was a major intermediary in bringing investors and the tug companies together in building barges along the lines described in this chapter. Maitland in fact had been the saviour of one deal when immediately following the sudden death of Harold Jones, Vancouver Tug had suddenly found

(continued on p.108)

PHOTO PORTFOLIO

The Stradiotti family has been in the towing business since they started as fish buyers in the mid-1930s. The third generation is now involved in what has been one of the most consistent success stories in the business. Their company became North Arm Transportation about forty years ago and ranges the entire coast with the largest fleet of ramp barges in the industry.

[97] **Lawrence L:** A tug with a distinctive appearance. Formerly the flagship of Lyttle Brothers Towing, North Arm has owned her for over twenty years, keeping the original name over most of that period. In keeping with other fleet renamings she is now **North Arm Voyager.**

[98] **Lawrence L:** Designed by William Brown, she was the first large steel boat built by George Fryatt's Belaire shipyard.

[99] North Arm Defiant, ex-Josee M, ex-Hamilton Baillie, originally built by Belaire for Chemainus Towing in 1977, incorporated small improvements on the lead ship of the class, the **G.D. Hemmingsen.** As **Josee M** she had seen a spell of duty on the East Coast, being brought back to Vancouver in a dockship. *(see chapter 13)*

[100] North Arm Diligent, ex-Guardian III, ex-G.D. Hemmingsen, was the first of the new breed of raised forecastle tugs, built to conform to new Transport Canada requirements which required that living accommodation should be above the main deck.

[101] N.A. Champion, ex-North Arm Champion, is now sold out of the fleet.

[102] North Arm Venture, a 42-foot tug, built in 1970.

[103] **North Arm Surveyor:** One of several 37' tugs built by Fairfield Fabricators in the mid-1960s, she was sold out of the fleet several years ago.

[104] A typical North Arm load of logging equipment travels upriver behind **North Arm Defiant.**

itself in a highly embarrassing position. To maintain its contractual arrangement with the pulp and paper industry it had committed to building a substantial number of barges at Yarrows Ltd., in Victoria.

In the confusion following the sudden death of Jones, the matter of dealing with estate taxes and paying for the barges loomed up quickly. Yarrows expected their final cheque against construction of each vessel at the time of handing the new barge over. There was no extended credit involved. Maitland and associates purchased 25 per cent of the capital stock of VanTug. He also took on the task of filling the void on the new chip barges and as each vessel came forward for handing over, he had an investor or group of investors ready and available to invest in each barge for tax shelter purposes.

How Maitland was compensated in each instance is not known. The one thing that was certain is that he improved his client base with all his investors and virtually secured his tugboat client as a captive marine insurance account. The tugboat operator became somewhat dependent on the Maitland connection for future finance, so it is hardly surprising that he was looked upon as a good friend.

Each charter provided that the tugboat company would look after the barge and keep it fully insured and employed within its contracts with the primary producer who might have been the Powell River Company, Crown Zellerbach, MacMillan, Bloedel, or another company. The arrangements were flexible so that a given barge would not be tied to one specific employment. They could move as the operator saw fit. Essentially what the operator guaranteed to the investor was a firmly contracted monthly payment of charter hire sufficient to amortize the financing over the period of the contract which was usually five years. At the end of the five years, the operator might purchase the barge at its written-down value reflecting a real market value as, after all, a five-year old barge still had as much as another 35 years of life ahead of it in real terms or real depreciation and not the artificially created zero value brought about by the fast write-off.

The alternative, and the one preferred by the tug boat operator, would be to pay charter hire at a rate of interest on the, by now, fully recovered investor's

stake in the barge, which of course would be a far lower monthly figure than that of the first five years.

The sale of the barge to the tugboat company automatically created a recapture situation. The investor at that time had fully written off his capital investment by the short route of accelerated depreciation, but would immediately nullify some of his gain through the sale of a capital asset which would draw back tax on a valuation based on its fair market value as a second-hand vessel. The answer was to either accept the far lower monthly return produced after the five year amortization period had expired, or else sell the vessel and roll the funds into a new replacement vessel, which of course is what happened in some instances. Tax shelter situations such as this were not a pure gift from a generous government but they are a tax deferment scheme when, after a series of rollovers, tax eventually becomes payable on the sale of the accumulated assets. A progressive investor could keep the process going theoretically as long as he wished until death finally caught up with him and the need for liquidation of his estate. As earlier noted the tax-sheltered provisions of a 100 per cent write-off over three years still apply and therefore constitute an available tax shelter, one of the few remaining.

Not everyone could be guaranteed to remain happy with this arrangement when it came time to accept a far smaller monthly return following the end of the five-year contract. Most would follow along because they had no knowledge of the marine market and therefore no alternative to what was not really a bad deal, so long as ownership continued they still had a reduced, but now fully taxable return on their fully paid investment. One investor group that was not prepared to accept this formula was the owner of four chip barges in the Vancouver Tug fleet. They came to Georgia Shipping with two of the barges and a suitable contract was worked out by which we would pay a higher rate of return than Vancouver Tug. Needless to say VanTug was less than happy about this turn of events. It left a bit of hole in their fleet until they could take delivery of new replacement barges.

We did one tow with these two vessels when we took the after loading gate out and took them up to

Holberg Inlet to load a special limestone required by Lafarge. Once back we promptly sub-chartered to Gulf of Georgia Towing Company who were happy to pay a premium for possession of two first-class chip barges. The two barges became a valuable addition to Gulf of Georgia's rental fleet at a time when there was a pronounced shortage of chipbarges and in turn gave Georgia Shipping another source of guaranteed income.

Incidentally, I have made reference here and elsewhere to the woodchip barge club of Island Tug, Vancouver Tug and Straits Towing. Mention of this is attributable to Maitland who used the term as an allusion rather than a firm understanding to illustrate his point when describing the working arrangements that existed between the tugboat operators and primary industry. This was taken literally and quoted by Donald Harley of the Union Insurance Society of Canton, one of the leading local underwriters, at the Association of Marine Underwriters of B.C. If there was such an understanding, it was entirely unofficial and did not exist in any formal way. The Competition Act virtually ruled it out. Don Elworthy, late of Island Tug, confirmed that they had never heard of any such arrangement, their attitude being that those who had the equipment went after the business, which was why the acquisition of the two ex-Vancouver Tug barges, from Georgia Shipping had importance to Jim Byrn at Gulf of Georgia. Byrn in actual fact already owned or controlled a number of chip barges* and when the timing was right he had the capability of calling in his chartered out units and going after a chip hauling contract.

In the 1960s and prior thereto, a logical source of mortgage money was either the Industrial Development Bank (IDB or one of its successor names such as Federal Business Development Bank), Roynat, a subsidiary of the Royal Bank, or one of the major finance companies such as Industrial Acceptance Corporation under five-year contracts. The lender took a registered first ship's mortage, an

---

* Despite what was noted in Tying the Knot, when discussing chip barge contracts, Gulf of Georgia did succeed in gaining a contract for chip barges to supply the Powell River mill during the last three years of its independent existence, 1974–1977.

---

assignment of freight earnings and the personal guarantees of the individual investors up to their proportional share of the loan. This avoided the unlimited liability otherwise usually incumbent in a loan to a partnership. With an interest rate of four per cent higher than the IDB rate of about six and a half per cent, we at Georgia Shipping, who used both IDB and Industrial Acceptance, thought we were paying a usurious rate.

The chartered banks avoided long-term commitments and would only advance money against a firm commitment for repayment out of the proceeds of a long-term loan. This was in every sense bridging finance, a banking process that has been well known, probably going back into the 19th century when the pulse of everything financial speeded up with the growth that flowed from the Industrial Revolution. Today, the banks are much more sophisticated. Medium- to long-term financing has been taken over by them which has in turn largely resulted in the disappearance of at least the finance companies who have been absorbed into banking organizations.

So much of modernday ship financing is handled by specialist accountants and lawyers, who work within the tax laws with the expertise needed to take full advantage of them. This has been brought about by the complexities of financing contracts, which in turn are tied directly to contracts of employment as one supports the other as collateral instruments. As the transportation industry has developed on the West Coast and vessels have become more complex and expensive, sale and leasebacks have become one avenue for raising capital as after all vessels have just as much potential in this regard as aircraft, vehicles and other industrial plant. This process has been resorted to by B.C. Ferry Corporation who, in 1976 and 1981, sold and have leased back all five of their large double-ended ferries and are known to have looked around for a similar arrangement on their three new aluminum catamaran ferries, although no final arrangement was ever reached, for reasons which can now be fully appreciated.

From a leasing point of view, a primary attraction beyond the straight commercial consideration of earning income on capital is the fact that, under a leasing contract, registered ownership of the prime asset passes to the leasing company, which then gains the benefit of accelerated depreciation if the vessel qualifies under the Income tax Act. This benefit would not normally be transferred without it being reflected to some extent in the benefit that the lessor returns to the lessee so that there is some advantage also to be gained in transferring the asset from the lessee's point of view.

In deep-sea practice, a major form of collateral is the firm term or time charter which is assigned to the mortgagor. To have the required strength, a term charter should at least run for the duration of the amortization period of the mortgage. Five years is the usual minimum but contracts for seven and ten years are far from uncommon. This type of financing depends as much as anything on the mortgagor's assessment of the strength of the charterer. Clearly in the case of a tanker, a charter from Shell, or Exxon, would have greater collateral strength that one originating with a minor oil company.

A method of corporate financing which has been used on the West Coast and elsewhere is the arrangement of a general wraparound debenture which when placed takes its collateral from a given set of assets or the entire fleet assets of a company. This has the benefit that, where advantageous financing is already in place, perhaps by way of an attractive first mortage, the debenture holder can register its security by way of a charge which becomes effectively a first mortgage on unencumbered assets and a second, or even third charge, on assets that are already encumbered. Usually these wraparound debentures form the security for a line of working capital credit at a floating rate with the highest rate being that shown on the registration document. Examination of registration documents reveals that in some instances when money has been very tight the interest rate has shown as high as 30 per cent per annum. That does not mean to say that this sort of rate is paid on a huge loan. What is paid is the applicable floating rate not exceeding pro rata of 30 per cent on the actual amount of the line of credit drawn for maybe a matter of days, perhaps to be sure that monthly payroll is met until the draw-down is extinguished. Needless to say when money is tight everyone tries to lean on their accounts payable as a means of using the other man's credit.

The strength of the large West Coast fleets is made up of many factors. Two that are obvious must be a clear plan of operation and an effective management and human resources structure to implement it. The ability to bring together the right mix of assets, to not only service the existing client base, but also to have the strength to efficiently develop extensions to the fleet in order that new business can be serviced are all critical factors in running a large marine business. Gone are the days when a strong individual with the strength of personality and leadership qualities could mastermind everything in the running of a fleet. Today, it needs strengths in directing quick regrouping of financial assets, the rewriting and negotiating of legal contracts and a banker who understands the nature of vessel owning and ship operations. It is perhaps because of the fact that a financial and legal team has such a powerful say in shipping generally that much of the earlier romance of shipping, which many of us remember with affection, has disappeared. Number crunching and legal strategizing have taken the place of many facets of traditional ship management as undertaken by people with seagoing experience. Leasing, as an example, is an exercise in making money, via ownership of assets, without the knowledge of hands-on shipping experience which is left to the lessee and in the whole process it has altered the personality of the shipping industries.

Vancouver as the centre of the B.C. marine transportation industry has, of course, developed a great deal of sophisticated expertise, although not on any basis comparable to world centres like London and New York where huge projects are financed by banking syndicates and big marine risks are insured by markets with massive capacity. Nevertheless, virtually all the component elements of what might be termed the Vancouver marine financial markets could be found within about one square mile in the downtown area. Today lesser pockets in the suburbs, house some of the ship management concerns, shipbrokers, bank head offices, marine insurance brokers and underwriters and, large accountancy and law firms. Modern communications enabler many businesses to function efficiently in lower rent areas.

There is an enormous pool of expertise with these various companies and then add to those the various professional and industry organizations such as the Chamber of Commerce, Council of Marine Carriers, the Law Society, the Association of Marine Underwriters, the Insurance Brokers Association, the Association of Marine Surveyors, the Vancouver Arbitration Centre and organizations which represent major industries such as the forest industry.

With all this expertise close at hand, some strange things are known to occasionally happen. "Legal beagles" and "number crunchers" are not always in touch with the time-honoured practices of the sea. A ship's master is in charge of his ship and the safety of the crew, his cargo and himself are all his responsibility in roughly that order. His acts, whatever they are, if held in question are usually only finally determinable in a court of law, but as one master remarked, "They can never fire you for the reason that you brought the tug and her tow safely to port." As he noted, it is amazing how many "experts" question the master's decisions after the event, particularly when they hinge on financial issues. Before the event it is always a matter of complying with the law and the safety of the ship and crew and the need to make quick command decisions. After the event, bottom line analysis can subject a master who has in every sense done his duty, to heavy criticism as the critics fantasize as to how they would have done it better.

Author's Note: A recent development is a new Canadian government initiative known as the "Structured Finance Facility." The aim is to generate employment in Canadian shipyards and to provide a financial incentive to purchasers of new Canadian-built vessels. Part of the value of a new vessel at 10 per cent of value is credited against the purchase price. A $2m vessel receives a credit of $200,000 in the form of an interest rate buydown, resulting in a significant saving and when the costs of delivery of a single vessel from a foreign yard are factored in, local building in a West Coast yard can still be attractive.

If a company has its own towing capacity and can bring a multiple tow across the Pacific, as has been done by Seaspan and Island Tug & Barge, it would be hard to beat their costs, but if one lacked towing capacity and employed a foreign flag dockship the cost of delivering a large barge could be well over a million dollars. The Structured Finance Facility may have the potential for helping smaller owners, who are still faced with the problems of replacement of aging equipment or need new to meet an employment obligation.

*   *   *   *   *

[104B] An Unusual Accident in Plumper Sound: In 1979, this foreign self-unloader ore carrier was discharging a heavy ore into a barge for transhipment. Careless handling by the ship's personnel caused the weight of the barge to hang on its lines until they snapped. The barge's starboard side went under, the port side flipped over and carried away the discharge arm of the ship's gear. Untangling needed extra heavy lift gear.

PART II

Chapter Eleven

THE INTERNATIONAL OIL INDUSTRY

THE GROWTH OF UNDERSEA EXPLORATION

There was an enormous readjustment in the world's flow of oil following World War II. The nature of the war ensured that the United States, Mexico and Venezuela became primary sources of oil to the Allied powers, particularly when events in the Middle East and Persian Gulf jeopardised the normal flow of oil through the Suez Canal and Mediterranean. Romania had also been a lesser source of oil for Western Europe but this country became the primary source of natural oil for Nazi Germany. Following Pearl Harbour the Dutch East Indies, Brunei and Burma, all normal sources run by Western oil companies were similarly cut off.

The United States, from being a net exporter of

[105] **Hurricane Hattie:** As a Caribbean hurricane approached, a drill rig courted disaster while being towed by **Sudbury II**. After removing the rig's crew, including an injured man, and as the storm intensified, **Sudbury II** tracked the rig for 400 miles through the hurricane and then reconnected to complete the tow successfully.

petroleum products to its entry into the Second World War in 1941, became an increasingly large importer as the demand on its own reserves grew with each passing year. As continental United States resources diminished, so also did Canadian continental resources in Alberta grow and gradually expand to include contiguous areas in B.C. and Saskatchewan. However, it was in the years immediately following WW II, in the shallow waters of the continental shelf from Florida to Texas that the American pioneer effort took place in developing undersea exploration and production technology. This was the forerunner to a worldwide exploration effort, which gathered impetus as crisis followed crisis in the Middle East.

Heavy industrialization throughout the Far East created an additional series of large customers for Persian Gulf oil. In general the Western world, particularly including Europe, gradually reduced its demands on coal and turned to oil and natural gas consumption for power generation, the diesel engine and the gasoline vehicle. In addition the petro-chemical industries consumed an increasing volume of oil and natural gas as feedstock material for all manner of plastics for industrial purposes and consumer goods.

For periods of time following the war, the world's economists and most governments worried about the possibility that oil would become an increasingly scarce commodity. The politically volatile Middle East became the leading oil reservoir of the world, but revolutions and regional wars demonstrated that this oil supply could become tenuous and unreliable.

The Anglo-Iranian confrontation in 1951, when Iranian Prime Minister Mohammet Mossadeq nationalized the British oil interests in the country, was followed by a wave of national assertion in other oil producing countries that threatened to undermine the security of Western oil sources. The multinational oil companies turned their attention to finding new offshore reserves in hitherto untapped

[106] Sedco 135F: Under construction by now defunct Victoria Machinery Depot. Claimed to be one of the biggest exploration rigs in the world at her time of construction in 1964–5, she has since been overtaken by vastly bigger ocean structures, including some in the following photos. Built for the Shell program in Hecate Straits, the specially rolled steel making up the main towers in the structure was fabricated in Vancouver and taken to Victoria by Gulf of Georgia barge. G of G seemed to have a close relationship with South-East Drilling and succeeded in gaining the primary towing contract using their **Gulf Joan.**

areas. Huge new sources were located in the North Sea, which made Britain and Norway net exporters of oil although they avoided joining the OPEC countries consisting of the Middle Eastern producers, Nigeria and Venezuela. Indonesian output soared, Alaska became another major producer as did China and Australia and many other areas of the world which had never been associated with oil production in the past.

More latterly, the Hibernia field situated in the Grand Banks area off the east coast of Newfoundland has been located and is now proving to be one of the prime undersea fields in the world. It was the first undersea field developed in Canadian waters and augmented the oil and gas industry, which had grown from very small beginnings with the original Alberta discovery at Pincher Creek in 1947.

This move towards undersea oil exploration gave rise to a whole new maritime industry, which started

[107] Sedco 708: The sheer massiveness of ocean rigs is well illustrated by this view of **Sedco 708** in Esquimalt inner harbour. **Seaspan Corsair** *(left)* and **Seaspan Cutlass** look like toy boats alongside. The rig must have been a towering sight visible from much of the city of Esquimalt. The displacement water mark on the supporting towers can be seen where the rust ends and the black starts. This also indicates how much of the rig is underwater when the rig is operating.

in the Gulf of Mexico. Different types of drilling rigs were developed, the first being the jackup type, which had retractable legs and could stand on the seafloor. Obviously, these could not work beyond a certain depth, so bigger, semi-submersible type drill rigs and production platforms followed. These were free-floating and the depth in which they could work was only limited by the depth at which drilling could be pursued. Concurrently a fleet of supply vessels and anchor-handling tugs to service the rigs followed. In addition there were hydrographic survey and geo-physical survey vessels which went ahead of actual oil exploration as so little was known at the time of actual undersea resources. When the rigs were small and only exploiting shallow seas, the service vessels were similarly small. Progress towards mid-ocean and deep drilling at great ocean depths was rapid and

the rigs quickly grew in size, along with the necessary service vessels which were really the equivalent of large tugs with high horsepower and large working decks aft of the towing winch.

The events of the Second World War in the Middle East and South East Asia with the Japanese invasion, the ejection of Anglo-Iranian Oil from Iran, the closure of the Suez Canal in the 1957 war, all pointed to the need to accelerate the development of deep-sea exploitation of oil reserves. This set off the large-scale construction of rigs and service vessels and, in turn, these developments aided the B.C. ship-building industry. After the surge of development in the 1960s through to the early '80s the deep-sea exploration business levelled off and subsided in many areas. The North Sea has probably now reached the limit of its productive capability and gas

[108] The drill rig **Ocean Bounty** leaves Nanoose Bay in tow of **Seaspan Regent.** The rig was evidently being removed to Esquimalt for repair. Big rigs like this have to be placed at temporary moorings with great care and always in a position affording maximum protection from the elements. Nanoose is very sheltered and has the capability of providing anchorage for very large vessels such as aircraft carriers.

fields have been developed in the Irish Sea. Ongoing exploration continues on the Chinese continental shelf, but Indonesia and South East Asia generally have been beset by political difficulties.

The supply of equipment in the way of drill rigs, production platforms and service vessels tend to keep in line with demand, so that any major return to undersea exploration and production is likely to be met with a shortage of available equipment, which will have to be overcome by new construction. Each area creates its own problems and vessels and rigs tend to some extent to be custom-built to meet the needs of a given area.

As everyone who lives in British Columbia knows, our provincial government has accumulated a massive burden of public debt. The attributed causes of this are beyond the scope of this book, but by 2002 the recently elected government was voicing its plans for an increase in oil and gas exploration off the B.C. coast. They see this as providing an answer to reducing this massive debt.

Needless to say this has brought heavy counter argument from the environmental lobby. They maintain that our pristine coast should be kept free of oil exploration and production, but given world supply challenges and the increasing reliance of the United States on Canada for its resources, the certainty of such activity is probably as inevitable as day follows night.

[109] A Drill Ship of the self-propelled type. This vessel was converted from a regular freighter, possibly of the war-built CI-MAV1 American-standard freighter, originally with a gross tonnage of about 4,500 tons. To assist stability the hull has had full-depth sponsons added over most of its length and the bow has been reinforced with a heavy outer skin, ideal for working through ice. The unidentified ship was in Esquimalt Roads, headed for the Arctic.

Author's note: For anyone interested in the history of international oil, I recommend the book The Seven Sisters: The Great Oil Companies and the World They Shaped *by Anthony Sampson. Even though it was first published in 1975, it provides a history since oil was first discovered at Titusville, Pennsylvania, in 1859 and gives an excellent opener to the state of world affairs and how they have affected the oil industry in the past 25 years. The seven sisters were Exxon, Shell, BP, Chevron, Gulf, Texaco and Mobil and between them they controlled world oil marketing then as they do now. Among our big four integrated companies only Petro-Canada is outside the circle of the seven sisters.*

Since the book was written Mobil has amalgamated with Exxon and Chevron has taken over Texaco. Gulf has been broken up and a French company, ELF/Aquitaine, probably now ranks as being one of the seven largest companies. Most of the dominant players in Canada are either subsidiaries of foreign companies or are otherwise associated with them. Discovering oil on B.C.'s coast is one thing, marketing it is another and without question some of the seven sisters will be heavily involved.

THE POTENTIAL OF THE B.C. COAST AS A PRODUCER OF OIL AND GAS

In the 1970s considerable drilling was undertaken in the Queen Charlotte Islands and offshore in Hecate Straits. These drill holes gave indications that there is a vast field underlaying the area which is estimated by the Geological Survey of Canada to contain 9.8 billion barrels of oil and 43.4 trillion cubic feet of natural gas. About one third of the oil is recoverable along with 90 per cent of the gas. The oil represents more than half of Canada's conventional oil reserves and 60 per cent of the country's gas, but primarily on account of environmental concerns development was frozen following completion of the Shell program in the late 1970s.

Hecate Straits and the Queen Charlotte sedimentary basin was explored by Shell although the details of the exploration were not released, but it is known

[110] Jeanne II: A suction dredge with a cutter head works at dredging up bottom spoil. Judging by the disturbed water astern of the dredge she is building up land in front of the reef. In the Beaufort Sea oil and gas play, artificial islands were created by suction dredges. In the background a great deal of dredged material has been placed on top of what appears to be original muskeg which made up the majority of the Mackenzie delta lands.

that oil and gas indications showed that there are reserves in quantity. It is also inferred that geology suggests large deposits of oil and/or gas exist at points in the Continental shelf including the Georgia basin between the mainland and Vancouver Island and the Tofino and Winona basins off the West Coast of Vancouver Island.

A quarter of a century later, with world oil prices being high and with heavy pressure on natural gas reserves, the present B.C. government has taken a fresh look at the potential and the hazards. Without seeking to become political about the subject, opening up these reserves to commercial exploitation could solve a lot of problems. From a financial point of view the province is carrying a hitherto unheard of provincial debt of close to $50 billion, much of it inflated as a result of such ill-fated projects as the

fast ferries and additional overspending in many other ways. Other industries, notably forestry, mining and commercial fishing have become compromised in a variety of directions, some of it through government meddling, but also on account of changing world conditions which have affected trade imbalances.

Environmental factors have to be allowed for, although it is expected that any move to open up the oil and gas industry will meet with the heaviest sort of opposition from those who wish to see a constant state of inertia and effectively a closing down of primary industry. This seems to be a feature of B.C., which draws more than its fair share of this kind of negativity. Since the drilling program initiated by Shell in the early 1970s there have been many important technological improvements. The international industry in fact has an enviable safety record with few recallable incidents of ruptured or runaway wells and where these have occurred the industry has demonstrated its ability to control and shut down such wells. A runaway well off the Farallone Islands in California in the '70s is probably among the worst such instances, with others occurring over the past 50 years or so off the Gulf Coast of the U.S., where undersea exploration first began and much of the technology of today was originally developed. Hibernia and the North Sea, being the two most modern and largest fields, have a good record. Drilling in the Beaufort Sea and the North Slope fields produced no major accidents.

The biggest generator of oil accidents at sea has been in the transportation sector with some spectacular losses. Even small vessels can create messy environmental losses which receive heavy publicity, but when losses occur such as the *Torrey Canyon, Amoco Cadiz, Exxon Valdez, Brea, Erika* and the latest sinking, *Prestige,* the damage can be catastrophic and the public has the right to be fearful. However, so long as we all want to drive our cars and use plastic products, ocean oil transportation is unavoidable. International conventions and agreements have sought to reduce the hazards and potential for loss with new tankers having double hulls which strengthen a ship and add an additional line of defence against spillage, but in the end double hulled ships will still be capable of fracturing, burning or foundering. New pilotage and ship handling rules have also been imposed in many world ports including Canadian, but the world has to go a long way yet as the *Prestige* demonstrated. Ordered away from the Spanish coast when in a poor condition following structural failure, the attitude of the Spanish authorities became one of "not in our backyard; go and make your mess somewhere else." The sunken ship is still polluting the very Spanish coastline they hoped to protect. What was lacking was a determination to get the ship into the nearest port of refuge, where the oil had a prospect of containment and recovery, even if there was some localized damage. Instead they arrested the master of the ship as the French did with the captain of the *Erika,* two years previously, as if the master involved

should bear full responsibility for many factors beyond his control. The master might be found responsible for navigational error, but such factors as suitability of the ship, structural strength, technical capability, type of oil carried, managerial decisions governing employment and so on fall into the field of responsibility of others.

The British Columbia tug and barge industry will receive a tremendous boost if it reacts quickly and positively to a wave of new development off the coast and on past performance it will. There is, of course, a great deal of international equipment in existence in the way of seismic survey vessels, drill rigs, pipe barges, and service vessels such as anchor-handling tugs and offshore supply vessels, but not all this international fleet can be remobilized at short notice as it is often committed for years ahead. When an important new field comes into play it often follows that new vessels have to be built to accommodate the need. This particularly applies to major rigs such as production platforms, which stay in place until a well is exhausted.

The tug and barge industry by its very nature should be able to adopt quickly to the technical needs that will arise, even if it means building some equipment possibly in China, or acquiring the types of vessels specific to offshore drilling and production. In 2000 Rivtow was purchased by Smit International, a company with much accumulated experience in every aspect of the ocean oil industry. It is thought by industry watchers to have been at least partially motivated by an expectation that an opening up of the coastal oil and gas deposits is fully anticipated following a change in public policy.

British Columbians with their high costs and burden of public debt look with envy to neighbouring Alberta and Great Britain. In the latter case the state of the economy was grim until North Sea oil turned things around, so that Britain has one of the world's strongest economies. As government is a prime beneficiary of successful oil and gas development, royalties could return B.C. to a public debt-free status in a relatively short period of time, given wise policies where priority is given to paying down the debt.

Chapter Twelve

GENSTAR'S INTERNATIONAL COMMITMENTS

Genstar Corporation found it expedient to set up Genstar Marine as a holding company, after the merger of Vancouver Tug Boat Company and Island Tug & Barge in 1970. The purpose was to hold the group's investments in Seaspan International, Vancouver Shipyards, Victoria Shipyards and other subsidiaries, to which could be added certain international joint ventures—an interesting phase in the history of the organization.

The succession of troubles in the Middle East which started with the Iranian ejection of the Anglo-Iranian Oil Company (later British Petroleum) from Iran in 1949, and saw a succession of conflicts between Israel and its neighbours, also focussed the attention of the Western powers on finding new oil reserves on the continental shelves of their own and other friendly countries.

The ouster of Anglo-Iranian also coincided with an increasing recognition that the Unites States was no longer self-sustaining as an oil producer. From being a net exporter to world markets in 1939 the position was in full reverse by 1949 and American imports were exceeding its exports, which caused it to focus on the Persian Gulf to a degree not known before. The era of international oil politics had arrived and took hold to an extent never before recognized. Heavy dependency on Arab oil, while still a fact of life, was seen as too much of a gamble and the Suez Canal was like a neck through which everything travelled, a neck that could be throttled too easily.

The first of a series of wars was that of 1956 when, following Egyptian nationalization of the canal, Britain, France and Israel attacked Egypt with the aim of toppling the strong man, Gamal Abdel Nasser. As virtual dictator of Egypt and a clear leader in the Arab world, Nasser had courted the USSR, joint ventured the construction of the Aswan Dam on the upper Nile, and thus let Russian influence into the vacuum of the Middle East with all its complex power politics and religious factions. It marked Nasser as being no friend of the West.

CLOSURE OF THE SUEZ CANAL

Instead of succeeding as the British-French and Israeli forces would have if left to their own devices, world opinion, led by the United States, frustrated their action, but not before Nasser had sunk dredgers and other vessels in the canal, effectively blocking it to all shipping for close to a year.

In the third Arab-Israeli war of 1967, the canal was again closed, this time for eight years during which four British, one American and eight European vessels remained trapped in the Bitter Lakes, hostages in effect to Arab-Israeli conflict. The crews were shipped home and eventually most of the ships became the property of the Mutual Protection and Indemnity Associations in which they were insured against such eventualities. So far as the owners were concerned they were total losses.

The trapped ships were a minor blip in terms of international shipping, but with the canal blocked the effect on shipping was tremendous. The main route from Europe to the Orient and Australia was now around the southern tip of Africa which doubled the distance for Europe-bound tankers from the Iranian Gulf to Europe. To compensate, new tankers took a radical jump in size and very quickly it seems, a succession of new ships took them into a size range when it became clear that, even with the Suez open, these VLCCs (Very Large Crude Carriers) and even bigger ULCCs (Ultra-Large Crude Carriers), would always have to use the Cape route.

In other words, the closure of the Suez changed the logistics of world shipping permanently. The canal, along with Panama, became less important, with bulk carriers reaching 200,000 tons deadweight and tankers reaching the 600,000-tdw mark, although today ships in these categories have retreated from these mammoth sizes particularly in the tankers.

THE FOUNDING OF OPEC

Up until the founding of OPEC, the organization formed by the oil-producing countries to coordinate the interests of these countries which included all the Arab producers as well as Iran, Nigeria, and Venezuela, the cost of crude had been low—in the region of $5–6 dollars per barrel at the loading terminal. OPEC drummed the price up to around $30 per barrel. The effect on the consuming countries economies was drastic and near runaway world inflation occurred.

There were two backlashes which eventually hurt the Suez and to some extent OPEC. As noted above tanker sizes grew rapidly as tonnage per ship sought to neutralise the adverse factor of distance, so that when traffic was eventually regularized with the reopening of the canal following the 1967 war, a huge volume of the world tanker-fleet was now too large to use the canal. To get some of this lost business back the Egyptians let a contract to an Italian firm to build a pipeline from Suez at the south entrance to the canal to a point near Alexandria on the Mediterranean side. Supertankers too big to transit the canal in fully loaded condition would discharge into the pipeline and then reload near Alexandria once through the canal in lightened condition. It returned some of the lost business to the canal, Egypt's biggest source by far of foreign earnings.

With oil now being more highly valued, the second backlash was the fact that much of the rest of

[111] **Petrobras XV1:** This shows the launch of this 15,000-ton semi-submersible drill rig at Cherbourg, France. The launch took a month from November 5, 1983, to complete. Here the giant rig is rolled onto **Genmar 104** and **Genmar 106**. Each barge had a loaded draft of 20' and dead-weight capacity of 17,000 tons on measurements of 400' x 100' x 25'. Each barge had six tracking skegs.

the world now had the incentive to find fresh reserves outside of OPEC. Most of the likely land resources such as the oil fields of Texas, Oklahoma, California, the North West Territories, Alberta, Saskatchewan and neighbouring areas had been developed. Europe had little oil except in Romania and the Southern USSR. Of the remaining continental land masses, the Netherlands Antilles, Indonesia, Brunei and Burma had developed oil industries and only China had significant unexploited land-based reserves, so attention shifted to the continental shelves which were believed to contain most of the world's remaining oil reserves.

Since the end of the World War II, the Americans had been developing technology which allowed them to explore the Mississippi Delta and shallow areas in the offshore Gulf of Mexico. The two most promising areas were the North Sea and Alaska with the adjacent Canadian Arctic in the Mackenzie River delta and the Beaufort Sea. Major discoveries in both key areas led to the development of giant oil and gas fields which greatly helped stabilization of the oil-based consumer economies of Western Europe and North America and also blunted the political threats poised by interference in the flow of Arab oil.

[112] **Petrobras XV1:** With the rig in place work continued to make it ready for the water by submersion of the two barges. Once in place, access ports in the twin hulls of the rig were opened up.

OFFSHORE OIL AND GAS

The process of development of these areas, to be joined by offshore fields in Australia, Indonesia, China, India, and the East Coast of Canada, meant a drastic increase in demand for drill rigs and offshore service vessels to undertake seismic work, provide supply services to the rigs and act as anchor-handling vessels or to provide towing services. The original vessels as developed by the Americans had high forecastles which contained most of the living accommodation and the navigating bridge behind which were located triple drum high capacity towing winches. Usually about half or more of the main deck area of the vessel aft of the winch was a large clear working area on which drill pipe and a variety of heavy equipment and stores were carried. Unusually large tanks integral with the hull carried drilling mud, diesel fuel and potable water as all had to be supplied to the rigs.

The entire process opened up a huge potential for towing companies around the world. While regular

tugs lacked the high stowage or on-deck carrying capacity of the offshore supply vessels, they often had the horsepower and towing capability. One of the first Vancouver tugs to find its way to the North Sea was Straits Towing's new *Gibraltar Straits,* which spent several years working with British and European vessels while stationed at Aberdeen. In chapter 15 I have told something of Nordic Offshore Services, Vancouver's only home-based offshore supply vessel company. The trend towards offshore exploration was well established when Genstar Marine came into being. Medium-size shipyards around the world capable of building large tugs were building a variety of offshore service vessels. Victoria Machinery Depot, as one of its last acts in business, built a huge offshore drilling rig, the *Sedco 135F,* while Allied Shipbuilders, Belaire and Star among local shipyards, benefitted from a succession of orders from the oil industry, many of which were designed by local naval architects such as Robert Allan, Arthur McLaren, William Brown and Derek Cove. Burrard Iron Works, Swann Winches and Kobelt Controls, among local firms of suppliers, benefitted internationally from much of this activity.

Allied was the first local builder in the field with two vessels for Tidewater Oil of the U.S. and others for the Arctic. Belaire Shipyards built 12 similar vessels for a variety of owners including Inchcape, FedNav and Nordic Offshore. Star Shipyards got into difficulties over its last contracts of this type and had to declare bankruptcy.

Genstar Marine and FedNav seemed to be natural partners, both being part of the Belgian "network." Just what FedNav's relationship was with Belgium is not known except that they had far more ships than

[113] **Genmar 104,** submerged to receive her load, a drill rig to be loaded at Port Arthur, Texas, for Lake Maracaibo, Venezuela, in 1987. The big pump rooms of these vessels were located forward under the forecastle. Venting and exhaust pipes can be seen in a cluster.

[114] **Genmar 104:** Now fully loaded, the semi-submerged barge will start pumping out her tanks to emerge looking like her sister in the next photo.

[115] Genmar 105, underway with the jackup rig **Interocean II** on a 77-day delivery voyage of 15,000 miles from Japan to Mexico.

[116] Genmar 105: Another type of load shows the barge fully laden with a dredge aft and a big load of pipe secured by stakes. She has a lot of unused dead-weight capacity in this instance. The ocean-going tug is the Panamanian **Suhaili,** owned by International Transport Suhaili.

[117] Jackup rig **Key Biscayne** is readied for loading aboard the semi-submerged **Genmar 102** in the River Amazon at Belem, Brazil.

[118] Genmar 102: Seaspan's Othello Nocente from Trail, B.C., directs operations from the control bridge of the barge.

[119] Bound for Western Australia, the tow of **Genmar 102** gets underway behind the Bugsier Company's 15,000-hp German tug **Titan.**

[120] **Penrod 72,** an 18,000-ton semi-submersible drill rig was converted to a production platform for the Green Canyon field in the Gulf of Mexico. The conversion took from August to December. **Genmar 104** and **Genmar 105** were used like a floating dock to lift the rig from the water and deliver it ready for offloading to the nearby Marathon LeTourneau yard at Brownsville, Texas.

most non-Belgian owners, built in Belgian yards and often owned at least at the outset, by a Belgian-registered joint-venture company. The precise arrangements between FedNav and its Belgian partner, Union Belge d'Enterprises Maritimes, S.A., have not been revealed except to say that they probably hinged on favourable financing arrangements and a Belgian need to secure its finances in a manner that suited their banking or financial legislation. FedNav has successfully grown its business through joint ventures, following a late twentieth century trend towards spreading the risk through syndication in one combination or another. Joint venturers, provided they have chosen their partners wisely, have gained and, given strength between the venture partners. With joint ventures have come sometimes greater knowledge and, by spreading the corporate wings far further than would have been done by staying with a rigid, traditional and "go it alone" policy, all have gained.

CANADIAN-AMERICAN JOINT VENTURES

Who initiated the joint ventures in which the two Canadian companies, Genstar Marine Ltd. and FedNav Ltd., came together with Crowley Maritime Corporation of San Francisco would be a good question, but it is a fair guess that FedNav had a major say based on its previous way of doing business. It was the way in which Nordic Offshore and FedNav came together in another joint venture described in chapter 15. Nordic could have drawn strength from its association with FedNav, but unsophisticated minds, lacking vision, at Nordic failed to realise this and did not take appropriate advantage.

In any event Genstar Marine, FedNav and Crowley formed Arctic Navigation Ltd. as a joint venture to service the needs of oil exploration in the high Arctic, most particularly the North Slope of Alaska and the Beaufort Sea. Of all the offshore oil and gas exploration plays that Genstar was associated with, the Arctic operations of Dome Petroleum, Husky Oil and other oil companies in the Beaufort Sea brought the greatest direct benefit to B.C. shipyards in the 1970s and into the '80s. A consider-

able fleet of anchor handling tugs, barges and ancillary vessels were built in Vancouver yards, including Allied, Belaire, Star and Burrard Dry Dock or its successor Versatile Pacific.

To coordinate their joint activities, the three North American partners formally organized Global Transport Organization, (GTO) then went into a joint venture, "Unitow," with the largest Belgian towing and salvage firm, Union Remorquage et de Sauvetage SA (Union Towing & Salvage Co. Ltd.), based in Antwerp and controlled by the George Letzer interests.

Union, with units in its fleet up to 18,000 hp, was right in the heart of one of the most competitive areas in the world for major towing companies, such as Smit and Bureau Weijsmuller of Holland, United of Hull, England, Bugsier and Unterweser of Germany, Svitzers in Denmark, as well as companies in Norway, Sweden, South Africa and France. Major shipping companies such as P & O, Wilhelmsen, Hansa, Maersk and others started supply and towing subsidiaries and some made investments in rigs. Suitable tugs, barges, supply vessels and rigs came from all over the world to participate in the North Sea boom and the big international oil companies and many smaller ones participated in the various oil and gas plays. In terms of oil riches, Britain and Norway gained the lion's share given the nature of North Sea geography and international standards of division of the ocean into national demarcation areas.

To undertake major ocean deliveries of barge cargoes, the North American partnership of Genstar, FedNav and Crowley had built ten large ocean-going barges (length, 400 feet, breadth, 100 feet). These vessels were submersible to allow float-on/float-off cargoes such as drill rigs, dredgers, etc. They were built in the Orient and Seaspan contributed its largest tugs, *Seaspan Royal* of 9,000 hp and *Seaspan Regent* of 5,500 hp, to the group. Over the next several years GTO did many jobs of ocean towing involving the movement of giant rigs, dredgers and pressure vessels, in some instances in tows that went halfway around the world, involving some of the biggest rigs in the industry. A few typical examples selected at random from an extensive list are:

* Carriage of dredging equipment aboard *Genmar 105,* from Bahrein, in the Persian Gulf, to Columbia for China Harbour Engineering Company.

* Carriage of jackup drilling rig *Zapata Sovereign,* aboard *Genmar 103* from the Arabian Gulf to Irian Jaya (Indonesia) for Zapata Drilling and Amoco Corporation.

* A cargo of 15,000 tons of massive breakwater stone aboard *Genmar 105,* from the Persian Gulf to a South Indian Ocean Island (Diego Garcia) for contractors, Woodward Dickerson Company for an air base extension.

* Transport of jackup drill rig *Key Biscayne,* aboard *Genmar 102,* from Belem, Brazil, to Australia for Key Drilling of Houston Texas.

* The lift of *Penrod 72,* an 18,000-tons displacement offshore drilling rig in what was believed to be the heaviest lift ever handled to September 25, 1986, using the method now described. Because of its huge bulk the rig, which was being converted from a drilling rig to a production platform could not be lifted in a conventional floating dry dock. The twin submersible barges *Genmar 104* and *Genmar 105* were sunk under the rig and when suitably placed, pumped out, lifting the rig clear of the water for the needed work. The barges took six hours to submerge as 18,000 tons of water took them to the bottom. The return to full flotation took another six hours following which the rig was moved a short distance to the Marathon LeTourneau yard at Brownsville, Texas, for the required repairs and alterations.

These illustrate the broad ranging and international nature of GTO's activities and also at this distance in time, how little the Canadian public knew of two of the country's major transportation businesses, Seaspan and FedNav in this trade. While no one had any need for shame or embarrassment, it was quite simply a form of transportaion which did not call for a public relations effort outside of the industry itself.

Crowley also provided units from its fleet, the *Gladiator* and *Ranger* each with a horsepower of 9,000, to a new joint venture publicized as EAST, an acronym for Euro-Arab Sea Trailers, which was brought to the group by FedNav to run a service from the modern port of Fos, near Marseilles, through the Suez Canal to Arabian ports of Yanbu and Jedah, with calls at Genoa, Italy.

The British ship agency firm of Gray MacKenzie & Co. of London had powerful connections throughout the East and was related to the P & O group. It had obtained a management contract to modernize Jeddah (also known as Juddah, Jidda and Jedda), which was woefully inadequate. For this purpose EAST was engaged to run its barge line from Europe to several Arabian ports with all manner of container cargo, steel and construction supplies.

Saudi Arabia was moving into the modern world in one giant step. GTO had two barges built in Japan for EAST. Named *Arab Falcon* and *Arab Hawk,* these vessels were purpose-built for the Fos-Arabian run and were provided with two additional overhead decks for containers mounted on a large fleet of leased trailers. The main deck and the No. 2 deck were loaded from shore-attached ramps, while No. 3 top deck was loaded via a built-in ramp that ran from the second deck to the top deck. With barge cargo it was invariably more a matter of available deck space rather than deadweight carrying capacity that counted. The barges had a maximum load capacity of about 18,000 tons so that even with three decks fully stowed with vehicles and containers there would usually be deadweight capacity to spare.

Meanwhile as EAST developed and the Arabian port development modernization went ahead, Vancouver was fully alert to the needs of its international interests. Each of the three participants in the Global Transport Organization loaned personnel to different phases as needed. Captain Sven Stokke, a former Norwegian deep-sea master, and Genstar Marine's vice-president and general manager, was Seaspan's nominee. Captain J. Bruce Garvey was the representative of FedNav. Al Watkins represented the interests of Crowley. Garvey in fact was relocated to Jeddah to take charge of the port improvement

[121] **Penrod 72.** The sheer massiveness of the rig can be appreciated in this view of it as it sat in the water before lifting. To submerge each barge had to take on 18,000 tons of seawater over a period of six hours.

[122] **Penrod 72.** The barges are readied for submersion to receive the rig. Stiffeners are in place from barge to barge so that they remain in a constant position with each other.

[123] Blocks are placed on the decks of the barges in the same way as they would be found in a dry dock. The rig's pontoons will lie along these blocks on both barges.

[124] Fully Loaded. The two barges pumped out all their ballast water once the rig was placed in the desired position over the submerged barges. Pumping out took another six hours.

[125] Dixilyn-Field 87. This jackup rig is seen here at a Gulf of Mexico port awaiting loading for a tow to the North Sea. The huge size of the legs dwarf the drill tower.

[126] The rig was loaded onto **Genmar 106** and is seen here getting underway for a 21-day tow behind the Bugsier tug **Simson.** These big German tugs with horsepowers around 15,000 make a impressive sight. With a fleet of around 30 tugs at the time of most of these tows, Bugsier ranks as one of the biggest international towing companies.

[127] Rigs laid up awaiting more favourable conditions at Port Arthur, Texas. The rigs are sitting with their legs on the bottom. Some of them never went back to work.

[128] **Genmar 103.** An excellent view, illustrating the totally clear cargo deck of these big barges. Bollards, mooring capstans aft and five big cleats along either side of the barges are set in recesses below cargo deck level. This way nothing stands proud above the cargo deck that would be an impediment to the loading of rigs or any other form of deck cargo.

operations. Under the direction of Captain Jim Stewart, Seaspan's Captain R.E. "Dick" Tolhurst purchased a Robert Allen-designed tug of 5,500 hp for Genstar Marine which had been built in Australia and renamed *Seaspan Raider* and the purchase from Crowley of the American-built *Seaspan Rogue,* of 7,000 hp. Both tugs were placed on Cayman Islands registry and went directly to the North Sea and placed in the joint-venture company of GTO and the Letzer interests—Union Towing & Salvage Co. Ltd. Later, when an assist tug stationed at Port Said was needed, the *Seaspan Raider* was transferred to EAST to help tows through the Suez Canal. On behalf of

Genstar Marine, Captain Stokke contracted for the construction of the Genmar-class submersible barges in Japan for delivery through the 1975–77 period.

Captain Fred Collins of Seaspan was loaned to GTO. He describes his experience and duties with EAST and another joint venture in which Seaspan, FedNav and Crowley participated, in the notes that follow. This venture was SATOL, the Saudi-Arabian Transport Organization, which set up lighterage operations on the Persian Gulf Coast of Saudi Arabia. Captain Collins' verbatim description more than adequately sets out the details of GTO's operation in the Mediterranean and Middle East:

In 1975, Gordon Mowatt, Charlie Watt and myself from Seaspan, along with Tom Orange from Crowley Maritime, were sent to Saudi Arabia to set up a lighterage operation on that country's Gulf Coast, headquartered at Dhahran.

Our lighterage operation was based at Ras Tannurah. The early stages used flat deck scows and a small tug to lighter cargo from anchored ships into the Aramco dock. This was a stopgap until proper barge berths were built to the north at Al Jubayl and to the south at Al Uqayra.

These berths were capable of handling 400' x 100' barges and heavy loads on the deck surface. I left after the first three months to return to Seaspan, North Vancouver.

Before I left I was sent over to Jeddah where our agent, Y.B.A. Kanoo, loaned me one of his younger staff members to act as my interpreter. The job was to work my way northward from Jeddah, looking for a suitable port for EAST's ro-ro barge operation. The young fellow who I first met at the office was dressed in the traditional Arab white robes and headress.

When he picked me up the following morning, gone was the traditional. In its place was a Levi shirt and jeans, driving a beaten up Sports Toyota. We looked in at several places, but the west coast of Saudi Arabia is for the most part unsheltered. At first I thought Sharm Yanbu, a large inlet north of the port of Yanbu would be best. The Saudi Coastguard loaned me an outboard so my young friend and I could sound the entrance and channel.

Following our survey, we were invited to a large tent where we sat on cushions in a large circle. Through the interpreter I soon found out that Sharm Yanbu was part of a principality. The sheik used it for recreation and barges would not be welcome.

The port of Yanbu was chosen. It required dredging and back fill. As well, routes had to be laid out for large semi-trailer trucks as the town streets were too narrow. Immediately following my trip to Yanbu and a debriefing at Ras Tannurrah I returned to North Vancouver.

In December 1976, I was transferred back to GTO at Port Said, Egypt. The ro-ro barge service was in operation and was having great difficulty meeting a schedule owing to the Canal Authority's reluctance to transit tugs and barges through the canal. This time my wife, Audrey, accompanied me and we set up housekeeping in a two-story apartment termed a "villa."

Tugs encountered in the Eastern Mediterranean were usually very old British or Northern European cast-offs. They were clumsy to handle and prone to breakdown. The canal was Egypt's main source of income and any accident or blockage was a real threat to their economy.

Crowley's tugs *Gladiator* and *Ranger* were modern, well-found vessels powered by twin 16-cylinder EMD diesels. Unfortunately to the Suez Canal officials they looked like tugboats and therefore were not to be trusted.

After many meetings it became apparent that we must have our own assist tug as the tug supplied by the Canal Authority for use as an assist was not at all satisfactory. The Crowley tug *Apache* was stationed on an interim basis. Once our vessels demonstrated their ability to control the barge, in most cases better that the larger ocean-going ships, we found ourselves being included in the first available convoy, north or south.

In the fall the Canadian tug *Seaspan Raider* relieved the *Apache,* staying until the operation closed down in the spring of 1979.

In the fall of 1978, my wife and self were transferred to Marseilles. Since 1976 we had built an Egyptian staff of two at Port Said with a representative in Cairo. From Marseilles I would travel to Egypt about once a month to coordinate the operation.

Fos, France, was built as a container port and is well-suited to the movement of trailer borne containers. A special ramp was built to accommodate loading the main and second barge deck, direct from the dock. The third or upper barge deck was accessed via fixed ramp on the barge. Proper connection to the shore ramp was maintained by ballasting or deballasting the barge trimming tanks.

Port de Bouc was our GTO office location for servicing the barge terminal at Fos. Staff consisted of two engineers and a very competent, bilingual French secretary, overseen by myself. Although our prime duty was managing the tugs and barges employed in EAST operations, we also took care of all GTO vessels in our area.

As 1978 came to an end, it was apparent that the EAST service was no longer as necessary to Saudi Arabia. By March/April 1979, schedule frequency was reduced. It was decided that EAST would continue operating using the smaller tug *Seaspan Raider* and outside chartered tugs. The two Crowley tugs *Gladiator* and *Ranger* were withdrawn.

The Port de Bouc office was closed and I was transferred to St. Johns, Newfoundland, where it was a wholly Genstar Marine operation. We supplied offshore towing and supply vessels, on short contracts to the offshore exploration industry.

None of these joint ventures had an indefinite life. Once the North Sea moved from an exploration to a production stage, priorities changed and the need for many of the vessels employed there diminished. It was the same with the Arabian venture—once the ports were brought up to modern standards the need for the barge service ended. The last to be disbanded was Arctic Navigation which lasted on a reduced scale into the early '90s.

Seaspan International was purchased by the MacCluhan Capital Group at the end of the '80s. With the change of ownership, new policies led to the decision to phase out of foreign joint ventures. The name "Genstar" and its derivative Genstar Marine were also phased out following dissolution of the Genstar connection and that corporation's dismemberment by its new owner, Imasco, a holding company controlled by British American Tobacco Company. *Seaspan Regent* returned to Vancouver to run alongside her near sister ship *Seaspan Commodore*. The tugs *Seaspan Royal, Seaspan Rogue* and *Seaspan Raider* and the large foreign-registered barges were sold foreign and thus this phase of one of the most interesting examples of a Canadian marine transport operation in foreign service and competition came to an end as an actual owner/operator.

However, it was not the actual end of Seaspan's interest in foreign operations. Two associated companies remain in active operation as part of Washington Marine Group's business which could now be described as the successor to Genstar Marine as the holding company for Seaspan International and the shipyards and minor group subsidiaries. Of the associates, one is Seaspan (Cyprus) Ltd., which offers a variety of services including project management, chartering, naval architecture and engineering. A sister company, Seaspan Shipbrokers, headquartered in Vancouver, has a representative office in Shanghai and offers a variety of services in vessel sale and purchase, chartering, cargo brokerage and marine consultancy.

While the ten barges were disposed of, two actually were transferred to Seaspan as the registered owner on Canadian registry. They became the *Seaspan 270* and *Seaspan 271* and engaged in carrying lumber to California, but with the fall off in exports *Seaspan 271* has been further converted to the carriage of limerock or gravel. The remaining Genmar barges were sold to Boa Ltd. of Trondheim, Norway, where they are engaged in international towing, as before, arranged by Seaspan Shipbrokers or Seaspan (Cyprus) Ltd. The connection with Boa is very close. The Boa Company concentrates on the ownership aspects for which purpose it has had new additional units built in China.

[129] **Genmar 103**, or a sister barge, discharges giant pressure vessels in a Saudi-Arabian port. With a clear deck, the right state of the tide, and an easy graded ramp lifted in place by a crane, unloading goes smoothly with the pressure vessels loaded on multi-wheeled trailers.

[130] **Seaspan Royal.** Seaspan's biggest ever tug, with twin Nohab Polar diesels giving a total 9,000 ihp, a bollard pull of 100 tons and a range of 11,000 miles at 14 knots, she was heavily employed towing rigs until a change of ownership and management reflected new policies. One of these was to stay closer to home and get out of international groups, which called for a different management style. Built in Vancouver, registered in Bermuda, she eventually passed to Mexican owners.

[131] Seaspan Rogue. One of two ocean-going tugs acquired from foreign sources. This one with 7,000 hp was built by the McDermott yard in the Southern U.S. With twin turbo-charged GM Electromotive 12-cylinder diesels she had a speed of 14 knots and a range of 12,000 miles, making her ideal for the medium-sized loads that were frequent. The other foreign-built tug was **Seaspan Raider** with 5,500 hp, built at Adelaide, South Australia.

[132] Seaspan 270, ex-Genmar 101. The lead barge was the slightly smaller **Seaspan 250,** one of two sisters originally built for Seaspan in Arctic service. For some years after the 1987 change of direction these two barges were engaged in delivering Doman lumber to the California market. **Seaspan Commodore** can be seen ahead with separate towlines out to each barge. In this picture the tow was just getting underway and as it proceeded they would work themselves into a full line ahead configuration.

BUILDER'S SKETCH OF ARAB FALCON AND ARAB HAWK

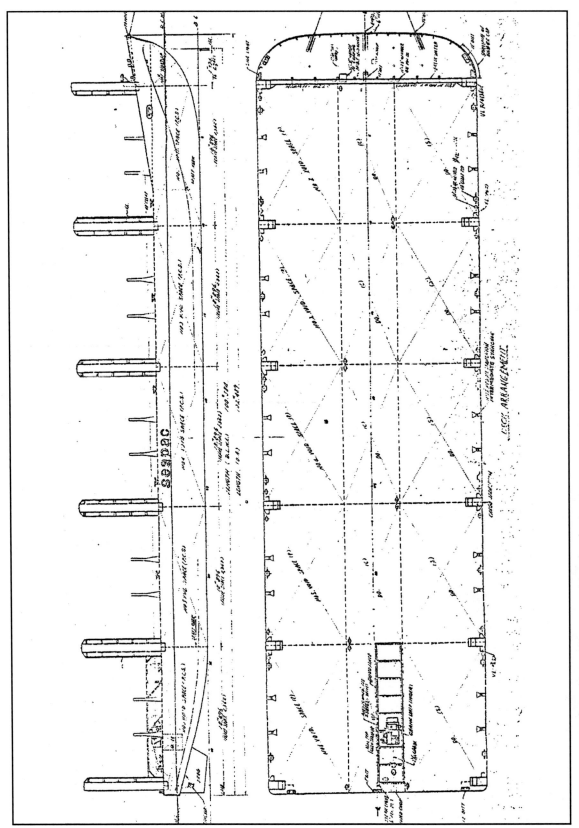

Arab Falcon and Arab Hawk, understood to have been the same as in the plan depicted here. They had hull dimensions of 336' x 98' x 21' and a capacity of 18,000 dwt. The giant stanchions were big enough to support two additional decks for the EAST barge line service.

[133] **Change of Direction:** After the new management regime centred around the Shields-led takeover of the Seaspan–Vancouver Shipyards group by the McCluhan Capital Group, the Genstar fleet was broken up. Seaspan's domestic operation acquired the **Genmar 101** (*photo #132*). The rest of the barge fleet, which had performed an enormous number of jobs with complete success, was sold to BOA A/S of Trondheim, Norway. Here Captain Sven Stokke, vice-president of Seaspan's Offshore Division, is seen standing on the left under the coat of arms of the famous Baltic Exchange in London, England, after a successful deal had been concluded with Ole Bjornevik, owner of BOA A/S.

[134] The Seaspan Offshore group became Seaspan (Cyprus) Ltd. As such it still operates in close association with Boa who added new equipment. One such was the powerful supply tug **Boa Power.**

[135] Boa Pride, a somewhat smaller unit in the fleet.

THE ARCTIC SEALIFT

Shipbuilding is outside the scope of this series, but the best intimate account dealing with the ships built in B.C. for the Arctic is contained in the book *Ships of Steel: A British Columbia Shipbuilder's Story,* by the late T. Arthur McLaren and Vicki Jensen. Art McLaren was right at the centre of this unique action, which started in the 1960s and petered out at the beginning of 1980s.

It was an extraordinary period when oil and gas exploration in the Arctic, particularly the Beaufort Sea and Mackenzie River delta saw large scale efforts to probe for oil and gas. In the end result huge volumes of natural gas were found but with the difficulty of getting it to market taking it out of the ground had to wait. Twenty to thirty years later, progress has been made and a new Mackenzie pipeline now seems to be in the offing.

The Arctic oil and gas play was unlike any other in Canadian petroleum history. It involved the dispatch of an armada of tugs, barges and special service craft of one sort and another, including dredgers, floating docks and icebreaking supply tugs. Each year vessels going there had to deliver themselves around Cape Barrow to fit the narrow time frame that was the Arctic open season.

The vessels came from an initial vast new building project that involved several B.C. yards as well as equipment from the U.S. and some giant barges built in Japan as well as a variety of river craft. Seaspan was a major participant in its joint venture with Crowley of San Francisco and FedNav of Montreal. They came together in the joint-venture company, Arctic Transportation Limited. In addition Seaspan provided much of the towing capacity in getting barges and their deck cargoes to their destination. The entire play was so vast that it would merit a book in itself.

The following photographs, mostly from the Seaspan archives, depict this fleet. It reminded any one who had experienced the vast invasion fleets of WW II of history repeating itself.

[136] **Pusher tug Matt Berry:** Built by the Vito shipyard in Delta, B.C., in 1973 for Northern Transportation Ltd. of Edmonton. Here she manoeuvers at Seaspan facility in North Vancouver. Sister ships **Henry Christoffersen** and **Jock McNiven** to the left will follow for loading on barges.

[137] **Jock McNiven,** after loading on a barge. With a length of 148 feet and a gross tonnage of around 770 tons they were sizeable, powerful vessels specially designed for shallow draft river work.

[138] A stern view of **Jock McNiven,** loaded on her barge.

[139] Sister tugs **Arctic Hooper** and **Arctic Taglu** were built at Allied Shipbuilders, North Vancouver, B.C., in 1978. With 2,250 hp they are important units today in the fleet of Sea-Link Marine Services of New Westminster, B.C.

[140] Part of the convoy is seen passing West Vancouver. Another view of the same convoy is shown in photo #3 in the introduction.

[141] **Arctic Tarsiut**, built at Hiroshima in 1981. With a length of 485', a beam of about 120' and a dead-weight capacity of about 24,000 tons, it was the biggest of a number of large barges built in Japan for Arctic service. In terms of size it outranked the Genmar barges photographed earlier in this chapter. With semi-submersible capability, she was designed to lift huge preformed concrete structures the size of the one shown here.

[142] **Seaspan King** stands by with a steadying line to the buoy in the foreground. **Arctic Tarsiut** has her chain bridle rigged and likely connected to the tug's towline ready to proceed to the Arctic as soon as final arrangements are completed. To the right, **Seaspan Chief** is readying another tow for the Arctic.

[143] **Seaspan Mariner** heads out with a tow that includes the accommodation ship **Sinniktarpok,** built in 1945 in the U.S. This is believed to be a sister or maybe the same vessel as the one in the chapter entitled "Misadventure at Twin Creeks" in *Tying the Knot,* Book 3 in this series.

[144] One of the triple-stacked barges confronts Arctic icepacks somewhere off the North slope of Alaska.

[145] **Henry Christoffersen,** having been floated off her submerged barge, is seen here doing the job she was built for as she pushes a triple stack of barges upriver. They will be separated by first sinking the lowest level barge, floating off the other two and then sinking the middle barge, to release the top one.

[146] **Arctic Taglu** *(left)* and **Arctic Pelly,** ex-**Federal VII** *(right),* laid up in winter ice, awaiting the next season. The centre tug has not been identified by the author.

[147] Typical river craft arriving behind a Seaspan tug. A shallow draft river pusher tug is loaded on deck along with a typical West Coast seiner. This combination can also be clearly seen in the foreground in the convoy picture #140. Why the seiner was sent to the Arctic is not now recalled.

[148] **Kap IV,** a river pusher tug owned by Kap's Transport stands by to handle a newly launched river freighter, the **Aurora Explorer** in her original configuration. She and her sister **Aurora Surveyor** were originally designed by William Brown as seismic survey vessels in the North West Territories. Since then **Aurora Explorer** has been much rebuilt and enlarged as a cruise/workboat sailing out of Menzie Bay, Campbell River, for Marine Link Ltd. as described in *Boomsticks & Towlines,* Book 1 in this series.

Chapter Thirteen

THE DOCKSHIPS AND THEIR ORIGINS

Having written in the previous chapter about the semi-submersible barges developed by Genstar and its co-venturing partners in offshore operations, it seems like a reasonable and logical extension of that subject to now make some observations about the handling of large and awkward cargoes by other means, prior to and since the development of these oversize barges. To the ship watcher few things are more fascinating than witnessing the handling of oversize loads, as the operators use the forces of nature as their helpers. These are combined with engineering and mathematical skills that appear to work miracles in moving everything from locomotives and heavy machinery to giant digesters, container gantries, drilling rigs and production platforms.

Admittedly, this chapter has little to do with Canadian offshore tug and barge operations except that while Genstar pursued its options in this field, it was theoretically competing with the heavy lift ships, mostly from a previous era, and the modern dockships whose technology largely stems from wartime developments in the Second World War. The word "theoretical" is used because while all handled heavy lifts they each occupied a differing sector of the market because of the different techniques used.

The heavy-lift era, more or less started with the need to transport such items as large steam locomotives from their European and later American manufacturers. The railway building era spread to colonies and developing countries as the development of railways became a worldwide trend. The biggest manufacturers up to the end of the steam era were British companies like Bayer–Garrett, Beyer–Peacock, North British, Vulcan Locomotive and Metropolitan–Cammell and the biggest markets were in countries like India, Australia, New Zealand and the South American and African countries.

[149] **Seaspan Careen,** described as a heavy lift, submersible dry-dock barge, has dimensions of 131.06 m x 48.77 m x 7.62 m with a clear 33.5 m between the towers and a lifting capacity of 30,000 metric tonnes, which compares to the 18,000 tdw of the biggest Dockwise vessel. It is also mobile enough to be able to do lengthy voyages in tow. It is moved as needed between Vancouver and Victoria, but is offered worldwide by Seaspan Cyprus working in conjunction with Boa A/S. It can do everything the Dockwise ships can do, except load overside because of the towers and it lacks the ability of self-propulsion.

[150] Dockwise and Dock Express were previously competing companies but they have now been brought together under the common brand name of Dockwise. Two basic types are offered, the "float-on/float-off" and the "float-in/float out." Here a float-on type, the **Swift,** is seen arriving at Vancouver with a delivery of eight new steel chip barges, built in China for Rivtow. The barges were each secured to the deck of **Swift** by welded connections which had to be burned off first, but once done the ship submerged and the eight barges floated off like a huge raft which was quickly broken up as Rivtow tugs separated the new vessels.

Starting in Victorian times locomotives were transported, perhaps four at a time with their tenders on tramp steamers, usually mounted on heavy cribbings to spread the load on the main deck on either side of the hatches, fore and aft. Ship's tackle utilized as heavy lift gear was unknown before the early 1920s, so heavy reliance was placed on floating cranes or dockside cranes in loading and unloading these ships. To this point three British companies, Clan Line, Ellerman Lines and T. & J. Harrison, had been able to handle most of the loads going to many overseas destinations, particularly Africa and India as they had developed ships with extra features to assist this traffic. These included reinforced decks and heavy lift derricks, but essentially they were only an intermediate step in the development of the true heavy-lift ships.

In 1926, Norwegian shipowner, Christen Smith A/S, went to the Armstrong, Whitworth shipyard at Newcastle, England, a company with a track record second-to-none as the builder of the major warships and passenger liners of that era. Smith placed the order for the first purpose-built heavy lift ship, *Belnor.* Using oversize derricks, gantries to spread the load and a system of compensating ballast and deballasting tanks in the hull, the ship could lean over, pluck say a smaller vessel out of the water or a locomotive off the dock and then right herself as the water levels in the tanks were adjusted and the derrick brought the load inboard. The reverse followed when unloading.

The design was a success and soon Smith, now operating under the brand name Belships, followed with more and bigger vessels. As the Second World

War progressed, Britain found that the Belships which had escaped the German invasion of Norway, were a valuable addition to the wartime fleet. They could carry tanks and heavy equipment more efficiently than most. Often they were called upon to handle locomotives as the need for the rebuilding of railways inevitably followed reoccupation of recovered lands.

The problem was that there were not enough of these specialty vessels, so the British Ministry of War Transport commissioned Vickers Armstrong to build more vessels that followed the Belships design. The war-built ships were constructed to a high specification and none were lost through war casualties. Liberties, Park ships and other war-built classes were also fit to carry heavy loads on deck, including tanks, and on many occasions such ships also carried heavy locomotives on deck. Thus there was an oversupply of heavy lift ships and Belships built no new versions of their pre-war design after the war. Another factor was the changing pattern of trade with important countries like India, China, South Africa and Australia becoming self-sufficient in manufacturing their own railway equipment.

During the war, with the growth of amphibious operations in the Mediterranean, Northern Europe and East Asia, another new type of ship evolved. This was the Dock Landing Ship, usually termed an LSD. Essentially it was a floating dry dock with propulsion and the ability to proceed under power at an operating speed of around 15 knots. These ships were designed in Britain with the idea that they could carry far bigger units than the heavy lift ships could conveniently handle. A typical load might be several larger class landing craft. The LSD could load far faster and could discharge its cargo quickly even in the open ocean if weather conditions permitted. The British design was adapted to American construction processes and the first self-propelled dockships were built in the U.S., who built a fleet of them during and after the war. The British built a smaller fleet towards the end of the war and the type has been continued in both navies since.

The dockships based on the original model could only load vessels lengthwise, loading through the open dock gate placed at the stern of the ships and then pumping out to lift the entire load in an enclosed deck, which was open to the sky. The submersible

[151] Here is **Swan,** a sister of the **Swift,** after submerging and releasing a deck cargo. She is pumping off her ballast water as the main deck forward starts to reappear.

barge developed by Genstar and its partners had the advantage that it could submerse sufficiently to allow the load to be floated over the cargo deck and thus be loaded athwartships with significant overhangs on either side. This permitted oversize loads that could not be loaded into the fore and aft design represented by the LSD type.

The principal operator of self-propelled dock-ships is Dockwise NV, a Belgian company and its Texan subsidiary, Dockwise Inc. of Houston. At last report they had 13 vessels in their fleet, some of which are developed from the LSD design and others are really self-propelled deck barges which can float cargo across the vessel. This gives them considerable flexibility in handling multiple loads of woodchip barges as Dockwise did for Rivtow in 1999 with a load of eight chippers. The design has also been very effective in delivering large container cranes, mostly built in China, and supplied to world container ports.

As noted in chapter 10, Genstar disposed of all its interests in large submersible barges, the buyer being Boa A/S of Trondheim, Norway who have built even bigger barges than the original Genstar units. Boa conducts an active business to this day and is ranked among the competitors of Dockwise NV. When

exploration of the British Columbia offshore oil and gas fields commences we can expect to see more of these semi-submersible ships and barges visiting B.C. as they deliver rigs and other installations. No doubt B.C. towing companies expect to benefit from the traffic generated by coastal tows, from say the delivery spot in Esquimalt Roads or English Bay to the coastal site. If units are towed in rather than transported, then the benefit of the towing will probably go to the foreign company that originated the tow from its point of departure.

An interesting combination is the *Seaspan Careen*, which can function as a seagoing barge just as readily as it can be used as a stationary floating dry dock for lifting and repairing damaged vessels up to the size of the largest units in the Seaspan fleet. The hull is clearly originally a large ocean-going flat-deck barge with all apertures sealed. Entry into the hull is facilitated through large vertical tanks, which serve as dock walls, erected on either side of the deck. The vessel is always submerged or raised in such a way that the hull remains horizontal at all times which is the same principle employed in the Genstar barges.

[152] Now in light condition, **Swan** lays at anchor awaiting her next assignment. Machinery aft and a small forward navigation bridge for use when loads obscure the main bridge aft, distinguish the type.

[153] **Dock Express 11** represents the "float-on/float-out" type as she is seen here delivering a new container crane to Vancouver. She was deeply ballasted before entering the harbour to allay any fears about fouling the Lions Gate bridge.

[154] **Dock Express 11.** A close-up view gives a better idea of the size of the ungainly looking load. The two red-painted erections behind the twin stacks are a part of the ship's gear, being mobile loading gantries that can move along the length of the cargo deck. Assisted by Seaspan shipberthing tugs, **Seaspan Falcon** can be seen at the ship's stern.

[155] **Dock Express 11** is seen awaiting unloading orders in the harbour while arrangements are made ashore to receive the new arrival. **Seaspan Hawk** attends at the bow.

[156] With the assignment completed, **Dock Express 11** leaves Vancouver harbour for her next job. This shot gives an excellent idea of the empty cargo deck and the watertight tailgate.

[157] **Dock Express 11** also functions as a yacht transporter in a steady trade developed by Dockwise. The opportunity was taken on this occasion for North Arm's **Josee M,** now **North Arm Defiant,** to hitch a ride from Fort Lauderdale, Florida, after delivering some barges there.

[158] **Dock Express 11.** An interesting shot of this unique type of vessel. They were not beauties in any way, but they are one of the most functional types of ships afloat.

Chapter Fourteen

THE SMIT INTERNATIONAL ORGANIZATION

The importance of including the following on the Smit International Organization arises because of its takeover in 2000 of Rivtow Marine. This puts Smit firmly into the North Pacific with important bases at Vancouver and Prince Rupert. Conversely this development also enlarges Rivtow's potential as it becomes a component of one of the world's major marine towing and contracting groups. Rivtow is not Smit's first acquisition in Canada as it did own a 50 per cent interest in Eastern Canada Towing, operating on Canada's east coast during the 1980s. This investment was subsequently disposed of. Going back to the post-war years of the 1950s and 1960s, Smit was in partnership with Island Tug & Barge Ltd. in transpacific towing operations based on Victoria, B.C., detailed earlier in this book.

In 1896 the Dutch tugs *Oceaan* and *Oostzee* towed a small floating dock with a lifting capacity of 1,350 tons, 5,308 nautical miles from Rotterdam to San Paul de Loanda, believed to be in Brazil. To give a little historical perspective to that year, that was also the year when the little Vancouver steam tug *On Time* was built to be chartered two years later by Harry Jones who founded the business that became Vancouver Tug Boat Company and loomed large in the history of B.C. towboating.

Shipping reference books give no note of when L. Smit & Company actually started, but they count their deep-sea towings from 1892. It is more than probable that the Smit business grew from the smallest beginnings on the canals and waterways of the Netherlands, an unknown number of years before that. The 1896 tow was the first of 76 successful similar deliveries of floating dry docks made between that first year and 1948 when L. Smit & Co's Internationale Sleepdienst published its first post-war booklet explaining its operations to that date. The author has held a copy of that booklet since it was published a little past the halfway mark in Smit's first century and it makes an interesting comparison with the current position of Smit another half-century later and what has grown into the

world's largest international towing organization with subsidiary operations in many countries.

Of all the European continental powers none has developed the unique commercial ties like those that exist between the Netherlands and Britain. Historically these go back to a period when Britain and the Netherlands were as often at war with each as they were in peace. Both were strong colonial powers and to gain advantage of each other's special situations they often formed commercial partnerships. The biggest ones existing today are Royal Dutch Shell and Unilever, both of which are worldwide names whose products are to be found in every region of the world. A more recent one, which touches us in British Columbia, is P & O NedLloyd, the Anglo–Dutch container partnership.

The recent acquisition of Rivtow by Smit is not the first time that we have seen the Dutch marine industries make an incursion into British Columbia. Back in the late fifties the Dutch shipping and tanker company, Phs. Van Ommeren, acquired Northland Navigation the last major conventional shipping concern on the West Coast. Northland had enjoyed the benefit of a federal subsidy covering its shipping services from Vancouver to Northern B.C., but when this was cancelled in the face of political pressure,

Northland wound down its coastal services and eventually retired from business and Van Ommeren withdrew. It was not the best of investment situations for the Dutch company and one has to wonder why they ever made it, given the political nature of subsidies and how they can become illusions for the unwary. In any event when Northland got out of the coastal business, the principal beneficiary was Rivtow which put in a barge service which functions to this day.

Another Dutch incursion was Louis Van der Veen who sold Stork–Werkspoor engines to the B.C. tug and barge industry. Because this was a big supplier of diesels for deep-sea shipping applications it did not follow that the line of diesels on offer would have the same success in tugboats. Stork-Werkspoor diesels had their brief fling and then withdrew.

In 1930, Smit owned 23 tugs and one sailing vessel. The latter's significance is not known, although it might have been a training ship of some sort. Following the depression the company started an upgrading program building more powerful diesel tugs. By 1940 when the Netherlands was overrun by the Nazi invasion the fleet consisted of 21 tugs. All ten of the larger ocean-going type escaped to serve the Allied cause, and the rest which were mostly of the river and harbour types fell to the Germans. Regular towing operations were suspended and at the end of the war, Smit was left with 13 boats, the bigger number of casualties being victims of Allied bombing. Of the personnel, 37 Smit men lost their lives during the war.

With the 1948 book Smit took a look at their own record, which is set out below. From 1892 to 1948 the company completed 7,966 ocean tows with a loss ratio of well under one per cent. From 1923 on, with improved techniques and higher horsepower tugs the loss ratio fell below a half of one per cent, an enviable record in anyone's language. By 1948 the ocean-going fleet had recovered to 15 units with three new tugs under construction. The largest unit remained the *Zwarte Zee* with an ihp of 4,200, followed by *Thames* at 3,000 ihp and *Rode Zee* at 2,000 ihp.

But world events were overtaking the colonial powers, and this included the Dutch with their huge holdings in what became Indonesia, which had generated wealth for Holland for three hundred years. It is no use criticizing the colonial powers as they were the spearheads of economic growth and colonization starting in the middle ages until the early years of the last century. The Dutch, like the British and French had to retrench and find new roles for themselves in world commerce, at the same time as patterns of world trade and political boundaries and ideologies were changing so radically.

As a side note, consider the relative 1948 position of the Cosulich interests and their River Towing Ltd. business. At that time Rivtow, as it came to be known in the '60s, was a small, aggressive and highly competitive river towboat company whose main business was moving logs in the Fraser River, with some scow towing of gravel. It is doubtful if they had a unit over 500 hp at that time and they had not broken out into coastal towing.

In the early post-war period offshore exploration for oil started in the shallow seas off the Mississippi delta, and soon extended itself out into the Gulf of Mexico. This is where the techniques, which became standard around the world, were initially developed. Jackup rigs became bigger as they stepped out into deep water and in due time the water became too deep for them and several types of semi-submersible exploration and production platforms developed. Then in the 1950s oil was found in commercial quantities in the storm-wracked North Sea, but the equipment needed was much bigger than that developed in the Gulf of Mexico. Just as the need for bigger scale equipment became apparent so also were higher horsepower tugs also required for anchor handling and towing duties.

The trend to bigger tugs grew as ships became bigger. A 3,000-hp tug could easily handle a loaded Liberty ship or a T2-size tanker in the 15,000-tdw size range. When tankers with a dead weight over 250,000 tons and up to 600,000 tons deadweight broke down at sea it called for tugs in the 16–24,000 hp range. Smits, like other owners in Holland, Germany, Belgium, Scandinavia, Britain, South Africa and elsewhere, swiftly developed the new generation of tugs required in the second half of the 20th century.

FROM THE HISTORY BOOKS

Smit International's roots probably go back to the 1860s. By the 1890s it was a major factor in international towing. The record of its international tows is an impressive one. The first table taken from their first post-war book gives details of their loss record, which is usually something that most companies do not publicize. The second sets out their history in one category alone as towers of floating docks. *(pp. 153-155)*

SMIT'S TOWAGES SINCE 1892

	STEAMERS	OBSOLETES	SAILING SHIPS	DREDGING MATERIAL	THAMES BARGES	LIGHTERS	FLOATING CRANES	FLOATING DRYDOCKS	OTHER CRAFT	TOTAL	LOSSES
From 1892 till 1923	344	387	not registered	663	1274	903	78	41	281	3972	36
(specification in previous issues)											
1924	34	9	13	36	85	52	5	4	—	238	
1925	15	5	7	70	100	27	6	1	—	231	2 dredgers
1926	15	6	2	87	110	11	7	3	—	241	
1927	17	16	4	86	121	19	9	1	—	273	2 dredgers 1 barge
1928	21	8	2	93	160	26	15	3	—	328	
1929	30	6	7	57	132	23	9	1	3	268	1 dock 2 barges
1930	32	9	3	45	85	19	9	1	4	206	
1931	22	12	2	115	65	16	6	1	—	239	
1932	11	7	1	63	55	5	12	—	2	156	2 dredgers 1 tug
1933	12	8	1	42	22	8	5	1	2	101	1 tug
1934	11	8	1	79	50	9	4	—	—	162	
1935	11	16	—	70	77	19	—	—	4	197	2 barges
1936	19	9	1	92	75	42	1	3	—	242	1 dredger
1937	40	25	—	67	95	48	12	1	1	289	2 dredgers 1 crane pontoon
1938	23	8	1	59	46	48	3	—	5	193	
1939	33	13	—	71	20	48	—	2	1	188	1 dredger
1940	10	—	—	28	—	13	—	1	—	52	
1940/1945	War period				No commercial towage						
1945/1946	52	5	—	70	—	15	14	2	56	214	
1947	31	18	—	91	—	18	27	3	8	196	
	783	575	45	1984	2572	1369	222	69	367	7986	55 = 0.689%

Since 1923 in total 7986—3972 = 4014 towages with 19 losses, is 0.473%.

LIST OF FLOATING DOCKS TOWED BY THE TUGS OF L. SMIT & CO'S INTERNATIONALE SLEEPDIENST AT ROTTERDAM

Number of Voyage	Year	Dimensions of Dock Length	Width	Lifting Capacity	FROM	TO	Distance in Nautical Miles by route followed	Tugs
1	1896	180' × 44'		1350 Tons	ROTTERDAM ...	SAN PAUL DE LOANDA	5308	Oceaan / Oostzee
2	1898	510' × 110'8"		12000 „	TYNE	STETTIN	753	Roode Zee / Zwarte Zee / Noordzee
3	1901	450' × 117'		12000 „	TYNE	PORT MAHON ..	2150	Zwarte Zee / Oceaan
4	1902	545' × 126'		17000 „	TYNE	BERMUDA	4065	Zwarte Zee / Oceaan
5	1903	300' × 70'		3000 „	CLYDE	ROTTERDAM ...	770	Zwarte Zee / Lauwerzee
6	1903	436' × 95'		7500 „	CLYDE	ROTTERDAM ...	770	Zwarte Zee / Lauwerzee
7	1903	430' × 92'		8500 „	TYNE	DURBAN	7864	Zwarte Zee / Oceaan
8	1904	203'4" × 57'4"		1200 „	HAMBURG	DUALA	4895	Oceaan / Zuiderzee
9	1904	295' × 85'		3000 „	TYNE	PORT-SAID	3565	Zwarte Zee / Lauwerzee
10	1906	208' × 98'		4500 „	ANTWERP	COPENHAGEN ..	670	Oceaan / Noordzee
11	1906	277' × 98'		6500 „	ANTWERP	COPENHAGEN ..	670	Oceaan / Noordzee
12	1907	340'6" × 81'		4000 „	TYNE	TRINIDAD	4577	Zwarte Zee / Lauwerzee
13	1907	425' × 95'		7500 „	TYNE	ROTTERDAM ...	291	Oceaan / Oostzee
14	1908	139' × 50'		400 „	TYNE	LAGOS	4636	Oceaan
15	1909	385' × 95'		7000 „	TYNE	CALLAO	10260	Zwarte Zee / Oceaan
16	1909	294'9" × 88'6"		7000 „	BREMEN	KIEL........	660	Roode Zee / Wodan
17	1909	140' × 51'		450 „	BARROW i. F....	BURUTU	4215	Thames
18	1910	550'6" × 136'		25000 „	BARROW i. F....	RIO DE JANEIRO .	5200	Roode Zee / Zwarte Zee
19	1910	219'4" × 60'2"		1200 „	CLYDE	BAHIA	4550	Oceaan
20	1910	152' × 88'		2000 „	FLENSBURG	HAMBURG	610	Thames
21	1910	152' × 88'		2000 „	FLENSBURG	HAMBURG	610	Thames
22	1911	310' × 90'		5350 „	BARROW i. F....	ABERDEEN	556	Zwarte Zee / Wodan
23	1911	365' × 81'		5000 „	TYNE	ROTTERDAM ...	291	Zwarte Zee / Wodan
24	1912	450' × 117'		12000 „	PORT MAHON ...	TRIEST	1266	Roode Zee / Zwarte Zee
25	1912	640' × 144'		32000 „	TYNE	MEDWAY	308	Roode Zee / Zwarte Zee / Oceaan / Oostzee
26	1912	600' × 135'		25000 „	BARROW i. F....	MONTREAL	4000	Zwarte Zee / Roode Zee
27	1912	358' × 81'		3000 „	TYNE	LAGOS	(lost)	Poolzee / Lauwerzee
28	1912	252' × 133'		10000 „	FLENSBURG	HAMBURG	610	Schelde / Donau
29	1912	252' × 133'		10000 „	FLENSBURG	HAMBURG	610	Schelde / Donau
30	1912	350' × 81'		3500 „	GREENOCK	SURABAYA	9025	Thames
31	1913	425' × 95'		5000 „	TYNE	CONSTANTINOPLE	3360	Zwarte Zee / Poolzee
32	1913	300' × 60'		1500 „	BARROW i. F....	BUENOS AYRES ..	6248	Roode Zee
33	1915	479' × 110'		4900 „	AMSTERDAM ...	ROTTERDAM ...	60	Oceaan / Poolzee / Wodan
34	1920	366' × 95'		4200 „	HAMBURG	ROTTERDAM ...	324	Witte Zee / Lauwerzee
35	1920	366' × 95'		4200 „	HAMBURG	ROTTERDAM ...	324	Witte Zee / Lauwerzee
36	1920	500' × 104'		10000 „	INVERGORDON .	SCHIEDAM	490	Humber / Schelde / Seine

Number of Voyage	Year	Dimensions of Dock		Lifting Capacity	FROM	TO	Distance in Nautical Miles by route followed	Tugs
		Length	Width					
37	1920	703′ × 170′		46000 Tons	HAMBURG	SCHIEDAM	324	Humber Schelde Seine Donau
38	1920	366′ × 95′		4200 ,,	KIEL	ROUEN	567	Zwarte Zee Lauwerzee
39	1920	366′ × 95′		4200 ,,	KIEL	HAVRE	500	Zwarte Zee Lauwerzee
40	1921	400′ × 92′		3600 ,,	HAMBURG	CHERBOURG . . .	531	Roode Zee Lauwerzee
41	1922	233′ × 66′		1600 ,,	HAMBURG	TARRAGONA . . .	2100	Humber
42	1923	500′ × 96′		8000 ,,	ROTTERDAM . . .	TANDJONG PRIOK	8700	Humber Poolzee
43	1924	250′ × 70′		—	TYNE	DARTMOUTH . . .	485	Humber
44	1924	262′5″ × 65′5″		1800 ,,	CADIZ	CARTAGENA . . .	300	Humber
45	1924	310′ × 77′		3000 ,,	TYNE	LAGOS	4332	Roode Zee
46	1924	361′ × 93′5″		4200 ,,	BREMERHAVEN . .	VALENCIA . . . . :	1954	Humber Seine
47	1926	480′ × 120′		20000 ,,	HAMBURG	SCHIEDAM	324	Roode Zee Witte Zee
48	1926	250′ × 74′		3000 ,,	ROTTERDAM . . .	CURAÇAO	4700	Roode Zee
49	1926	115′ × 109′		section of 40000 ,,	QUEENBOROUGH	SCAPA FLOW . . .	530	Poolzee Hudson
50	1926	656′ × 187′		40000 ,,	PORTSMOUTH . .	ROSYTH	500	Zwarte Zee Witte Zee Roode Zee
51	1928	305′ × 78′		3000 ,,	ROTTERDAM . . .	SURABAYA	9000	Gele Zee
52	1928	390′ × 172′		middle-section and end sections of 50.000 t.	TYNE	SINGAPORE	8500	Roode Zee Zwarte Zee Indus Schelde
53	1928	465′ × 172′			TYNE	SINGAPORE	8500	Witte Zee Humber Java Zee Oostzee
54	1929	365′ × 81′		4000 Tons	AMSTERDAM . . .	CURAÇAO	4700	Roode Zee
55	1929	510′ × 110′		11000 ,,	HAMBURG	ROTTERDAM . . .	(lost)	Humber Witte Zee
56	1932	584′ × 117′6″		17000 ,,	TYNE	WELLINGTON . .	13000	Zwarte Zee Witte Zee
57	1933	200′ × 72′		1600 ,,	CADIZ	PASSAGES	1000	Noordzee Donau
58	1936	478′ × 88′		6000 ,,	PALERMO	BANDAR SCHAPUR	4640	Humber
59	1936	531′ × 95′		7500 ,,	SPEZIA	MASSAUA	2450	Humber Ganges
60	1936	229′ × 31′		1000 ,,	ROTTERDAM . . .	LENINGRAD	1115	Indus
61	1937	563′ × 118′		15000 ,,	BERGEN	OSLO	370	Humber Witte Zee
62	1938	350′ × 88′		4000 ,,	MIDDLESBOROUGH	DURBAN	8000	Roode Zee
63	1939	680′ × 144′		31000 ,,	PORTSMOUTH . .	ALEXANDRIA . . .	3000	Zwarte Zee Thames Witte Zee
64	1939	391′ × 85′		5000 ,,	SABANG	SINGAPORE	600	Roode Zee
65	1946	150′ × 50′		250 ,,	GREENOCK	ROTTERDAM . . .	818	Witte Zee
66	1946	280′ × 102′		1800 ,,	SHEERNESS	SÖDERTÄLJA . . .	971	Zwarte Zee
67	1946	468′ × 100′		7500 ,,	HAVERTON HIL ON TEES	STOCKHOLM . . .	936	Zwarte Zee
68	1946	210′ × 64′		400 ,, (concrete)	LONDON	VLAARDINGEN . .	177	Schelde Ebro
69	1947	550′ × 135′		17000 ,,	BERMUDA	MONTEVIDEO . . .	7080	Zwarte Zee
70	1947	69′ × 100′		1500 ,,	HAVERTON HILL ON TEES	STOCKHOLM . . .	936	Ganges
71	1947	215′ × 61′		750 ,,	CAPETOWN	LA PLATA	4650	Witte Zee
72	1947	478′ × 88′		6000 ,,	ADEN	TANDJONG PRIOK	4030	Zwarte Zee
73	1948	215′ × 61′		750 ,,	BOMBAY	SORONG	4600	Tyne
74	1948	215′ × 61′		750 ,,	KARACHI	LA PLATA	9400	Poolzee
75	1948	215′ × 61′		750 ,,	VIZAGAPATAM . .	LA PLATA	9700	Witte Zee
76	1948	215′ × 61′		750 ,,	COCHIN	LA PLATA	9100	Tyne

In total 76 dockvoyages, covering 237.681 miles.

155

In this same time period, the concept of the transnational corporations took hold in a far bigger way. Inspired by moves to break down trade barriers and open up worldwide markets to easier trade between nations, the process of merger and amalgamation has gathered speed. Supporters of the trend see it as a logical outgrowth of the need to improve standards of living for the poorer nations; others see it as a new form of business imperialism by which the rich become richer at the expense of the poor. However it is looked at, some of the trend appears to be a rather mindless exercise in grabbing naked power and the best defence for some appears to be a matter of gobbling up the competition before it eats up the gobbler.

Smit appears to have made a major policy decision to be implemented after the war and as quickly as peacetime conditions permitted. This decision, even if it could be defined as something highly specific in the confused conditions immediately after the war, was to grow its business by all means available to it. The company had been a leader in its highly specialized field for decades, but like all leaders it was capable of being toppled from its leading position. Let us a pause for a moment and take a look at what they were faced with.

Hitler's invasion of the Low Countries took place in 1940. It separated Holland from its East Indies Empire and possessions in the Netherlands Antilles. The Caribbean area was one of vital importance to Britain which now stood alone against Germany, so it would be a virtually instantaneous action by which Dutch possessions, Aruba and Curacao, in this area moved from neutral to combatant status.

The situation was somewhat different in the East Indies with its several thousand islands and hundreds of isolated communities covering a vast area which stretched from Burma at its northern extremity, touched the Philippines in the east and stretched down to the northern tips of Australia. It was a

[159] **Zwarte Zee,** built prior to WW II, was the most powerful tug in the Smit fleet with 4,200 hp. Here she rests after delivering a 17,000-ton dry dock from Bermuda to Montevideo, Uruguay, in 1946. Smit's ocean tugs escaped the Nazi invasion of Holland in 1940 and became valuable additions to the Allied war effort at sea. New tugs were built after the war and horsepowers rose rapidly as ships increased in size.

complete colonial oligarchy, with an Imperial Dutch army and navy and all the usual trappings of the occupying power which had been on the scene for upwards of three hundred years and, in the manner of the colonial era, the Dutch, like their other European confreres in colonialism, had little reason to assume that they would not be there for several hundred more years.

[160] **Smit Rotterdam** and her sister **Smit London,** each with 26,000 hp, are part of a total fleet of over 500 vessels of which eleven are in the 14,000–26,000 hp range. Compare the power of these giants with **Rivtow Captain Bob** at 6,000 hp, the most powerful tug in B.C. which successfully towed a fully laden 90,000-ton tanker in the North Pacific. These units now carry the name Smitwijs on their sides and in their names to indicate the link up between Smit and its biggest Dutch competitor, Weijsmueller.

Japan shattered that illusion when it attacked Pearl Harbour on December 7, 1941, by which time the Dutch East Indies had been effectively cut off from the mother country for over a year. During that year, life for the colonial Dutch had gone on more or less uninterrupted and its valuable resources of oil, rubber, copra and many other raw materials had benefitted those who had the means to ship the resources out, primarily the British, neutral Americans and the Japanese until trade embargoes were imposed following Japan's taking of French Indo-China, some five months prior to Pearl Harbour. Because normal trade patterns had been distorted the East Indies was a rich storehouse of stockpiled materials when the Japanese invaded and for a while Japan had a field day as it transferred all manner of strategic materials as fast as its ships could carry the cargoes.

Smit was not particularly involved in the shipping activities of the Dutch colonies in the East. Its sphere of operations was Western Europe and the North Atlantic. Here it maintained salvage stations at Queenstown, Southern Ireland, St. John's, Newfoundland; Horta in the Azores; Coruna, North West Spain; Douarnenez, Northwest France; the Hook of Holland and Flushing. J.D. McLaren & Company were Smit's agents in London and were able to give any information required about the position and availability of any of the company's tugs, on a daily or even hourly basis if needed. This accords with earlier descriptions of the international nature of the London ship charter and marine insurance markets.

The outbreak of the European war soon affected all such peacetime arrangements, but the invasion of the Netherlands quickly settled all Dutch salvage tugs which were not caught in Holland on to the Allied side, and a valuable addition they were to be working alongside British Admiralty and eventually

[161] Smit Mississippi is one of five "M"-class ship berthing tugs with 5,200 hp, a bollard pull of 60 tons and twin azimuth stern drives. The shipberthing division of Rivtow is the one that is closest to Smit's general run of business and probably the one where they will maintain the most competitive pressure with an ever-increasing identification with Smit at B.C. ports.

[162] Smit Pioneer is one of three semi-submersible dockships, similar to those in the Dockwise fleet earlier described. However, employment differs with the Smit ships being more likely involved in heavy ocean engineering jobs as the photo indicates with a heavy-duty crane mounted on a tower astern.

[163] **Giant,** a 24,000 semi-submersible barge, has a major part of a production platform assembled on board in Denmark for Norsk Hydro. This would have been added to a floating structure in the North Sea.

U.S. Navy tugs. Some of the Dutch tugs were to be engaged in towing Mulberry harbour sections to Normandy, among many other tasks.

The British and Americans built large fleets of deep-sea salvage type tugs which meant that when the war was over many of them were classified as "war surplus" and put up for disposal. The better ones went into commercial service, which had the effect of increasing competition. On the other hand the aftermath of the war left a huge clean up of wrecks to be undertaken and equipment like dredgers and dry docks to be towed to harbours that had been neglected for years.

To add to all the confusion following the war, the

Netherlands was faced with an outright insurrection in its East Indies possessions. This quickly became a nasty war, which the Dutch could not win, particularly as the prevailing mood of much of the world was to see an end to colonial empires. Unfortunately what the world sometimes gained in return was something far worse than the old colonial regimes.

After the colonial possessions of the Dutch, British, French and Portuguese were given their independence or, in some instances as with Indonesia had forcibly taken it, the old trade patterns started to rearrange themselves. Much of this was due to encouragement by the Americans and Soviets of the new post-colonial regimes and the U.S./Soviet

159

agendas for gaining power and strategic influence at each other's expense. Inevitably it led to conflict, much of it on the African continent. One of the most noteworthy was the French-British and Israeli attack on the Gamal Abdel Nasser regime in Egypt which was the last display of such action by the old colonial powers without the approval of the Americans. Nasser filled the Suez Canal with sunken dredgers and sundry marine equipment and it seems reasonable to suppose that companies like Smit participated fully in its eventual clearance.

In the meantime interest in offshore oil exploration was picking up and in the '50s the first oil and gas fields were located in the North Sea. Germany, Holland, Denmark and Belgium all had sectors allocated to them, based on the length of their coastlines. This was fixed by international convention with the biggest gainers being Britain and Norway on account of their long North Sea coastlines and it was in their sectors that the biggest discoveries were made. The war and its immediate aftermath, along with the withdrawal from Empire, had devastated Britain's finances so the inflow of oil and gas royalties were a fortunate offset which came to Britain in a timely fashion and gradually redressed the adverse balance of her national finances. Norway was not a wealthy country either, earning its living largely through its shipping and fisheries industries. Both countries became net exporters of oil and gas and both prospered on account of this new found wealth.

The Smit organization, now functioning as Smit International, has grown with changing world events. It has acquired subsidiary and joint-venture companies around the world and maintains regional head offices in Houston, Texas for the Americas region, Singapore for Asia, Capetown, South Africa for Africa with its international head office in Rotterdam also serving the European region. Subsidiaries or joint-venture companies are consolidated in each of these regional offices. Rivtow, for example, comes under the jurisdiction of the Houston office.

What seemed to be a fairly frequent pattern of operation for Smit was to enter into a partnership or joint venture with a minimum 50 per cent interest

being help by Smit. Later one of three things could happen; either Smit would buy out its partner or, sell its interest back to the partner, or the two would sell out jointly to another party. It might have been a way in which the two parties came together to see if they were compatible, rather like a trial marriage. One major such move was the acquisition of a 50 per cent joint interest in a very large U.K. towing organization, Cory Towage Ltd., which serviced all the major U.K. ports. Cory was a subsidiary of Ocean Transport & Trading Ltd. of Liverpool, which had grown out of the famous Alfred Holt's Blue Funnel Line, a pillar of British shipping. They came together forming Smit & Cory International Port Towage after Cory was the successful tenderer to service the Canadian East Coast oil port of Port Hawkesbury. Later Ocean wished to retire entirely from marine activities and sold its interest to Australian interests who wanted the entire operation, so Ocean and Smit sold their interests together.

In 1987 Rivtow listed its entire fleet as consisting of 275 vessels of all types, but when Rivtow was acquired by Smit it consisted of 110 vessels from the fleet flagship *Rivtow Captain Bob* of 6,100 hp down to diminutive small towboats used in the Fraser River and adjoining Pitt and Harrison lakes. At least half the total number would have been barges from 17,000 tdw down. Rivtow had trimmed a number of its operations down from the acquisitive years of massive expansion when the slogan was "Where there's water, there's Rivtow." When Cecil Cosulich was in the chair at Rivtow it seemed to outsiders that it was expansion for expansion's sake. This took the company into the Mackenzie River system and the Beaufort Sea as well as many little places on the B.C. coast and interior. Isolated operators like Frank Hole in Quatsino Sound were approached and could have walked away with a good paper profit provided that he was prepared to accept notes in lieu of cash. It was a period when Rivtow's finances were frequently stretched to the breaking point as has been told in some detail in *Tying the Knot,* in this series.

When John Cosulich, the son of Cecil, took over his avowed purpose was to trim the fat and sell off operations not central to the main business of Rivtow and at the same time strengthen the treasury. He encouraged the development of worthwhile new activities such as competing for ship berthing in Vancouver with their successful new subsidiary, Tiger Tugz. The area of operations had been centralized on Vancouver with a second important region around Prince Rupert, Stewart and Kitimat. Rivtow looked after ship berthing and towing at Prince Rupert and Kitimat and also took out a high proportion of the logs from the area aboard its log barges.

The log barges were not confined to serving that area. In fact they ranged the entire coast as did their competitors. In the south a solid core business was the woodchip and hogfuel operations serving the mills at Crofton and Harmac near Nanaimo. The company also handled a proportion of the pulp and paper business, but in all categories in southern B.C. and railcar barging it was number two to Seaspan. Rivtow had never been in the railcar barge business and did not hold any of the major oil distribution accounts.

In a sense Cosulich's purpose was to prepare the "turkey ready for the oven," in the form of a strong balance sheet with well-identified profit centres. It roughly followed the precedent set by Thomas Stephens in his reorganization and clean-up of the sprawling MacMillan, Bloedel operations, preparatory to its takeover by Weyerhaueser. A major difference was that Rivtow was a private company wholly owned by the Cosulich interests and like all privately owned businesses, succession in key managerial positions was a matter that had to be to the fore. When Smits came calling, Cosulich was able to show a strong balance sheet with a considerably renewed fleet solidly employed in its main trades of log barging, harbour towing, woodchip transporation and general towing including its coastal freight run to northern coastal points.

Smit in return picked up a solidly entrenched base in British Columbia, second in the market place to the number-one operator Washington Marine Group and its main operating subsidiary Seaspan International. This alone fitted Smit's corporate concept of being number one, or a healthy number two, in every department of its activities. It admittedly moved into some activities in log and woodchip barging which were new to it, but that would be unavoidable and not unusual as every tugboat company worldwide responds to serving its local market in sometimes unusual conditions. On the face of things its timing for a purchase might have been somewhat off in that since taking over at Rivtow, the forest industry has plummeted in the face of regressive American anti-free trade actions against Canadian lumber and this in turn will affect all forest-based operations. On the other hand a far bigger plum, which suits Smit and its experience, is the probability of extensive offshore oil and gas exploration activities on the B.C. coast with a new provincial government now in charge which favours business development.

A look at the Smit fleet, which includes joint ventures as well as Rivtow's 110[1] vessels, reveals a fleet of 516 vessels, as at April 1, 2001. The fleet list follows on p.162.

The fleet list follows on p.162.

1. In the three years since Smit took over at Rivtow there are indications of many changes in the Rivtow fleet. By 2003 it was largely out of log towing and was giving up its freight barge run to Prince Rupert. A large part of the tug inventory had been disposed of or else was in the resale market. There is every indication that the business is being scaled down considerably. In view of the state of the coastal lumber industry and its poor prospects for the near future, it is anticipated that there will be considerable further consolidation in the log towing, log barging and forest products sector.

SMIT FLEET LIST

Ocean-going tugs	14,000–26,000 ihp	11
Ocean-going tugs *	4,000–10,000 ihp	5
Anchor Handling tugs	3,300–10,000 ihp	8
Anchor handling tug/supply vessels	8,000 ihp	5
Diving support vessel	1,900 ihp	1
Utility vessels		7
Ocean-going salvage vessels		5
Inland salvage vessels		4
Floating sheerlegs, seagoing	400–3,000 ton	9
Floating sheerlegs, inland	100–400 ton	5
Multipurpose offshore installation vessel		1
Self-propelled, semi-submersible heavy transport vessels		3
Pull barges		3
Barges, seagoing	24,000 tdw	3
Barges, seagoing *	10–14,000 tdw	8
Barges, seagoing *	1–8,000 tdw	56
Barges, inland	100–1,000 tdw	104
Coastal/harbour tugs *	3,000–6,000 ihp	95
Coastal/harbour tugs *	1,000–3,000 ihp	70
Harbour/Inland tugs	100–1,000 ihp	43
Harbour/Inland pusher tugs	480–2,800 ihp	11
Miscellaneous craft, workboats, launches, etc. *		59
TOTAL worldwide fleet		**516**

* Classification containing Rivtow units shown with an asterisk

The selection of pictures, all courtesy of Smit International, portray an enormous range of work vessels and assignments. One point that deserves mention is that critics of the likely gas and oil exploration program that is anticipated in British Columbia coastal waters conclude that our coast has some of the stormiest waters in the world and that loss or damage to vessels and pipelines is inevitable with huge consequences for the environment.

Such a possibility cannot be ruled out anywhere in the world, but let us keep a sense of proportion in such matters. There is probably no ocean area of the world that exceeds the ferocity of the North Sea and yet the safety record has been exemplary in every way. The same goes for the Bass Strait between Tasmania and mainland Australia and the Grand Banks off Newfoundland and there are many other

equally exposed areas. So long as we all wish to run our motor cars, fly planes and use plastics of every kind, mankind must win an increasing proportion of its oil from undersea areas.

What speaks loudest of all, is Smit's long record of successful towage/salvage operations. There are many other companies internationally that have pulled off notable feats, but none exceed Smit in terms of time, size or success ratio. It was notable that Smits was chosen to head the team that raised the recently lost Russian submarine *Kursk*. At a more local level, Smit was awarded the contract for raising the recently overturned log barge *Seaspan Rigger* as well as Rivtow's own *Powell Carrier*. What greater compliment could be paid to Smit when their main competitor, itself with a record of success going back to the Island Tug & Barge years, comes to them for

[164] Balder. Big rigs like the one in the previous picture require massive assistance to be put together. The **Balder** is typical and can lift 12,000 tons with her huge cranes.

[165] The Hereema Company is a Dutch-based ocean engineering concern which works closely with Smit and others in the industry. Here the **Balder** is seen with Arctic Transportation's ice-breaking tug **Arctic Nutsukpok,** which was built by Allied Shipbuilders in North Vancouver.

[166] Major ship raising projects are a specialty of Smit. Pictured here is a major job involving heavy lifting gear. Smit was involved in the raising of the Russian nuclear submarine **Kursk** in 2002 and is currently engaged in 2003 in removing the wreck of the Norwegian **Tricolor.** Locally Smit also successfully handled the righting of the Seaspan log barge **Seaspan Rigger.**

[167] Smit uses the joint-venture device to the maximum extent and as a tool for international expansion. Always watchful for favourable opportunities, the large-scale replacement of old undersea cables by modern fibre optics communication cables is a worldwide process. They have, for example, formed a joint venture with Oceaneering International of Houston, Texas. The vessel depicted here is **Ocean Hercules,** Smit's contribution to Smit Oceaneering Cable Systems. Oceaneering added all the cable laying equipment as their contribution to the joint venture.

assistance in this incident? It's a certain sign that the international insurance markets, who ultimately will pay most of the bills recognize the pre-eminence of Smit in this field.

VANCOUVER HARBOUR TUGS

Mention was made in *Tying the Knot,* Book 3 in this series, of how C.H. Cates & Sons, the Vancouver harbour ship berthing monopoly was finally joined in competition by Seaspan and was then united with Seaspan within the Washington Marine Group. Little mention was made in previous volumes of how a third entity, Tiger Tugz, a division of Rivtow Marine, joined the competitive fray and really there is not much to actually say on this initiative. Captain John Cosulich, then president of Rivtow, saw an opportunity when Seaspan and Cates were fighting it out for an all too brief period. When Seaspan was planning

on taking over Cates in an internal rearrangement there were some worries at Seaspan as to whether the Competition Act might come into play and spoil an otherwise attractive series of moves to finally unite Cates and Seaspan.

To the relief of some, Rivtow's introduction of itself as the provider of ship berthing services at Vancouver took away the possibility of anti-competition action and as before the Seaspan buyout by Washington, there were two genuine competitors in the business again.

While the subject matter in this brief photo essay has nothing specific to do with the international oil industry, the decision to place them here was governed by the big interest of Smit in harbour towing, plus space restraints.

The following selection of photos shows the ship berthing tugs at Vancouver through the three ownerships involved:

CATES TUGS

[168] Charles H. Cates I (old)

CATES TUGS *(cont.)*

[169] Charles H. Cates V (old)

[170] Charles H. Cates I (new), Z-Peller type

[171] **Charles H. Cates V** (new)

[172] **Charles H. Cates IV**

CATES TUGS *(cont.)*

[173] **Charles H. Cates XIX**

[174] **Charles H. Cates X**

[175] **Charles H. Cates III,** Z-Peller type

[176] **Charles H. Cates IV** in Seaspan colours with WMG logo

[177] **Charles H. Cates VIII** with tow post, no winch

[178] **Charles H. Cates XVIII** with winch

SEASPAN TUGS & WESTMINSTER TUGS (A DIVISION OF SMIT HARBOUR TUGS)

[179] Seaspan Discovery

[182] Seaspan Falcon

[180] Seaspan Falcon

[183] Westminster Chinook

[181] Seaspan Hawk

[184] Westminster Hunter

TIGER TUGZ (A DIVISION OF SMIT HARBOUR TUGS)

[185] Tiger Shaman

[186] Tiger Sun

[187] Tiger Sun, shows off extreme beam in this type

[188] Tiger Pride

Chapter Fifteen

VANCOUVER'S ONLY LOCALLY OWNED OFFSHORE SUPPLY COMPANY

Only one drill rig was built in B.C. and that was at Victoria Machinery Depot in Victoria. This rig was used initially in the exploration program in Hecate Straits. There were no purpose-built service vessels available on the West Coast, but Gulf of Georgia Towing Company, obtained the contract to service the rig with regular tugs and suitable barges from its fleet. With offshore supply and anchor handling tugs, several British Columbia yards benefitted in a significant way as has been mentioned earlier.

What follows had much to do with coastal shipping history and could have led to the formation of a powerful Vancouver-based offshore supply vessel company with future involvements in B.C., possibly the Arctic, and certainly in overseas developments for oil as an international industry.

The players involved were Federal Commerce & Navigation Ltd. of Montreal (now universally known as FedNav Ltd.), a large and successful deep-sea shipping concern, and Anglo-British Columbia Packing Co. Ltd. (ABC), then associated with the Bell-Irving interests of Vancouver.

The author at the time was employed by Bell-Irving and in turn was friendly with Bruce Garvey, manager of FedNav's Vancouver Office. Mr. Garvey and I discussed the possibility of launching a Vancouver-based international offshore supply company over a cup of coffee, in just the way that so many big deals are conceived. His principals at FedNav were interested in getting into the business and expressed a wish to find a financial and operating partner.

ABC had retired from active involvement in the B.C. fishing industry having sold its canneries and associated interests to B.C. Packers and Canadian Fishing Company. Originally incorporated in England, ABC had its head office in London and it was to the British company that the proceeds of sale flowed. ABC did however, retain its interest in a herring processing plant at Caraquet, New Brunswick, and it was for that plant that a number of the larger vessels under contract to ABC in the B.C. fishery had transferred themselves to fish for herring out of Caraquet.

In 1970 management control of ABC was transferred to Vancouver and with it came its substantial cash surplus of funds available for investment. ABC made a number of investments, through my intermediary, buying among other companies Swann Winches, a well-known name around the fishing and towing industries. Swann was then managed by Arthur Burgess, an entrepreneur with an engineering background. Burgess, with his sales manager, Dennis Shears, was actively promoting Swann products in Western Canada, Halifax, Nova Scotia, Texas and Singapore.

Among the contacts made by Shears on behalf of Swann, was an American offshore services company called the Seal Fleet Inc. of Galveston, Texas. Two of its employees were Chris Louth and Thomas E. Cook III. Louth was an operating man and his associate an accountant. Both wanted to set up their own firm in the rapidly expanding offshore service and supply field. Burgess introduced them to me at the same time as I had had discussions with Garvey.

I brought the entire package to the attention of ABC who had Peter Brown, a Bell-Irving relative, and Mel Newth, a New Zealand chartered accountant with a considerable financial ability, act in their behalf.

The end result was that ABC agreed to form a 50-50 joint venture with FedNav. For its own purposes it acquired Nordic Shipping Ltd., a shell company, which I had brought with me from the windup of Georgia Shipping Ltd. Nordic by a simple change of name became Nordic Offshore Services Ltd. The joint venture successfully competed for a Mobil Oil contract on the East Coast requiring three vessels which would be built for the purpose as at that time there were virtually no unemployed offshore supply ships round.

Louth and Cook joined and became president and vice-president of Nordic Offshore respectively. Peter Brown, Mel Newth and myself were appointed directors along with other Bell-Irving nominees. Among other expectations I had was that of bringing a potentially large insurance account to our associated Bell-Irving Insurance brokerage. It was the old intercorporate connection or wheels-within-wheels routine.

Upon confirmation of the Mobil contract, tenders were invited for two 174-foot supply ships and one 160-foot supply ship. Belaire won the contract for the two larger ships and Star Shipyards in New Westminster secured the contract for the smaller vessel. The vessels were designed by William Brown, a local naval architect, who turned out designs which were typical of international thinking in such ships at the time. The engines came from English Electric in the U.K.

Supply ships of this type had extra capacity triple-drum towing winches and had to have considerable on deck area to carry pipe, drill stems and containers with underdeck capacity for cement, diesel fuel and potable water for transfer to the rigs. In every sense they were tugs equipped with high fo'c'sles and bridge superstructure with generous crew accommodation placed as far forward as possible to leave available the long working deck aft for their carrying purposes.

With the securing of the Mobil contract the search for further contracts intensified as, if the new venture was to be sustained and expanded, firm contracts of employment were the collateral needed to justify taking on additional commitments. I was sent on two trips to South East Asia. The first was exploratory to test the waters using Swann Winches office at Johore as a base. I came back with an overall optimistic report of potential. Nordic engaged a man to act as our representative there. His work was effective and resulted in a second trip for myself accompanied by Newth to place contracts for two pipe barges with the Westbank shipyard for which we had a suitable undertaking from the Indonesian subsidiary of Union Oil of California.

Everything was coming together very well. A firm long-term charter contract from Union Oil was a highly bankable piece of collateral and a building block for further growth. We were due to sign contracts the following day, but Newth leaning in the direction of caution decided to phone Vancouver first. To our consternation we were told to hold everything, they had been trying to locate us. Nordic Offshore had signed firm building contracts with Belaire and Star Shipyards for more supply ships on speculation, but with the hope that work would follow.

I felt like we had in some way been set up particularly when told to drop the Union Oil deal and any further action in Singapore. It was almost as though we had been sent to Singapore a few days earlier to hang out to dry while someone back in Vancouver made the decision as soon as we had left to take this precipitate action. Speaking for myself, this behaviour left me feeling very uneasy and undermined my confidence in the potential for this new enterprise in which I had played a considerable role, at least in its formative stages, and it was not a good portent for the future which rapidly unfolded upon my return to Vancouver. It became obvious that a tug-of-war had been going on for some time. Louth and Cook had an agenda which would have led to them taking over everything over time, while ABC with its interests in Singapore saw the idea of a Singapore marine operation as a logical next step in its build-up of the Swann business. Added to all that it was obvious that management at the top in ABC which held the moneybags, was not up to the task.

[189] Mary B VI: The third and smallest of the first trio built in 1972 for the FedNav/Nordic joint venture which had won a service contract from Mobil for work in the Hibernia field off Newfoundland. The two larger boats in the first trio were **Cathy B** and **Janie B.** *(see plan p.176)* **Cathy B** was chartered by the Canadian Coast Guard, who later purchased **Janie B** and renamed her **George E. Darby.**

[190] Federal VI was originally intended to be one of the second group of offshore boats for the FedNav/Nordic joint venture. When the local backers of Nordic got into difficulties, having ordered the vessels on speculation, FedNav set up Federal Offshore to take delivery of **Federal VI, Federal VII** from Star Shipyards. Meanwhile Nordic Offshore had ordered **Nordic IV** and **Nordic V** from Belaire which were similar ships to **Cathy B** and her sister. Later the two Nordic vessels were leased to Zapata Offshore as **Hudson Service** and **Baffin Service** and then passed to the Canadian Coast Guard.

Even though I was a director I actually never had any say or even attended a single director's meeting. The company was run by a committee comprising the two Americans, Brown and to the extent of keeping an eye on the cash supply, Newth. What was forecastable was that ABC with certain other ventures it was into, was in the process of overextending itself. The company had to pull its horns in at top speed. In fact the bank put a manager of its own in to take charge and he acted with a heavy hand. I resigned and fully reverted to my duties in the insurance brokerage of which I was managing director while Mel Newth returned to Bell-Irving Realty from which he had been loaned. All the other heads rolled, FedNav bought out ABC's interest in the vessels which were completed by the two yards, but Star went bankrupt. I never did hear the exact details of what went on during the two or three days between our departure from Vancouver and our date with Westbank shipyard, but I suspect that Star had offered Nordic a price "it could not refuse," in a last-ditch effort to save itself. There were certain highly forceful elements in Nordic Offshore who would not have hesitated to upset the Singapore trip in favour of a deal such as I believe Star offered, but in the end it was all for nought. Newth and I had obviously been sent to Singapore to hang out and dry, although I doubt that the Bell-Irving faction saw it that way at the time.

The only satisfaction I got out of the entire deal was to be able to say at the end of it, "I told you so," as I had all along preached the gospel of firm collateral employment contracts. This might have been slower, but it was a firm foundation. Parcelling out speculative building contracts covered by banking money in an industry in which we were still neophytes, coupled with the high-pressure tactics of our two American friends with all their supposed expertise, was not the way to go. I was no doubt influenced by the history of Georgia Shipping where we fought for almost every morsel of business without any collateral contracts.

Thus ended Vancouver's only brush with a local ownership of offshore supply ships directly engaged in the oil exploration business, although some of the locally built Arctic supply tugs later found their way back into local ownerships for employment as tugs in the coastal trade, but that was not associated with the oil industry.

The names chosen for the ships have an origin of sorts. In an effort to please the top men at Mobil the names of their wives or daughters were chosen, thus *Cathy B, Janie B,* and *Mary B VI* came into being. It sounded like a collection of fishboats, whereas a proper naming system established from the beginning would have given the ships and their owners an identifiable personality. I was surprised that FedNav, a large established company, went along with the notion, but with so many supposed experts running the show it was perhaps inevitable that they would eventually drive the whole enterprise on the rocks. *Janie B* did have a longer life under the Canadian flag than her sisters. She was acquired by the Department of Transport, partially rebuilt and renamed *George E. Derby.*

All the actors involved in this local melodrama are now either dead or retired and I doubt if there are more than just a few outside this small group who will even remember this brief initiative. That is, other than Bill Brown, the naval architect who designed the vessels, George Fryatt of Belaire shipyard who built most of them and myself, who at least gave Nordic Offshore Services its name and tried to steer it along a safer path that could have assured its future prosperity.

SIDE ELEVATION AND DECK PLANS OF CATHY B AND JANIE B

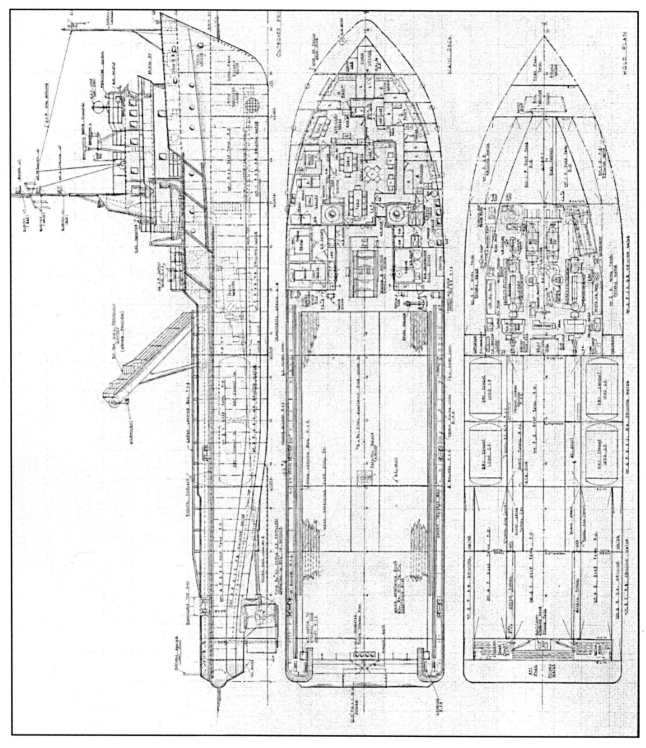

From the board of William (Bill) Brown, naval architect

FLEET LIST FOR FEDNAV/NORDIC JOINT VENTURE

Cathy B became **Janie B**	1972	Belaire SY N. Vancouver	184'9" oa x 45' x 16'6" 885.13 grt, 4,000 hp
Janie B became **Cathy B** later, CCGS **George E. Derby**	1972	same	same
Mary B VI became **Arctic Tuktu**	1972	Star SY New Westminster	171' x 38' x 15' 3,280 hp

The undernoted four vessels were the four that were ordered "on spec" and are set out for the record:

Nordic IV became **Hudson Service** later, CCGS **Grenfell**	1973	Belaire SY	similar sister of **Cathy B,** except for twin stacks further aft
Nordic V became **Baffin Service** later, CCGS **Jackman**	1973	Belaire SY	similar sister of **Janie B,** except for twin stacks further aft
Federal VI became **Arctic Mallik**	1973	Star SY	sister ship to **Mary B VI**
Federal VII became **Arctic Pelly**	1973	Star SY	sister ship to **Mary B VI**

Note: *All vessels were reported to have been acquired by FedNav upon completion or, with the second group of four, while under construction. Up to the early 1980s* Nordic IV *and* Nordic V *were still registered to Nordic Offshore which was struck off the register in 1983. FedNav never acquired Nordic as a corporation and again this is unexplainable. No one today has any recollection as to why* Janie B *and* Cathy B *switched names in the late 1970s.*

[191] **Canmar Supplier:** Two of four of the B.C.-built sisters offshore supply ships constructed for Dome Petroleum. Allied built the first vessel, followed by Vito with **Canmar Supplier II,** Burrard Dry Dock and Yarrows with the **Canmar Supplier III** and **Canmar Supplier IV.**

[192] **Ocean Foxtrot** is seen here in 1995. She was built by Cochrane & Sons at Selby, Yorkshire, England, as **Polar Shore.** A little larger than the FedNav/Nordic ships she is full ice strengthened. Owned by Quebec owners for a period she eventually became **Canmar Supplier VII** in the Dome Fleet.

[193] **Robert Lemeur** is seen here when owned by Grenadier Energy, Calgary, in the 1990s. Originally built for Dome, she was described as a tug/supply vessel. Built by Burrard–Yarrows in 1982 and with a length of 258 ft and a dead-weight capacity of 4,450 tons she was far bigger than most offshore service vessels of the type.

[194] **Alaska Husky** typified the smaller offshore supply vessels which mostly originated in the Gulf of Mexico, where offshore oil exploration first started after WW II. Usually with a length of about 120–30 ft, the engines were placed well aft with exhaust uptakes as seen here. The North Sea demonstrated that something bigger and more robust was needed as shown in other vessels illustrated here. The vessel shown here actually had dimensions similar to FedNav/Nordic vessels. She was owned by Foss Launch & Tug Company, Seattle, and was built in 1966.

[195] **Satro 21.** Local shipyards and naval architects enjoyed a busy time in the 1960s and 1970s building offshore supply ships for foreign owners. **Satro 21** was built for Soc. Aux. Industria de Petroles SATRO of Brazil. Belaire built this Brown-designed vessel.

[196] **Hudson Service.** The former **Nordic IV** was one of the seven vessels that grew out of the FedNav/Nordic offshore joint venture. Zapata Offshore resold the vessel to the Canadian Coast Guard six years after she was built and renamed her **Jackman.** CCGS then sold her back into commercial service in 1992. Her sister, **Baffin Service,** ex-**Nordic V,** became the CCGS **Grenfell.**

[197] **Canmar Supplier,** built by Allied as the first of a quartet already mentioned is shown here on trials before being handed over to Dome Petroleum. Allied built more ice-strengthened tug/supply ships than any other local shipyards.

[198] **Lady Alexandra.** Allied was also a full participant in the export of vessels for foreign owners. **Lady Alexandra** was the last in a quartet built for IOS of Britain, a subsidiary of P & O. Her name had a sentimental connection to the early history of the McLarens at Allied but, as Arthur McLaren related in the book *Ships of Steel,* the contract almost broke the shipbuilder. Building North Sea-style vessels was a different proposition from the Gulf-style mud boats which Allied had previously built for Tidewater.

Chapter Sixteen

CONCLUSIONS

1. What does the future hold for the West Coast Marine Transportation Industry?

The industry is made up of up to six primary elements. Three are the ferry system, the tug and barge industry and the building and repair industries. The fourth, outside of the scope of this study, normally has a bearing on the entire mix in the form of commercial fishing, but that is in severe decline, even if offset in some degree by fish farming and its future growth. The fifth, really a subdivision of the third identified above, is the deep-sea ship repair business which grows out of the activities, largely of Vancouver and other coastal ports, in international trade. A possible sixth may be found in association with tourism through which mini-cruise ships specialize in eco-cruises and the like and they, along with other specialty craft of one sort or another, may become a bigger industry.

Pure public necessity drives the ferry element of the marine transportation industry and secures its future. The parameters of public transportation overlap to affect the tug and barge industry where roll-on, roll-off barge services are provided by private operators for freight purposes only. The ferry system has an important bearing on the shipbuilding and repair element without which the latter could be in a sorry mess as a whole. In fact, the ferry corporation itself has developed severe shortcomings due to poor planning and ongoing political interference, without the intervention of the shipbuilding industry contributing to it.

Taking into account all the factors previously described, the future of the tug and barge element of marine transportation on the B.C. Coast is not bright.

It is not going to come to a sudden end, but where the forest industry goes, so also does the tug and barge sector follow to a large extent. The forest industry is in a state of malaise and its recovery from more political interference and environmental attacks, sometimes weak vacillating governments in Ottawa and Victoria, taxation policies, bureaucratic over-indulgence have produced a jungle of regulatory obfuscation. Higher costs of doing business all contributed to by the foregoing, plus the U.S.–Canada softwood dispute, along with frail markets in South and East Asia and competition from cheaper producers leaves more questions than there are adequate answers.

In the world of globalization and free flows of capital, one thing is certain—as water runs downhill, investment capital moves to whatever sector of the world economy provides the most attractive set of circumstances and this goes for Canadian capital as much as that of any other nation. National symbols of ownership, be they flag, name or domicile, mean less than they did and it is a trend that is forecast by many, to continue to progress to its final theoretical conclusion—a one world economy where national frontiers become meaningless.

However, most of us can only have faith that the forest industry will survive and live to prosper again, albeit in a drastically altered form, with fewer corporate units but more efficient manufacturing facilities, an ever greater reliance on plantation wood and a reduced dependency on original forests, particularly first growth which seems to lead to nothing but confrontations with environmentalists. The non-availability of much first growth timber even on a careful selection basis means that the available cut is further reduced. The attitude of many environmentalists that standing timber will stand forever ensures that the natural progression of rot and disease will take its toll of otherwise healthy timber which could have had economic value. An example is beetle infestation in Tweedsmuir Park where huge areas are being laid waste, but could at least be removed as useable timber while it has economic value, before the infestation reaches the point when trees die and rot away where they fall.

By the beginning of the twentieth century tug-boating was becoming well established as an industry in its own right and not merely an auxiliary for towing cannery vessels and inbound or outbound sailing ships. The expansion of tug and barge companies followed in the wake of sawmill development and the development of logging camps. Improvements in tugboats with larger more powerful vessels and improved towing capability, increased carrying capacity in barges, all enabled logging operations and pulp and paper manufacturing facilities to be extended to all sectors of the coast. Important, but lesser needs in terms of volume developed concurrently in such fields as aggregates, building materials, petroleum products and general freight including railcar barge traffic. In the final analysis, most of their volume has grown concurrently with and as part of, or associated with, the growth of the forest industries.

Many of the boats built in that period (1890–1920s) were owned by rugged individualists to whom the idea of today's large corporate concerns would be anathema. However, individualists alone were not enough to guarantee progress in the industry so the towing companies started to form as a means of concentrating capital and limiting personal liability. They also developed a corporate structure, which gave a greater guarantee of succession within the company. This process gathered speed in the 1920s and was well underway by the 1930s and saw the establishment or re-establishment of several of the large companies which made up the bigger operators who emerged prior to and following the Second World War.

As we have seen, the opening of the Panama Canal and WW I gave a great impetus to tugboating.

The last steam tugs came out of B.C. yards in the mid-20s. The process of dieselization started in the same period as steam gradually fell out of favour. It was a process that accelerated when diesel tugs of U.S. wartime construction and diesel engines became available as war surplus, after WW II. Conversion from steam to diesel was still a viable proposition until the Canadian Vessels Construction Assistance Act provided for shipbuilding subsidies. In spite of higher first capital cost the economics of the diesel engine were indisputable with superior fuel utilization and reduced manning requirements, but it probably took up to 30 years for the steamer to finally be phrased out.

The post-war period defined the companies which were to rank among the industry heavies and make their contribution to future major mergers in the industry and, who among the industry were to remain as small operators. Aside from personal qualities and the strength of the capital resources of the big companies, a defining moment came when the forest industry seemed agreed, either tacitly or by a form of natural progression through possession of the requisite equipment, that three companies, Island Tug & Barge, Vancouver Tug Boat Company and Straits Towing, were to be the contract providers of woodchip barges to service the increasing number of pulp mills built or projected for the coast. This was probably the most important contractual development to that date of the sort needed to underwrite further growth of these three majors.

Essentially, this was a classic example of what would be called in ocean shipping terms "a contract of affreightment," by which the tugboat operators knew that they had to have a barge under the pouring spout, or conveyor, at a sawmill that was under contract to supply all its woodchip bi-product to one of the major forest companies. It was like a pipeline from sawmill to pulp mill and it was essential to keep it filled. The award of a long-term contract from a major forest products producer had greater collateral value when the need arose to support favourable, back-to-back, long-term financing on terms not available to more speculative types of employment and operators.

This was also probably the defining moment

[199] Hecate Prince. In spite of the concentration that has taken place in the industry smaller companies can still find a niche and prosper. Gemini Marine Services is the main carrier of fishfeed for the aquaculture industry.

[200] GMS 620: Built at Vancouver Shipyards, North Vancouver, this covered barge measuring 200' x 50" utilized the new Federal finance package for the shipbuilding industry. Gemini, which started up when fish farming became a serious industry in the mid-1980s, couples it with **Hecate Prince.**

when the separation from the ranks of the smaller operators became more pronounced and, while there are well-founded, solidly financed, smaller companies, the opportunity to become an integral part of the coast's major heavy industry of pulp and paper had passed. The other two members of the big five, River Towing Ltd. and Gulf of Georgia Towing, almost certainly realized this and, while they had largely missed the boat in competing for an allocation of the woodchip contracts, they were not idle in the unfolding of their own plans as we saw in earlier books in this series. River Towing became Rivtow Marine and merged with Straits Towing to form Rivtow–Straits and Gulf of Georgia, which did successfully get into direct contracting in the chip barge business, became by merger, the third major component in the Seaspan organization.

At Seaspan, the heavyweight in the towing industry, the stage was set in 1995 for the third change of ownership when U.S. tycoon Dennis Washington came to British Columbia acquiring first Cates Towing Ltd. of North Vancouver, which enjoyed the shiphandling business of the Port of Vancouver, and then the railroad assets of B.C. Hydro & Power Authority. The acquisition of Seaspan was to have a far-reaching effect as Washington Marine Group was formed and in steady succession added further marine assets to their key holding in Seaspan. In spite of the fact that much Canadian capital has flown to tax free or tax reduced economies, this fact has not deterred the Washington group from coming into Canada and replacing Canadian beneficial ownership.

One has to wonder if it is so attractive to American capital, why does Canadian capital continue to flee from the industry? No specific reason other than high Canadian taxation has been offered, but undoubtedly the disparity between the Canadian and American dollars has been a major factor in allowing the purchase of Canadian assets cheapened by our 60–65 cent dollar in terms of the U.S. dollar. It also seems reasonable to suppose that as much as anything it remains a matter of positioning for the twenty-first century when, by a process of fairly rapid evolution, the Canadian economy will be gradually integrated into that of the U.S. and ultimately absorbed as we lose the last vestiges of independence. A cartoonist might use the Canadian grape and place it alongside the American grapefruit as it inexorably rolls forward with its greater mass and extraordinary strength and crushes the grape. For those who place national independence ahead of pure personal gain it is a disheartening process to observe.

So far, this has resulted in the Americanization of by far the biggest group of prime marine transportation assets on the B.C. Coast. This is not the first time we have seen an American incursion into what a lot of the public take pride in viewing as an alert, active and efficient Canadian industry. It might, on the other hand, be seen as part of the globalization process. With the industry dominated by one big operator, we keep away from the final stage of total monopoly, so long as some other operator has some small part of the particular segment of the industry.

An important question surrounding the future of Rivtow was answered by its sale to the Dutch Smit International towing group, which is the largest international player in the industry. Prior to that happening in 2000, any move made by Rivtow to divest out of marine transportation, in any way in favour of Washington, might have led to an impass. The Washington Group could have found itself being ordered to divest itself of some of its assets to a third operator in the interests of maintaining competition. That eventuality has been avoided by the sale to Smit. We also have several other family controlled towing businesses and some new entities appeared on the scene in the 1990s to prove that new capital formation is still feasible. However, control by the second generation might generate closer grouping. Or, there may be one or more mergers between these smaller companies to bring about management economies, create greater critical mass and reduce competition. It may also be a means to retire as painlessly as possible.

Rivtow's current dispersal of towing assets runs concurrently with expansion of several of the smaller companies who are picking up ex-Rivtow vessels and finding work for them, which is not easy given the current state of the forest industry economy.

[201 & 202] **Ocean Warlock.** Another smaller company which occupies a special position in the trailer barge business is Mercury Launch & Tug. **Ocean Warlock** with 1,900 hp represents a significant new investment at a time when times are hard for many in the industry.

2. What is the scale and scope of public investment in the marine transportation industry and what benefits does it create?

Historically there have been six instances of a public stock market flotation among the local marine industries. Two, Burrard–Yarrows and its successor Versatile Pacific Corporation and Western Canada Steamships Ltd. are outside the immediate scope of this study. The others were Union Steamships of British Columbia Ltd., Pacific Coyle Navigation Ltd., and Straits Towing Ltd. It was via the stock market that the McKeen interests at Straits Towing were able to gain control of Union and Pacific Coyle. Straits was the operating vehicle of Senator Stan McKeen and his colleague Fred B. Brown. Stock flotations had some degree of popularity in the early post-WW II period up to the time of the big mergers in the early '70s. They provided a vehicle for transferring a part of the previously privately held investment to the public, at the same time recouping capital to the vendors without relinquishment of control. At least in theory they also created a market valuation of the companies concerned, but for the most part this did not work as market capitalizations were too small and the market too limited. However, times and priorities change, but these flotations have now all passed into the limbo of history.

There is no public investment in the tug and barge sector today. In fact, given the character of the private owners of tug and barge assets, it is unlikely that any sort of welcome mat would be laid out to incoming public investment. There has also been public investment in the sense that there were tax benefits, building subsidies and ploughback of discounted escrow funds that followed in the post-war period. They were of an attractive nature, created to fit the special circumstances of the post-war period.

Outside of the tug and barge industry, the biggest post-war shipbuilding customer has been the publicly owned B.C. Ferry Corporation which, since 1959, has had a succession of passenger ro-ro ferries from B.C. yards. It has progressively taken over all the major and smaller routes and has opened some new ones. Growth has been ongoing and parallels the growth of the coastal economy.

3. Do the companies that now control the bulk of the tug and barge business have loyalty to the concept of a Canadian shipbuilding industry, or will all the new building business follow the bottom line and end up in the low-cost economies such as China?

Rivtow in its early days did operate as a small yard near Hope. Additionally it did at one time control at least two shipyard businesses with a capability of building units for its fleet, but it now appears to be clear of that connection so that the only consideration remains the bottom line. In the case of the barge hulls built for Rivtow, Seaspan, Fraser River Terminals and Island Tug & Barge (II), the delivered costs including all import duty and taxes paid, resulted in a saving estimated to be in the region of 30 per cent less than the price for a duplicate built in British Columbia.

In the case of the Washington Marine Group and its Seaspan subsidiary it appears to be supportive of a Canadian shipbuilding industry, but only to the extent that the Washington group control significant shipbuilding assets of their own which might be hurt if all shipbuilding for Canadian owners moved offshore. At the time of ordering the Chinese-built vessels, Vancouver Shipyards, North Vancouver, the primary shipbuilding unit of the Washington Marine Group, was heavily committed to the construction of the three aluminum catamarans for B.C. Ferries, and claimed to have no available capacity to meet its requirements for new barge hulls. That overlooks the distinctively different processes used in aluminum and steel construction and the fact that they had set up a special unit for aluminum production.

This statement was clearly made for public consumption as at least two shipyards in Vancouver are under-utilized. The dormant Vito yard sits there waiting for a project having built the two superstructures for the two "Spirit-class" vessels, a particularly large job of prefabrication. At last report a new tenant is now building yachts at this location.

The "Spirit" ferries were the biggest example of modular construction undertaken in B.C. with no less than three yards contributing to the hulls. Modular construction of the largest ferry and barge hulls was

[203] Ocean Wrestler: Sea-Link Marine Services has been involved with this ocean-going type tug of around 6,000 hp since 1998. Registered to Bevis Associates in the Cayman Islands, she was built by Beliard, Chichton in Ostend, Belgium, in 1972. The sea-kindly lines of this vessel are notable compared to the awkward lines of many other modern vessels.

made it clear that it has every intention of moving to open bidding for major reconstruction and new building contracts to foreign shipyards. This is clearly with an eye on Asian countries who led the way in international shipbuilding. Very naturally it has brought considerable protest from both shipyard managements and local labour unions and, while no one can question the quality of B.C. shipbuilders and their ability to make good on their contracts, there is every reason to be concerned about quality supervision and delivery and redelivery costs when dealing with overseas yards. It is a lot like comparing apples and oranges when assuming that the building of simple barges guarantees the same level of satisfaction as the construction of large and complex ferries and their delivery here.

well within the ability of B.C. yards and capacity clearly exists to build locally.

The bottom line was therefore the sole consideration on the face of things and, unless considered on a solely philosophical basis where support of a local industry was the only consideration, it is hard to quarrel with the management decision to give the orders to the lowest bidder—a Chinese yard. After all none of these companies were doing anything other than spending their own money in the way which best suited their own needs, and that is a fundamental principle of a free market economy.

As to whether more newbuilding business will go to China, the answer seems to be clear. More orders will follow, as has actually happened, if the same delivery parameters of lower cost and adequate quality continue. Obsolescence is a factor in all local fleets. The cost of new replacement equipment when fully factored in means that operators can quote the lowest rates available to the industrial customers whose own bottom line, in some cases, has been severely eroded, their costs being entirely relevant in meeting their own competition.

As at August 2002, the B.C. Ferry Corporation, under directive from the provincial government, has

4. Is there a case for a renewed shipbuilding subsidy in Canada, given that tug and barge operators are already faced with an ongoing need for replacement of obsolete carrying capacity?

The barge fleet contains a large number of units built at least 30 years ago with some within this group now being over 40 years old. Barge hulls simply wear out, despite the best efforts possible in maintaining their fabric. Contact, loading and unloading damage weaken the structure of a hull over time. Some hulls look like a patchwork quilt after having been patched where plate has eroded, despite proper attention to electrolysis. Continuing service would be an impossibility without ever increasing attention to this factor. With advancing age, maintenance becomes an increasing cost factor, which cannot be justified beyond a certain point. Many locally owned barges are approaching this point and the several which were delivered to China for scrap as part of the building deal had clearly reached the point where further service in B.C. could not be justified.

Given the competition factor from China, the re-establishment of a national shipbuilding policy provokes two schools of thought. First, it can be claimed that a subsidy is desirable in order to meet the national interest in having a viable shipbuilding industry in being and maintaining through it a sufficiently large pool of skilled management and labour. The opposite point of view is that national barriers are slipping, globalization is well under way and the likely absorption of the Canadian economy into the American follows as a natural consequence of NAFTA. That being the case industries must be competitive or suffer the consequences. It follows that if Canadian shipbuilding cannot compete then it will simple go out of business so why prop it up with artificial crutches?

If the Canadian economy is absorbed into the American, then presumably Canadian shipbuilders will be able to compete freely on American business, this giving them the benefit of a larger protected market. Or is that just wishful thinking?

It is recognized that the provincial forest industry is in a lot of trouble, some of it being of its own making. So much of the inventory of standing timber has now been removed from future utilization that Alaska, lacking any manufacturing capacity of its own for pulp and paper is now a prime supplier of pulpwood delivered by B.C.-owned tugs and log barges to coastal B.C. mills. There is nothing wrong with that as an exercise in legitimate trade, although it does indicate how the raw meterials harvesting base is now greatly extended geographically due to factors earlier explained.

Without this source there is a danger of pulp and paper mills becoming part of their own rust belt. It seems inconceivable that public policy can permit this most basic of basic industries, so far as British Columbia is concerned, to reach the point when the major companies simply have to write off their manufacturing capacity and walk away from the province, for example as at Gold River. Some might say it is not going to happen, but insolvency can lead to that. If replacement operators cannot be found, as seems entirely likely, then the manufacturing facilities are reduced to scrap value, again as at Gold River and at the Skeena mill, Prince Rupert. In the latter

case a new owner has taken over at tremendous cost to the B.C. taxpayer, with no guarantee of success.

One might ask, if the forest products industry is in such a parlous state why bother replacing barge fleets? That is a fair question, but the truth is the forest products industry can only survive on a profitable basis, otherwise a vast part of the provincial economy goes down the drain with it. The forest products economy is better able to survive if it is supported by a first-class, high-quality and economic tug and barge industry, again on a profitable basis. To take any other attitude than "the bottom line" ultimately seals the fate of both industries.

The need for a reintroduction of the shipbuilding subsidy is now critical for the health of what remains of our shipbuilding industry. It does not have to be on the same open-ended basis as existed from the '50s to 1985 when it was finally phrased out, but it does need to be reintroduced on a measured basis with a ceiling of a certain number of units per year with replacement having priority. This could be a "scrap and build" program, where a formula would ensure that a given tonnage of worn-out hulls would be replaced by new, but a mechanism should also be in place which would allow new entrepreneurial enterprise. Some method of apportionment would also be needed, otherwise it becomes a certainty that the biggest "kid on the block," with its larger fleet, potentially bigger replacement problem and near absolute monopoly in today's local large shipbuilding market, would grab most of the benefits leaving the crumbs for the smaller competitors.

If a Canadian solution is not arrived at, as a part of our need as an independent nation and, if our political masters in Ottawa fail to shake off their eastward view of everything, all the work and the jobs entailed go to China or whatever new country comes on the scene with a better price and delivery. The truth of course is that geographical convenience ensures that B.C. yards will remain a factor in ship maintenance and repair work, but with the concentration of ownership among the tugboat companies even this is circumscribed by the fact that most of the facilities are now owned by the Washington group.

Shipbuilding subsidies are justifiable in a high-cost economy as happened in Canada from the 1950s on, if it is a matter of jump-starting the economy. The ripple-down effect extends to a great many businesses and people and the commensurate tax return probably eventually recovers most if not all of the basic subsidy. One source has estimated that the recovery by way of taxation represents as much as 22 per cent of the cost of a new vessel. The provision of an operating subsidy is a different matter, which to my knowledge has only ever been applied in Canada on a limited basis and is not suggested now. An interesting fact of life is that foreigners can have a field day in acquiring Canadian assets by simply setting up a Canadian corporation with 100 per cent foreign beneficial ownership. Foreign control of an American shipping corporation engaged wholly or partly in U.S. domestic trade which includes their coastal and intercoastal shipping is precluded by the Jones Act, a particularly protective piece of U.S. Federal legislation dating back over 80 years. Likewise under the same act only American-built vessels including tugs and barges can participate in intercoastal or state-to-state trade under any U.S. ownership.

A recent development, which came about through the political efforts of the Hon. Brian Tobin when he was in charge of the Industry portfolio in Ottawa, is termed a "Structured Finance Facility." So far it has been little used. It has assisted the construction of a new covered barge for Gemini Marine Services and possibly some chipbarges recently built at Vancouver Shipyards for Seaspan. Effectively it amounts to a 10 per cent subsidy derived through an interest rate buy down. It was of value to the covered barge owner in this case but how effective it will be in helping renew the B.C. fleet generally still has to be determined.

5. In the global village concept of world economics and shipping operations, will shipbuilding overseas for the Canadian coastal transportation industry be the thin edge of the wedge which allows foreign operators to compete for our business on even or preferred terms?

There appears to be a tendency for politicians and bureaucrats to pigeon-hole sectors of the world in such a way that they do more damage than good. A classic example was the relegation of the British shipbuilding industry to the status of a "twilight" industry. This was an action of Margaret Thatcher's Conservative government following denationalization of the state-owned shipbuilding industry created by an earlier socialist government. In effect it closed the door on any form of assistance to an industry which had been at the centre of British industrial might for the previous 200 years. Interestingly enough, since WW II British shipowning reached its zenith when Labour governments were in power, an anomoly when considering the record of left-leaning governments in the B.C. economy.

A similar move occurred in Sweden for somewhat different reasons associated with the development of the highest cost, fully welfared state in Europe. The end result is that most European orders that are handled within Europe go to Italy, Germany, Norway, Finland, Spain and Poland, some of which are high-cost economies. The decline in British shipbuilding also has been somewhat concurrent with the decline in that country's merchant navy, a logical consequence of the retreat from Empire. However, the latest statistics released from the U.K. indicate that once again a Labour government having removed some of the legislated hurdles has brought British merchant shipping up again from 21st place internationally to 8th as at 2002. That tends to confirm that government meddling with shipping should be confined to adopting enabling legislation and not to view the industry as a cash cow to be milked by way of taxation at every turn.

One can see the slotting of certain industries into given sectors of the world economy. Already the automobile industry is now dominated by American, Japanese, and German ownerships. Korea is less of a factor, which is weakened by the state of the South Korean economy. The majors have been busy gobbling up the smaller remaining independent manufacturers wherever they can be found. There is no longer a single surviving independent British automaker, but auto manufacturing thrives in Britain with its factories modernized or built anew and owned by German, American and Japanese makers. The recent merger of Chrysler into Daimler-Benz of Germany points the way to a world split up between six to eight major auto manufacturers, most of whom have been busily picking up any smaller competitors.

Do we want the same thing for what remains of our domestic coastal shipping industry? In Canada, we have failed to ever have a sensible long-term national shipping and shipbuilding policy, much better than a band-aid solution. Now it is probably too late. Shipbuilding and development initiatives have to come from Ottawa, but we have seen the effects of weak, vacillating government policies on the West Coast. When B.C. Ferries was considering new tonnage a few years ago, a loud and vociferous complaint went up from one American yard that under NAFTA they should be allowed to bid for the B.C. business. The scream would have been even louder (from the U.S.) if, through some presently non-existent loophole, a Canadian shipbuilder found itself able to bid on an American building contract. Considering that the B.C. Ferry Corporation is owned by the people of B.C. the political fallout might have been deafening if such a move had ever been given serious consideration. However, unification of the North American economies may yet see Canadian shipbuilders bidding successfully for American business as they do now for U.S. ship repair business.

Since the First World War, the United States has had a highly protectionist shipbuilding policy which has shielded its builders from foreign competition. In Canada a policy of reserving coastal shipping for Canadian flag ownership has helped to develop a vibrant industry for the benefit of the country. This has been breached by allowing the encroachment of total American beneficial share ownership into our biggest coastal shipping operation, to which have been added other smaller healthy businesses.

This is not the first time there has been an incursion by way of buying shares in an existing company. After all Vancouver Tug and Island Tug & Barge, were effectively foreign owned at the time of their merger. It is however, the first time when it has been on such a mighty scale to the extent that until recently only the presence of Rivtow relieved it of the label of monopoly in several sectors of the industry. As someone said, Rivtow was the biggest family concern in the business and it was a private company. A crisis can arise when one day a company

is faced with succession problems, always a greater risk in closely held private companies. In many instances the only way to ensure an adequate transference of power and ownership is to sell out to a competitor. It was not hard to anticipate that a future sale, if ever consummated, would probably be to a large American operator. That would effectively complete the transfer of an entire industry to American ownership, save only a handful of small firms, thus driving another nail into the coffin of Canadian independence.

Since these notes were originally prepared, the news that Rivtow has been sold to a large Dutch-based international towing company has been greeted with considerable relief.

6. Is West Coast coastal transportation a twilight industry destined to follow the fate of Canadian deep-sea shipowning in the new world of removing trade and protection barriers?

This could happen given current government attitudes. We have seen how the Federal government to all intents and purposes abandoned the West Coast shipbuilding industry when future naval construction all went to St. John Shipbuilding and Drydock at St. John, N.B. (now also closed) and Davie Shipbuilding Company at Levis, Quebec. As a sop, it awarded the contract for development of the proposed Arctic nuclear super-icebreaker to Versatile Pacific (formerly Burrard Dry Dock) in 1988 and then cancelled the contract after much development work had been done, but before the keel had been laid. Not one of the seven large West Coast shipyards, which contributed so much to the Canadian war effort in the Second World War, remains in being and with the eventual closure of Davie Shipbuilding much the same position applies on the East Coast.

Among intermediate and smaller yards, it is much the same story, although to assess these, one needs to compare the position when shipbuilding was booming under the influence of incentives such as the CVCA Act. Of the intermediate yards with a capability of building larger tugs and, in some instances barges, there are now only about five with this capability in physical terms compared to double that number 30–40 years ago. With orders only likely from the two big operators, Seaspan and Rivtow (who are now favouring China), possible orders from the two large cement and aggregate companies, Ocean Cement (Lehigh) and Lafarge and a sprinkling of possibilities from about six independent companies, the future for independent shipbuilding in B.C. is bleak indeed.

Outside of the big companies and the more alert smaller operators, no one seems to have an original new idea of knowing what to do. The Federal Government gives the appearance of always being asleep at the switch in terms of the fact that our entire barge fleet could be replaced by Chinese construction. It has difficulty in replying to even a constructive letter of enquiry and provincial politicians are more interested in counting the vote-making potential of each of their moves.

Meanwhile the Americanization of the Forest industry proceeds apace. On the one hand the industry has suffered the consequences of a throttling U.S. imposition of import quotas on Canadian lumber into the American market at the same time as first, Pope & Talbot Inc., a Portland, Oregon, firm has taken over Harmac, originally a MacMillan, Bloedel facility, and secondly, Weyerhaueser has acquired all the remaining assets of MacMillan after that company had divested itself of its pulp and paper and shipping divisions.

The biggest speculation after the forgoing was as to the future of Fletcher Challenge after its aborted effort to reorganize itself into a transpacific conglomeration of pulp and paper mills around the Pacific rim. This reorganization would have stripped it of its large cash reserves and shipped them to the debt laden New Zealand parent. However, as we learned in the year 2000 Fletcher Challenge became a subsidiary of the large Norwegian pulp and paper concern Norske Skog A/S which again saved a prime Canadian asset, the embarrassment of selling out to the Americans.

In the meantime the World Trade Organization, an international function with extraordinary dictatorial powers, rules on trade matters with little regard for sovereign powers. If not invented by multinational corporations, it certainly seems like a natural in its capacity to assist the multinationals. It is claimed that its open door, no borders policy, is a win-win situation for everyone, but given the relative size of different economies, who among Canadian capital sources would have had the strength to buy out, say Weyerhaueser, a company several times larger than MacMillan, Bloedel?

The same applies to the multiple interests of the Washington group. Like the iceberg, what the public sees usually after the event probably is a fraction of what is hidden as fresh moves are made to extend the octopus of control. Washington already controls almost the entire large-ship capacity, for building and drydocking at Vancouver and Victoria. Large ship in my definition means barges of a length exceeding say 200 feet and tugs over 2,500 hp. He has nominal competition from Allied Shipbuilders, Mackenzie, Sylte and Port Alberni Engineering (Point Hope has just declared bankruptcy). This by Competition Bureau standards appears to relieve B.C. shipbuilding of the stigmatizing label of monopoly.

No one can blame Dennis Washington for the woes of our maritime industries. He sees things through American eyes, which have always been acquisitive in the modern style of American-dominated world capitalism. He, I don't doubt, sees the inevitable absorbtion of the Canadian economy into the American and is positioning himself for the future. From an American standpoint there is nothing wrong with that and it is probably too late to counter it, but at least we should try to understand the forces that are likely to shape our lives in this new century.

It is not that much different with the tug and barge industry. Rivtow keeps Seaspan's position clean in some sectors in terms of monopoly. Second-line composite tug and barge companies beyond this are Island Tug & Barge Ltd. (II), Pacific Towing Services, Sea-Link Marine Services, North Arm Transportation and Gemini Marine Services. It likely pays Washington not to push these smaller competitors out of business. It makes sense to hand out river barge-handling work to what are primarily log towers like Hodder, Harken, Catherwood and others.

The choice for further acquisitions is now very limited and even a small one might finally rock the boat in Ottawa.

[204 & 205] Seaspan Tempest (and her sister **Seaspan Venture**) represent new investment for Washington Marine Group as part of an ongoing renewal program as many older units reach retirement age, including some of the big vessels in the fleet. The hulls were built in China and engine installation and finishing done at Vancouver Shipyards. It seems to point the way for most new construction in the WMG, i.e., offshore basic construction, with finishing in Vancouver. These two are general harbour tugs with 1,200 hp which likely means that they can lend a hand with ship berthing when needed.

SERIES BIBLIOGRAPHY

Aspinall, Craig. *The Story of Island Copper.* Madeira Park: Harbour Publishing, 1995.

Baptie, Sue. *First Growth: The Story of British Columbia Forest Products Ltd.* Vancouver: BCFP and J.J. Douglas, 1975.

Bowen, Lynne. *Boss Whistle: The Coal Miners Vancouver Island Remembers.* Lantzville: Oolichan Books, 1982.

Campbell, Kenneth. *North Coast Odyssey: The Inside Passage from Port Hardy to Prince Rupert.* Victoria: Sono Nis Press, 1993.

Clapp, Frank. "British Columbia's Early Log Barges." A two-part article in *The Sea Chest, Journal of the Puget Sound Maritime Historical Society.* Includes refs to John C. Coughlan.

Clyne, J.V *Jack of All Trades: Memories of a Busy Life.* Toronto: MacClelland & Stewart, 1985.

Drushka, Ken. *Against Wind & Weather: The History of Towboating in British Columbia.* Vancouver: Douglas & McIntyre, 1981.

———. *HR: A Biography of H.R. MacMillan.* Madeira Park: Harbour Publishing, 1995.
* Several books by this author on forestry-related matter are valuable reference sources.

Fisher, Robin. *Vancouver's Voyage: Charting the Northwest Coast.* Vancouver: Douglas & McIntyre, 1992.

Gibson, Gordon. and Carol Renison. *Bull of the Woods: The Gordon Gibson Story.* Vancouver: Douglas & McIntyre, 1980.

Gillespie, B. *Guild On Stormy Seas: The Triumphs & Torments of Capt. George Vancouver.* Victoria: Horsdahl & Schubart, 1992.

Hacking, Norman. *The Prince Ships of Northern B.C.* Surrey: Heritage House Publishing, 1995.

Hallock, Richard. *Pick Up Sticks: A History of the Intercoastal Lumber Trade.* Vancouver: Cordillera, 1995.

Heal, S.C. *The Maple Leaf Afloat, Volumes I & II.* Vancouver: Cordillera Publishing, 1991 and 1993. Ref. Tugboat companies, lumber and log carriers and B.C. Ferries.

———. *Conceived in War, Born in Peace: Canada's Deep Sea Merchant Marine.* Vancouver: Cordillera Publishing, 1992. Includes refs. to John C. Coughlan, as pioneer Vancouver shipbuilder and shipowner.

Jenkins, Geraint. *Evan, Thomas & Radcliffe, A Cardiff Shipping Company.* Cardiff: Welsh Industrial and Maritime Museum. With ref. to the 64th method of vessel finance and ownership.

Lillard, Charles. *Seven Shillings a Year: A History of Vancouver Island.* Victoria: Horsdahl & Schubart, 1986.

McKay, John. *The Hudson's Bay Company's 1835 Steam Ship Beaver.* St. Catherines: Vanwell Publishing, 2001.

McLaren, T.A. and Vickie Jensen. *Ships of Steel: The Allied Shipbuilder's Story.* Madeira Park, B.C.: Harbour Publishing, 2000.

Norris, Pat Wastell. *High Seas, High Risk: The Story of the Sudburys.* Madeira Park, B.C.: Harbour Publishing, 1999.

Perrault, Ernie. *Setting the Course for a Century, 1898-99: Seaspan International Ltd.* (a corporate profile) North Vancouver: Seaspan International, 1998.

Rushton, Gerald. *Whistle Up the Inlet: The Union Steamship Story.* Vancouver: Douglas & McIntyre Ltd., 1972/78.

Sheret, R.	*Seamen, Ships and Cargoes.* Victoria, B.C.: Western Isles, 2001.
———.	*Smoke, Ash & Steam.* Victoria, B.C.: Western Isles, 1997. Ref. West Coast steam engines and boilers
———.	*Tugs, Booms & Barges.* Victoria, B.C.: Western Isles, 1999. Ref. Log, boom and scow construction and handling methods
Taylor, G.W.	*Timber: History of the Forest Industry in B.C.* North Vancouver, B.C.: J.J. Douglas, 1975.
Wyngaert, Francis J.	*The West Howe Sound Story, 1886–1976.* (Published privately by Mr. Wyngaert, at Gibsons, B.C.: F. J. Wyngaert, 1980.
Wilson, James E. and S.C. Heal.	*Full Line, Full Away: A Towboat Master's Story.* Vancouver: Cordillera Publishing, 1991.
Wright, Peter Leckie.	*Risk and Responsibility: A History of the Insurance Industry of British Columbia.* Vancouver: Insurance Brokers Association of British Columbia, 1998.

CORPORATE PROFILES

Ocean Odyssey, Vancouver: Published by Vancouver Tug Boat Company, circa 1968.
Ocean Highway, Victoria, B.C.: Published by Island Tug & Barge, circa 1967.
Genstar Marine and Seaspan Overseas Operations, (promotional pieces published by Genstar, circa 1970s).

ANNUAL REPORTS OF:

Canfor Ltd. (Canadian Forest Products)
CBR (Parent Company of Tilbury Cement)
Doman Industries Ltd.
Fletcher Challenge Ltd.
Heidelberger Zement
International Forest Products Ltd. (Interfor)
MacMillan Bloedel Ltd.
Timberwest Forest Corpn.

Photograph Credits *(by photograph number)*